WELL-BEING

In search of a good life?

Beverley A. Searle

First published in Great Britain in 2008 by

The Policy Press
University of Bristol
Fourth Floor
Beacon House
Queen's Road
Bristol BS8 1QU
UK

Tel +44 (0)117 331 4054
Fax +44 (0)117 331 4093
e-mail tpp-info@bristol.ac.uk
www.policypress.org.uk

British Library Cataloguing in Publication Data
A catalogue record for this book is available from the British Library.

Library of Congress Cataloging-in-Publication Data
A catalog record for this book has been requested.

ISBN 978 1 86134 887 6 hardcover

Cover design by The Policy Press.
Front cover: photograph supplied by kind permission of Benny Hansson.
Printed and bound in Great Britain by MPG Books, Bodmin.

To Emma and Kim

Contents

Appendix: Regression tables

List of figures and tables

Figures

Tables

Acknowledgements

This analysis is based on data from the British Household Panel Survey (BHPS). The BHPS data is made available through the Economic and Social Research Council (ESRC) Data Archive. The data was originally collected by the ESRC Research Centre on Micro-Social Change at the University of Essex. The original data creators and the UK Data Archive bear no responsibility for the analyses or interpretations presented here.

The original analysis presented in this book was undertaken for a PhD funded by the ESRC; work was completed with the support of the ESRC and Durham University funded research.

This book could not have been completed without the invaluable support of Susan J. Smith. Thanks are also expressed to the editorial team at The Policy Press and the anonymous referees for their critical and stimulating comments.

Finally, I am forever indebted to my parents, Bill and Shirley, for their encouragement and support throughout, and to Paul for unconditional support and belief.

ONE

Introduction

It's official: Money can't buy happiness.

(Herper, 2004)

A statement that no one without money really believes, but one that is nonetheless increasingly becoming evidence based. That is what this book is about.

So does money matter? The simple answer is, not as much as we might expect it to. Increases in income may improve mood for a short while but over the longer term the initial 'high' mellows out as the new-found wealth just becomes a part of everyday living and desires and expectations lead to feelings of inadequacy and dissatisfaction. So if money is not the answer, then what is? This book will answer this question by considering the evidence along three key themes: firstly, by providing a critique of the economic idea that the richer societies are, the more people can consume and the happier they will be; secondly, by considering the social idea that unequal societies are unhappy; and thirdly, by proposing the 'welfare' idea that well-being is part of a quest for contentment which has a range of dimensions, and is not based only on the acquisition of wealth.

One of the principal ways of understanding well-being has been the adoption of 'utility' by economists, which equates wealth and consumption with satisfaction. So, whether this is through clothes, furniture, a season ticket, a lottery win or promotion, every time something new is purchased or income is increased well-being will be enhanced. There is no doubt that western nations have become richer, lives have been enhanced and standards of living have increased, but people are no happier as a result. Increased choice and increased consumption opportunities have not always brought greater satisfaction, with the flip side of the hedonic consumer coin being the anxiety, distrust and disillusionment that results from an unequal distribution of the profits and benefits born of capitalism.

This is not to say that all market activity, and its related economic growth, is detrimental (Reeves, 2002a) − nor that capitalism is unworkable in the move towards sustainable development and the associated measures of well-being (Porritt, 2005). Some developments have been beneficial, through improving quality of life where goods and services have become available to those who might not otherwise have access (Frank and Cook, 1995; Reeves, 2002a). It is undoubtedly true that, for developing countries, economic growth is associated with an element of happiness. But the key point is that there are limits to the extent to which well-being will be enhanced through such means, and there is a certain point at which the correlation between GDP per capita and well-being seems to break down (Reeves, 2002b; Schyns, 2002; Layard, 2003). Economic success needs to be set against the social and environmental waste and detriment it causes (Scitovsky, 1976; Hirsch, 1977; Talberth et al, 2007) with decades of affluence in itself presenting new challenges to sustaining future well-being (Offer, 2006).

This idea that capitalism, while bringing about wealth, will not necessarily enhance well-being is not a new concern. At the beginning of the twentieth century Newman (1931) recognised that industrialisation had the capacity not only to resolve problems, but also create more. It is perhaps not surprising, then, that his conclusion that positive changes to well-being had been achieved insofar as 'the comfort, contentment and happiness associated with health have been enhanced and increased' (Newman, 1931, p 179) was a little premature. Such a testament to industrialisation has not stood the test of time. Happiness levels have more or less remained stable throughout the twentieth century – in western nations generally, economic prosperity has not led to any greater experience of happiness over the last 50 years (Layard, 2003, 2005).

So if the economists got it wrong, what is the key to well-being? Do all the trappings of modern society – owner-occupation, work, money, 4x4, more money, promotion, bigger house, more money – in fact improve people's well-being? Or does the constant drive to 'achieve' and 'improve' one's lot in a consumer society lead to constant disappointment, where self-perpetuating 'needs' can never be fulfilled?

The assumption that 'more of everything for everyone makes anyone better off' (Little, 1950, p 44) does not hold water where more of everything becomes normalised and where everyone's standard increases at the same rate so that no one will necessarily *feel* better off. Picture: 'if everyone stands on tiptoe no-one gets a better view' (Hirsch, 1977, p 5).

This reflects the social idea that underlying well-being is the inequality in society. There is an increasing general consensus that a sense of well-being does not arise from objective material possessions but from subjective resources and social comparisons. From this viewpoint well-being becomes a function of relative social standing; an expression of comparisons of ourselves to others. The benefits of economic growth – or higher national GDP – then, are misjudged, as satisfaction does not arise from the extra income gained but from the fact that our income increased more than the 'Joneses' (Scitovsky, 1976).

Few people would be shocked to find that poverty is indicative not only of a deprivation of resources but also of a deprivation of well-being. What may come as a surprise, though, is that those who enjoy a higher standard of living are also at risk of an increased likelihood of experiencing reduced subjective well-being – that actual levels of affluence and *feelings* of affluence run in opposite directions. This, according to Campbell et al (1976), is one of the 'quirks of social comparisons' where an increased awareness of alternative circumstances causes people to be more critical of their current position (pp 137–43).

For Hirsch (1977), dissatisfaction is inevitable. Rising standards will fail to bring about happiness where, despite increased effort and rising standards of living, everyone is still only entitled to the same slice from the overall pie. Expectations may rise in line with increased wealth and quality of life, but the limited number of places at the top of the social hierarchy mean the rewards are restricted. People expect some gain in return for their hard work and effort, but instead they are increasingly finding that more resources are needed to maintain the same levels of satisfaction that had previously been gained through fewer resources. So for Hirsch, the principles of economic theory are fundamentally flawed because the material pie keeps on growing while the positional economy is fixed, leading to social waste, frustration and disappointment.

This is further exacerbated where individual efforts are set against a backdrop in which certain sectors of the economy are growing disproportionately faster than others. Increases in GDP per capita imply that everyone in society is better off, but exploration of the evidence at the micro level shows otherwise. For example, although the proportion of homes of a non-decent standard has reduced from nearly half (45%) in 1996, latest figures show a third of all households still live in homes which do not meet the government standard for decent housing (DCLG, 2006a); the proportion of British households living on an income deemed below the official Organisation for Economic Cooperation and Development (OECD) poverty line may have reduced from 26% in 1994/5 to 15% in 2001/2 – but in 2001/2, 11% of households still experienced persistent poverty; and while average incomes rose by 19% between 1994/5 and 2001/2, those in the top income decile saw a 21% increase as compared to 13% for those on the lowest incomes (ONS, 2003).

Clearly, while there are people who are benefiting from economic growth, there are also those who are not. Frank and Cook (1995) take up this argument, suggesting that advances in production methods, communication and information create a 'winner-take-all' market, and a powerful elite who are insulated from competition and are able to set their own terms 'in a world increasingly unrestrained by inhibitions about greed' (Bok (1993) cited in Frank and Cook, 1995, p 6). The difference between first and second place then grows rapidly, where rewards are based on relative rather than absolute performance, and – in line with Hirsch's theory – the attraction of a few highly paid jobs within limited areas of the economy leads to socially inefficient market incentives and wasteful consumption. The active pursuit of advancement has brought about a situation where too many consumers are investing in 'positional goods', creating an 'economic arms race' whereby 'if you don't buy the weapons you are at a disadvantage, but if both sides buy weapons they do worse than if neither had' (Frank and Cook, 1995, p 11).

The key argument here, then, is that despite the underlying assumption that economic growth – in part pursued through consumption behaviour – does not necessarily enhance feelings of well-being, what matters to our health and well-being is the psycho-social impact of an unequal society, as opposed to the absolute material living standards (Wilkinson, 1996). Goods and services are bought not for the utility they may provide in themselves but as a means of achieving an end gain – one that will give one person an advantage over another.

As a consequence we have become trapped on the 'hedonic treadmill' (Brickman and Campbell, 1971), believing that our dissatisfaction and unhappiness will be alleviated by the pursuit of more income and a move up to the next rung of the social ladder. But the fact that the ladder exists – and increasingly the rungs between the top and bottom are becoming wider apart (Orton and Rowlingson, 2007a; Dorling et al, 2007) – dampens the effect of the progress made, and the realisation that there are more rungs to climb leads to disappointment and negative feelings.

What has come to be associated with happiness and satisfaction has, then, become somewhat flawed. Seeking power, success, wealth and status has underestimated what is of true value in life. Increasingly caught up in the rush to reach the next deadline, goal or rung of the ladder, there is never actually the time to enjoy – or perhaps even notice – what has been achieved. So the next question is, if not happiness, what should we be aiming for? The final theme poses the engagement with the 'welfare' idea that well-being is part of (or perhaps should be) the quest for contentment. This idea embraces the notion that well-being has many dimensions – not just wealth, or a single measure of satisfaction or happiness – but is complex in nature, comprising different aspects for different people. Individuals and their perceptions of well-being are based not only on their own current circumstances but on how these circumstances compare with past experiences; the circumstances of those around them; and their expectations of the future – all of which are embedded in the prevailing philosophy and resource availability of the society in which they live. So are people's levels of happiness influenced by the same things throughout their lives? Is the pursuit of happiness a realistic and sustainable goal? Or is the true measure of well-being embedded in a wider set of emotions or feelings of contentment?

Where economic theory aligns consumption to satisfaction, and social theory suggests it is the inequality of societies that makes people unhappy, the rest of this book will unpack the different elements of our lives and ask 'what is important to well-being?' In so doing it will consider the 'welfare' idea. It will argue that money and material goods are not the route to happiness – they are not the only markers of 'success', but success and well-being are bound up in our lives in complex and sometimes surprising ways.

The uncoupling of economic and social advancement has stimulated a renewed interest in what makes people happy or satisfied. Theories have been – and continue to be – developed to try to explain why it is that increased production and consumption has resulted in a stagnation, rather than enhancement, of happiness or satisfaction at the national level. This book provides an explanation for this phenomenon with regard to Great Britain. Firstly, it provides a brief description of historical developments in the analysis and understanding of well-being. Secondly, it describes the findings from empirical research exploring the relevance and importance of various components of people's lives for their well-being. Finally, through drawing together the different themes that emerge, it provides some enlightenment as to why economic development has become detached from psychological fulfilment. The empirical research underpinning this study advances the knowledge on subjective well-being, showing what factors are associated with positive well-being and identifying the circumstances and changes in people's lives that improve (or hinder) their overall quality of life and sense of well-being; and seeks to establish whether the cycle can be broken – is there a point at which intervention can bring about positive changes in individuals' self-reported well-being?

This will be achieved by focusing on the factors influencing positive subjective well-being among the adult population of Great Britain between 1991 and 1999. Britain provides an interesting case study – not least because of the rich source of data available for this country – but also on account of the social and economic change that occurred during this period, associated with a changing political ideology and growing concern over the inequalities fuelled by the dominance of a particular kind of capitalism.

The 1990s brought a change to the political landscape of the United Kingdom. The election of a Labour government – following 18 years of Conservative rule – reflected a change in political ideology, away from a New Right ethos of fragmentation and competitive individualism to a New Labour 'Third Way' of cooperation and coordination (Giddens, 1998). But despite the rhetoric, the system underpinning British politics was still based on a neo-liberal free market economy where increased quality of life was associated with the expansion of the materialist market – a system which came under increasing criticism, since it failed to acknowledge the social limits to growth whereby only a few individuals have the real opportunity to improve their position. The inequalities that existed during the 1990s have already been touched upon in respect of housing conditions and wealth distribution. Britain in fact led and sustained the trend of inequality – the U-turn (Alderson and Nielson, 2002) – in the more developed world, giving precedence to a powerful elite who are insulated from competition and able to set their own terms, leading to soaring executive pay for a few and with little opportunity for those left behind (Frank and Cook, 1995). The disillusionment with the dominance of 'the economic' of society grew increasingly visible during the 1990s, through the development of movements, protests and demonstrations against capitalism and globalisation (Dobson, 2002). This period of the twentieth century thus marked a shift in attitudes globally that was galvanised by a common enemy – the capitalist system. The boom of the 1980s was followed by the 1990s recession (Figure 1.1) which, together with the collapse of 'eastern' economies that had adopted western-style capitalism, fuelled concerns with the established political system.

Market mania was in retreat – people became critical of the excesses of the 1980s, rejecting free market ideology and privatisation. In 1996 a group of around 10,000 demonstrators occupied a stretch of the M41 in west London – organised by a new group established in the UK called 'Reclaim The Streets' – an event that had gone global by the end of the 1990s (Dobson, 2002). Mass demonstrations, disrupting establishment meetings and protesting against international companies

Figure 1.1: Retail Price Index (annual percentage change) 1979–99

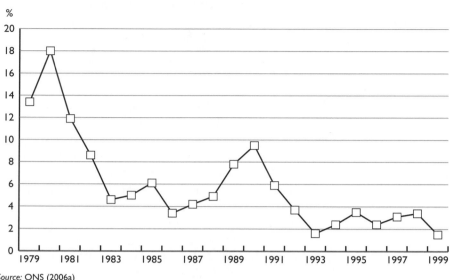

Source: ONS (2006a)

who put 'profits before people' were increasingly seen as the 'accepted method of struggle' against a common enemy, the capitalist system (Dobson, 2002; Rees, 2001). At the same time the insulation around the powerful elite (Frank and Cook, 1995) was being chipped away by angry protests against boardroom excess (Court, 2003; Stewart, 2003; Treanor, 2003).

This disillusionment with capitalism and increased concern over the damage that excessive consumption was causing to society and the environment not only manifested itself in highly visible public demonstrations, but also adapted through a more subtle – but nonetheless visible – approach as individuals were collectively making decisions about simplifying their lives and replacing economic and materialistic desires with satisfying and meaningful values (Voluntary Simplicity,[1] 2002). Out of this demonstrative period of protest, a post-consumer ethos was emerging against a backdrop of inequality. Identities were being redesigned, based on environmental and post-economic concerns and a 'cultivation of non-materialistic sources of satisfaction and meaning' (Etzioni, 1998, p 620).

As part of this simplifying movement individuals sought means of improving the quality of their own lives, and of those around them, through adopting alternative methods to those espoused by the economic system. Although established in the United States, a global phenomenon was growing as people began to voluntarily simplify aspirations and desires (Voluntary Simplicity, 2002), an ideology that was not overlooked by people in the UK as schemes flourished towards the end of the twentieth century. The growing popularity of Local Exchange and Trading Systems (LETS) saw the establishment of a dedicated website in 1991 that provided guidelines for setting up local exchange schemes (LetsLinkUK, 2006) which operate on the principle of 'time banking' – using voluntary time as an alternative currency (Parker, 2002).[2] For other people the attraction was to be associated with a community that emphasises the spiritual and environmental aspects of working and living (Cook, 2002)[3] – means by which people were, and still are, seeking to improve their well-being by being willing to change their attitudes towards their 'real' needs and the means by which they acquire resources and use them.

The establishment and development of such schemes implies that alternative measures of success are now being sought outside the realms of the economic panacea. While public protest since the 1990s has made such feelings visible, and the introduction of alternative monetary systems and lifestyles gives a certain pragmatism to such ideals, the difficult issue is how to measure the change in attitudes to what is of value in life, and ultimately what influences subjective well-being.

The rest of the book seeks to address these issues. Chapter 2 begins by addressing the two key strands of concern; it charts the historical development of economic and psychological understandings of well-being, and sets out the sociology that underpins these theories. This chapter also updates the debates, turning attention to the more recent preoccupation with positive psychology and happiness. The chapter argues that early theories were restrictive in their understanding of well-being, through a tendency to focus on negatives – namely, deprivation, exclusion and poverty. However, as will be discussed, economic and psychological research has made an important contribution to how well-being can be seen in a positive as well as a negative state – and they are not necessarily the mirror image of each other. Levels of satisfaction are not just related to objective conditions, but involve a complex process of perceptions of past and present circumstances, and the opportunities available as compared with other social groups. Well-being has become synonymous with quality of life and the possession of resources necessary for the satisfaction of needs, wants, desires and participation in activities enabling personal development, and self-actualisation and satisfactory comparison between oneself and others (Shin and Johnson, 1978). This chapter will also show how these conceptualisations have, in turn, been borne out by the development of comprehensive sets of indicators by which well-being can be measured both spatially and temporally.

Chapter 2, in short, shows that while steps have been taken towards understanding individual well-being in terms of more than material wealth, the tendency to define positive well-being as an absence of negative measures (namely, poverty) paints us half the picture. In this picture, positive well-being is secured by tackling the root causes of social exclusion rather than enhancing resilience or cultivating contentment. In order to bring about an improvement in the well-being of society, it is necessary to understand not only the circumstances of those with poor well-being, but also the circumstances through which positive well-being emerges. The focus on poor well-being becomes a 'heuristic', a shorthand description for all people in the same circumstances. However, my research shows that there are some surprising circumstances within which well-being is experienced. This is the theme of the next two chapters of the book.

Chapters 3 and 4 present findings from new empirical research on the adult population of Great Britain – defined here as those aged 25 and over.[4] The data are contained in the first nine waves (1991–99) of the British Household Panel Survey (BHPS), which are described in detail in Chapter 3. This chapter also explains how subjective well-being has been conceptualised and operationalised within this research. It explains the distribution of subjective well-being over nine years at the national level before examining in finer detail the circumstances under which individuals report positive subjective well-being. While Chapter 3 describes the conditions under which positive well-being is experienced, Chapter 4 describes in detail the factors associated with maintaining and promoting subjective well-being. It reports the findings of new statistical analyses with reference to socio-economic, social, health and spatial factors as well as levels of satisfaction with different aspects of life. The findings suggest that improving and maintaining high levels of well-being are not directly associated with affluence. So what are the factors associated with positive well-being? Do they change over time? Can changes in circumstances change well-being outcomes?

One of the main problems for this kind of empirical research is the vast amount of data that needs to be analysed and subsequently reported. The findings presented in Chapters 3 and 4 are based on a combination of more than 80 variables, for over 9,000 individuals across nine years. Following Tufte's (1997) ideas, the results have been presented in 'friendly' diagrammatic formats within the text, with the full statistical results reserved for the Appendix. Tufte (1997) suggests data can serve as an image where the idea, word and drawing add up to a coherent and vivid whole. The act of arranging information also becomes part of the process of interpretation, giving new insights into the data. In line with Tufte's thinking, the images used in the analysis chapters are designed as an aide memoire, and in no way are they meant to trivialise the importance of the statistical findings. The images have been designed to provoke an emotional response to otherwise 'dry' data. Only the minimum of data necessary to emphasise the key findings is presented; in this way the contrasts are emphasised and 'the mind is able to actively work to detect and generate links, clusters and matches . . . small differences can send clear signals' (Tufte, 1997, p 80).

Figure 1.2 is an example of the imagery used. The image on the left represents only those factors that significantly increase the odds of having high subjective well-being and are represented by someone who is on top of it all and can sit back and relax. The image on the right represents only those factors which significantly reduce the odds of having high subjective well-being and are represented by someone who feels everything is stacking up on top of them and they struggle to keep it all together.

The final two chapters (5 and 6) review the findings and draw conclusions that pave the way for well-being research. Chapter 5 sets out some of the principal issues that have emerged through studying high subjective well-being directly,

Figure 1.2: Example of the presentation of results

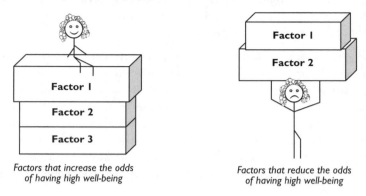

Factors that increase the odds
of having high well-being

Factors that reduce the odds
of having high well-being

and considers the implications for the direction of future well-being research. It will address theoretical and methodological aspects of constructing a measure of well-being, suggesting that improvements at the national level will only be possible where subjective well-being is supported by social justice and not driven by economic growth.

Returning to the first two themes of this book – the economic and social ideas – Chapter 6 opens up the debate on the 'myth' of economic progress and national well-being. It turns the spotlight onto social comparisons and what we perceive as success, considering as it does the implications for enhancing well-being. So, if economic measures do not capture well-being, then what should a measure of well-being look like? Chapter 6 answers this question by revisiting the 'welfare' theme. It addresses the complex make-up of well-being and considers whether happiness and satisfaction are what we should be striving for, or whether there is a more realistic and sustainable ideal.

The book may raise more questions than it is possible to answer. However, through researching positive well-being directly, it aims to go some way towards gaining a better understanding of a social phenomenon that we all aspire to, but empirically know little about.

Notes

1. 'Voluntary simplicity' refers to the choice, out of free will (rather than being coerced by poverty, government austerity programmes or being imprisoned) to limit expenditures on consumer goods and services, and to cultivate non-materialistic sources of satisfaction and meaning (Etzioni, 1998, p 620). A Voluntary Simplicity Movement became established in 1996, with a dedicated website at: www.simpleliving.net/main/.

2. In Gorbals, Glasgow, a new currency has been devised called the Lipton. Based on the time-banking scheme that was established in the UK in 1997, Liptons can be earned through doing voluntary work in the community. One hour of voluntary work equals one Lipton, which can then be exchanged to buy back an hour of someone else's time.

The scheme has reportedly led to greater bonds of friendship and trust, and improved self-esteem for those involved. The fact that everyone's time is given the same value means that people can gain access to services (for example plumbers, carpenters, childcare) that they might not otherwise be able to afford under conventional monetary exchanges.

3. The Findhorn Foundation, near Inverness, Scotland was established in 1962. It currently consists of a community of around 500 people whose aim is to live a more spiritual life and devise ways of putting less strain on the environment. The community has gained an international reputation, providing consultancy services on energy-saving methods, spiritual education, and developing human resources. Since it was established there has been growing interest in and commitment to these philosophies. During the 1990s the number of people and organisations associated with Findhorn began to outgrow the Foundation itself, culminating in the creation of the New Foundation Association in 1999 (www.findhorn.org).

4. This is mainly because it is considered that different factors will be related to the subjective well-being of adults as compared to those of children or young people. People under 25 may still be in education or experiencing the transition from young person to adult, and this has implications for their subjective well-being – not only in respect of bodily changes, but also their changing identity as they experience work, relationships or living away from parents for the first time (Jones, 2002; Seavers, 2002). As such, it is considered that the subjective well-being of this younger age group may be affected by different factors from those aged 25 and over. Many of the factors selected for analysis in the research reported here would not be applicable to those under 25, and analysis of their subjective well-being would benefit from separate research containing a different set of variables from those selected here.

TWO

The enigma of well-being?

A light shade had been pulled down between the Black community and all things white, but one could see through it enough to develop a fear-admiration-contempt for the white 'things' – white folks' cars and white glistening houses and their children and their women. But above all, their wealth that allowed them to waste was the most enviable.

(Maya Angelou, 2001, pp 49–50)

Introduction

Money matters, but for those fortunate enough to live in the modern developed 'western' world, it is no guarantee of well-being. Over the past 50 years happiness has reportedly not increased in line with GDP (Layard, 2003) and several theories have been developed that seek to explain this poor relationship. The growing despondency with the consuming capitalist philosophy of the 1980s fuelled a change in British and other attitudes into the 1990s and new lifestyles and measures of success were – and still are – being sought.

The idea of measuring successful – positive – outcomes developed from the psychological perspective of self-actualisation (Maslow, 1954). This was the idea that positive well-being was derived from the fulfilment of goals that lie along a hierarchy from basic needs to desires, a key concept being that engaging in activities that lead towards goal fulfilment in themselves may be deemed intrinsically rewarding, giving rise to the positive emotional outcomes associated with the experience of 'flow' – a sense of well-being that follows from reflecting on what has been achieved in doing an activity (Csikszentmihalyi and Rathunde, 1992; Csikszentmihalyi, 1999). These ideas are based on the 'eudaimonic' perspective of well-being and draw upon an Aristotelian view – that living a life of virtue is of greater worth than seeking out pleasure – the focus being on meaning and self-realisation and the extent to which a person is fully functioning (Ryan and Deci, 2001).

An alternative approach is the 'hedonic view' based on the philosophy of Aristippus – that the maximising of pleasure is the fundamental goal in life and means of achieving happiness (Ryan and Deci, 2001). Based on this idea the notion of well-being has become defined as the attainment of pleasure and the avoidance of negative emotion or pain – the components of happiness (Diener and Lucas, 1999). From this early philosophical theory there developed an increase in studies concerned with global elements of 'general happiness' as they relate to psychological, mental or subjective well-being (Gurin et al, 1960; Bradburn and Caplowitz, 1965; Diener, 1984; Veenhoven, 1984; Cheng and Furnham, 2003). What such studies began to show was that positive and negative feeling states, while not being correlated, were both individually correlated to general measures of happiness (Bradburn and Caplowitz, 1965). Further studies have supported these findings and concluded that predictors of happiness have implications for the development of individuals' subjective well-being in respect of sociability and activity (Costa and McCrae, 1980; Argyle and Lu, 1990; Cooper et al, 1992), relationships (Argyle, 1987; Furnham, 1991) and self-esteem (Campbell, 1981; Baumeister et al, 2003), and that how people feel about positive and negative aspects of their lives contributes to how they feel about life as a whole (Andrews and Withey, 1976).

Happiness as a measure of subjective well-being or as a focus for the ultimate good in life has, however, been disputed. For example, Ryff and Keyes (1995), adapting the argument put forward by Becker (1992), suggest that feelings of happiness may arise in people who otherwise live 'ugly, unjust and pointless lives' (Becker, 1992, p 725); while separate research shows that most people report themselves to be happy (Taylor and Brown, 1988) even when they have been abused or unemployed (Diener, 1993), leading to a questioning of the 'scientific attention lavished on happiness and positive effect, particularly at the expense of other aspects of positive functioning' (Ryff and Keyes, 1995, p 725). The main argument against using 'happiness levels' is that it only measures a part of subjective well-being, being limited to a subjective or emotional element related to the attainment of desires. As such, it does not address the more functional aspects of well-being such as autonomy, self-acceptance, mastery and personal growth (Ryff and Keyes, 1995).

Despite such criticisms, studies of happiness are once again 'coming of age' with a maturity associated with a new positive psychology. There is 'a proliferation of new measures, based on clear definitions, strong theoretical frameworks and rigorous methodology' (Kashdan, 2004, p 1225), further supported by research that shows there is a neural basis (that is, objective measure) of positive emotion (Davidson, 1992; Davidson et al, 2000). Happiness studies are no longer the preserve of philosophers and therapists but have become a discipline in their own right (Bond, 2003). More recent themes seek to measure the satisfaction individuals derive from their behaviour but attempt to set this within their social and psychological environment, which in turn determines the stressors to which people are exposed and the resources they have available to cope with such stress. As such, new measures combine both *conditions* and *experience*. In contrast to previous methods, the new happiness measures are extending beyond the boundaries of happiness, satisfaction or quality of life and are merging to provide more holistic measures of subjective well-being.

Although there is no overall consensus on whether 'happiness' or 'self-fulfilment' is the best measure of subjective well-being, what these arguments have developed is the principle that subjective well-being is not simply the opposite to psychological disorder, or the absence of negative factors, but is a multifaceted entity in its own right, arising from complex relationships involving both the individual and their environment. Maslow's hierarchy of needs suggests that motivation is the key to self-actualisation and that we need to study the 'relationship of all motivations to each other' (Maslow, 1954, p 69). In addition, although an individualistic model, the experience of self-actualisation is conditional on certain stable forces in society being met; freedom, justice, honesty and orderliness must exist in order for basic needs to be satisfied (Figure 2.1). An important element in achieving positive subjective well-being, therefore, is an ability to manage one's life in respect of ones surrounding world (Ryff and Keyes, 1995) by immunising against bad fortune through having the ability to understand events and be in control of the damage they do (Becker, 1992).

Modern concepts of well-being are beginning to address these complexities, in recognition of individual lifestyle choices set within the context of personal, political and social controls. The Oxford Happiness Questionnaire developed by Hills and Argyle (2002), for example, not only taps into people's emotional state, but also addresses issues related to psychological well-being such as ability to make decisions, feeling satisfied, being healthy, showing an interest in other people, having a sense of life achievement and being in control. Seligman has devised a questionnaire of 'Authentic Happiness' which also measures happiness beyond present mood state by tapping into cognitive evaluations of satisfaction and appreciation with the whole of ones life (Seligman, 2002). The European Union (EU) and OECD are developing programmes with the aim of monitoring

Figure 2.1: Hierarchy of needs based on Maslow's theory of self-actualisation

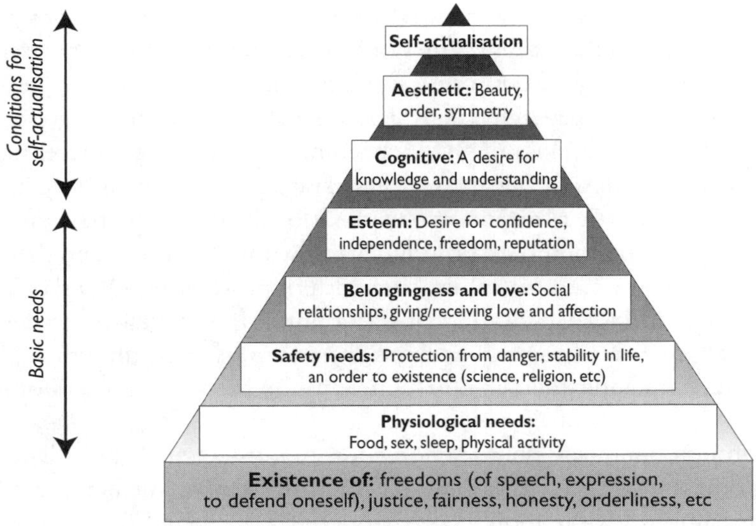

Source: Maslow (1954)

and analysing current state, and changes, of living conditions and the quality of life in different nations.[1] The European Values Survey (first carried out in 1981) and the World Values Survey established in 1990 contain data from nationally representative surveys on sociocultural and political change, and have produced evidence on what people want out of life, their values and beliefs,[2] while the Australian Unity Well-being Index is described as 'a new barometer of Australians' satisfaction with their lives, and life in Australia' and is designed as a 'complementary indicator of national performance and progress to the dominant economic measures' (Cummins et al, 2003, p 1).

In order to understand the rationale behind such developments, it is interesting to consider the wider conceptualisations of well-being and how the factors underpinning its operationalisation have influenced which measures have been selected. This chapter considers these themes in the light of the psychological and economic underpinnings of well-being and the sociology that qualifies them. It also sets the scene for the conceptualisation and measurement of well-being within these different disciplines. Finally, it describes how new methodological tools within the social sciences have enabled more complex and detailed analysis, adding further definition to the character of well-being. It does this by addressing the economics of well-being; the politicisation of well-being; the question of how well-being has become associated with identity and choice; the role of stress and coping; and looks at social well-being as a relative concept.

The economics of well-being

Traditionally measures of national well-being have been developed in the vein of 'hedonic' philosophy. Within the utilitarian theory of welfare economics there is a clear focus on the maximising of pleasure. Based on Jeremy Bentham's 'greatest happiness principle', where 'when one seeks to maximise those satisfactions which are the effects of economic causes, then one is maximising a part of happiness' (Little, 1950, p 8), utility is taken to mean satisfaction.

This theory assumes that individuals derive satisfaction from the goods and services they buy, and that this satisfaction becomes reflected in the prices people are willing to pay for those goods and services. Based on two principles, utilitarian theory further assumes that consumers behave rationally (whatever the consumer does is in their own best interests, otherwise they would not do it) and that they are maximisers (they aim to gain as much wealth or possessions – translated into satisfaction – as possible). By viewing satisfaction in this way, well-being became conceptualised as consumer activity and was deemed measurable through national accounts which include measures of consumption, namely, Gross Domestic Product (GDP).

To this end, the unmeasurable phenomenon of satisfaction (and well-being), was inferred from observable measures of economic activity. Furthermore, there was an expectation that the more people bought the more satisfied they would be, implying that economic growth (an increase in GDP) would bring about increased national (and individual) well-being. However, not everyone benefited from economic growth to the same extent and, far from there being an equal advancement, economic development became synonymous with increased inequality, with the focus of well-being turning to those who were falling behind – that is, those deemed to be in poverty.

Set within the context of a prevailing ideology of laissez-faire and the optimism associated with material progress (Rose, 1972), these early statistics – collected through social surveys – revealed that the economic growth associated with industrialisation and urbanisation had a negative impact on society – bringing mass poverty and health and housing problems. So despite developments in the economic realm, research was showing that poverty was evident in the 'midst of urban plenty' (Pfautz, 1967, p 6) and the plight of the industrial poor – revealed by pioneering city studies (Mayhew, 1861; Rowntree, 1902; Booth, 1902/3) – showed the inadequacy of the established philosophy in solving such problems. With this concern there developed an awareness on the part of the state of the need to identify trends and causation of poverty.

The existence of poverty, despite economic progress, led to the fundamental principles of economic theory being called into question and social (and government) concerns turned towards those whose well-being was not increasing, in particular the activity of those people whose consumption patterns were below those deemed adequate for sustaining a reasonable standard of living. This aspect of well-being was first captured by Seebohm Rowntree through the creation of an objective (absolute) measurement of poverty – a poverty line (Rowntree, 1902). The poverty line was based on the 'minimum [income] necessary to maintain families' in relation to food, rent and household sundries (Rowntree, 1902, p x), and personal and social expenditure (Rowntree, 1941; Rowntree and Lavers, 1951). This correlation between income and standard of living dominated conceptions of poverty in the first half of the twentieth century (Bradshaw, 2001), with the abolition of want (poverty) being achievable through economic means and the provision of 'adequate' income (Beveridge, 1942). As such, economic concerns with well-being measured a deviation away from a 'normal' or acceptable standard of living, and were in fact measuring deprivation.

During the latter half of the twentieth century, however, concepts of poverty were changing. There was a focus on citizenship and social exclusion, recognising that poverty constituted more than a 'physical lack of basic necessities' (Bradshaw, 2001), but was socially determined and represented a lack of resources that prevented participation in society. Developments in the measurement and operationalisation of poverty moved towards a need to address social as well as material circumstances, whereby the alleviation of poverty was concerned with an enhancement of conditions that brought about improvements in subjective well-being.

The key concept of the economic approach is that well-being (or rather its absence) can be accounted for in terms of economic indicators, and that a lack of well-being can be overcome through adjusting economic conditions. This approach does not, however, take account of the different circumstances in which people experience poverty. In line with the social idea, poverty may be an expression of comparisons with others as much as it is about actual levels of wealth. Not only does poverty undermine well-being, but so too does inequality.

In developing the work of Rowntree, Peter Townsend gave rise to a notion of a relative measure of poverty. Townsend argued that people's experiences of poverty differed according to how their needs were conditioned by the society in which they lived. Poverty represented a 'lack of resources to participate in activities and obtain the living conditions and amenities which are customary, or are at least widely encouraged or approved, in the societies to which [people] belong' (Townsend, 1979, p 31). Three types of deprivation could therefore be experienced by degree: objective (actual conditions); normative (what is acceptable or not acceptable in a society); and subjective (feelings, perceptions of poverty) (Townsend, 1979).

Essentially, what Townsend showed was that income (a purely economic-based approach) as a measure of standard of living was flawed. As such, he sought to measure individuals' resources as opposed to just income and identify a style of living as opposed to consumption patterns, thereby exploring standard of living in terms of quality as opposed to quantity measures (Townsend, 1979).

Following on from Townsend's original analysis of poverty in the UK during the 1970s, three further studies were conducted during the 1980s (Mack and Lansley, 1985) and 1990s (Gordon and Pantazis, 1998; Gordon et al, 2000), which showed the state of poverty in Britain based on the concept of 'subjective' poverty – so for the first time lay perceptions (as opposed to academic or politically based notions) were the means of measuring poverty by identifying socially perceived necessities as determined by the public's view.

Analysis of all four of these studies (Table 2.1) shows a clear difference over time between the number and type of items perceived as necessities, a fact that would lend support to poverty being a relative concept. Gordon et al (2000) report that differences between the surveys not only represent changes in taste and technology but are also indicative of changes in attitudes towards social needs and social exclusion. For example, in 1999 fewer items were chosen as necessities by young people (16–30 years) than by older people, suggesting that young people have become less materialistic. Also, more respondents thought a hobby or leisure activity, or having friends/family round for a meal, was a necessity in 1999 than did in 1983 and 1990, suggesting that social activity and social participation are seen as important elements in life (Gordon et al, 2000 (table 12, p 44)). Gordon et al (2000) conclude that such differences – this change in what is valued in society – 'show how exclusion is not just about a reduction in income but also includes the effects of not having social interaction or participation, namely, *factors important to subjective well-being*' (p 54, emphasis added). These ideas developed the understanding that well-being may be influenced by much broader aspects of individuals' lives than a narrow focus on financial resources, and led to the

Table 2.1: Changes in perception of necessities 1979–99

Poverty in the UK 1979	Breadline Britain 1983	Breadline Britain 1990	Poverty and social exclusion 1999
Indoor amenities: toilet, sink, bath + cooker	Indoor toilet and bath (not shared) Self-contained accommodation	Indoor toilet and bath (not shared)	
	Heating to warm living areas	Heating to warm living areas	Heating to warm living areas
	Damp-free home	Damp-free home	Damp-free home
	Bed for everyone in household; each child aged 10+ of different sex in own bedroom	Bed for everyone in household; bedroom for each child aged 10+ of different sex	Beds and bedding for everyone
	Carpets in living/ bedrooms	Carpets in living/ bedrooms	Carpets in living/bedrooms
		A decent state of decoration in the home	Money to keep home in a decent state of decoration and replace worn-out furniture
Fridge	Fridge	Fridge	Fridge and deep freezer or fridge freezer
	Washing machine	Washing machine	Washing machine
		Dishwasher	
	TV	TV	TV
	Telephone	Telephone	Telephone
		Video	
		Computer	
			Repair or replace broken electrical goods
		Insurance for contents of dwelling	Insurance for contents of dwelling
	Garden		
	Car	Car	
		Regular savings of £10 per month for 'rainy days'	Regular savings of £10 per month for 'rainy days' or retirement
			A small amount of money to spend on self weekly, not on family
Relative or friends to visit (or visit them) once a month	Friends/family for meal monthly	Friends/family for meal monthly	Friends/family to visit (or visit them) once a month
	Public transport for one's needs	Fares to visit friends 4 times a year	Visit friends or family in hospital
			Visits to school, eg sports day, and collect children from school
Afternoon/night out fortnightly	Night out fortnightly	Night out fortnightly	
		Restaurant meal monthly	

(continued)

Table 2.1: Changes in perception of necessities 1979–99 (continued)

Poverty in the UK 1979	Breadline Britain 1983	Breadline Britain 1990	Poverty and social exclusion 1999
Children's birthday parties	Celebration on special occasions, eg Christmas, birthdays	Celebration on special occasions	Celebration on special occasions and attend weddings/funerals
	Present for friends/family once per year	Present for friends/family once per year	Present for friends/family once per year
	Hobby/leisure activity	Hobby/leisure activity	Hobby/leisure activity
Annual holiday away from home	One week's holiday away from home without relatives	Annual week's holiday away from home without relatives	Annual week's holiday away from home without relatives
		Holidays abroad annually	
Children's friends round once per month	Children's friends round once per fortnight	Children's friends round once per fortnight	
	Outings for children once per week	Outings for children once per week	
		Child's participation in out-of-school activities	
		Child's music/dance/ sports lessons	
	Toys and leisure equipment for children, eg bicycle	Toys and leisure equipment for children	
Fresh meat most days	Meat/fish every other day	Meat/fish (or vegetarian equivalent) every other day	Meat/fish (or vegetarian equivalent) every other day
At least one cooked meal per day and cooked breakfast most days	Hot meals per day (3 for children, 2 for adults)	Hot meals per day (3 for children, 2 for adults)	2 meals a day
Sunday joint most weeks	Roast joint or its equivalent	Weekly roast/vegetarian equivalent	Weekly roast/vegetarian equivalent
		Daily fresh fruit and vegetables	Daily fresh fruit and vegetables
	Warm waterproof coat + 2 pairs all-weather shoes	Warm waterproof coat + 2 pairs all-weather shoes	Warm waterproof coat + 2 pairs all-weather shoes
	New, not second-hand clothes	New, not second-hand clothes	
	A 'best outfit' for special occasions	A 'best outfit' for special occasions	An outfit for special occasions
			Appropriate clothes for job interviews
	Dressing gown	Dressing gown	
	Packet of cigarettes every other day	Packet of cigarettes every other day	
			Dictionary
			Medicines prescribed by doctor

Sources: Townsend, 1979; Mack and Lansley, 1985; Gordon and Pantazis, 1998; Gordon et al, 2000.

continued development of measures that sought to capture the increasingly changing condition of people's lives.

Where it was established that inequalities existed in society at the beginning of the twentieth century, recent research suggests that little progress has been made. Economic growth over the second half of the twentieth century has apparently not been matched by increased levels of happiness (Layard, 2003, 2005). It is recognised that wealth and resources are not equally distributed throughout society and the differences in well-being are being understood within a relative framework. Actual income levels were (and still are) deemed a poor indicator of well-being and what becomes important is how we compare our circumstances with those of other people, whereby relative (or perceived) wealth is more likely to be associated with variations in well-being.

Although much attention has been paid to standards of living in respect of those who fall below an acceptable level, relatively little attention has been given to measuring affluence, or those whose resources are well above an acceptable standard of living. It is only through focusing on both extremes of the economic spectrum that an understanding of inequality – and how it undermines well-being – can be developed. In recognition of this Townsend (and more recently Orton and Rowlingson, 2007a) argues that any measure of relative poverty needs to include the rich as well as the poor. Through the acquisition of wealth, some groups in society secure a disproportionately large share of available resources, putting them in a position of power where they can influence public attitude as to what is an acceptable standard of living, and consequently what constitutes deprivation:

> The rich are not only favoured by the system, and exploit it. They actively shape its standards and values. They set fashions which become the styles sought after by the mass of the population. Over a period of time luxuries which they enjoy become the necessities of society …They foster the values which preserve their own status and induce deference. These values are values which condone, if not positively uphold, degrees of inequality and poverty.
>
> (Townsend, 1979, p 367)

Although research is seeking to develop a measure of subjective poverty in terms of perceived necessities, this of itself is encased in an economic paradigm of necessity as determined by the affluent. Where economic growth raises standards, this also raises the 'norm' of what is acceptable (Frank and Cook, 1995), so that while measurement against a socially determined norm is a legitimate consideration when measuring poverty, it should also be noted that it can create a 'false sense of poverty' where the comparisons are being made against a 'norm' based on excessive comfort. People may consider themselves poor by comparison against those who have gone beyond consumption for necessity to consuming luxuries, to the point where their needs are saturated (Scitovsky, 1976).

Thirty years later, such arguments still hold true. It is suggested that desired standards of living among average households have risen so far above the actual standards affordable by those on average incomes that people feel constantly deprived of the 'good life' (Hamilton, 2003). The limited understanding of relative living standards means that *feelings* of poverty run higher than levels measured through other observable means such as economic resources (Bradshaw, 2001). Wealth then becomes the 'social problem' because it causes poverty (Orton and Rowlingson, 2007a); poverty and insecurity are not discrete issues but arise through the existence of inequality and a sense of injustice that undermines well-being.

The discrepancies between *feelings* and *observable* measures suggest that social welfare and well-being are more complex entities than a binary – affluent (well-being)/poverty (ill-being) – divide. Well-being is a function of relationships and comparisons with domains other than economics. The traditional focus on economic progress measured as GDP is, arguably, only indicative of changes in one subsystem and 'it cannot be assumed that a positive movement in the economic sub-system results in a positive movement of other sub-systems' (Clarke and Islam, 2002, p 4). Increases in economic growth may mean more is produced and consumed; however – as discussed in Chapter 1 – it does not necessarily follow that everyone is better off. Developments are not evenly distributed between or within countries, and where economic progress is evident more money or resources may be needed to maintain the same position in society.

The standard of living may rise over a given period, but if everyone's standard increases at the same rate, then no one will necessarily *feel* better off. Where progress and advancement in society means moving to a higher place compared to those around you, this unsettles economic theory, since satisfaction will depend on a person's comparative position and not on the utility associated with consumption. So while increased GDP per capita gives the impression that everyone is better off – not everyone is (or perceives they are) benefiting to the same extent.

A system that relies on material growth will not necessarily realise an increase in well-being for all individuals where the stratification of a society is fixed (Chapter 1). As individuals rise up the social ladder in the name of economic progress, this leads to an increased demand – and overcrowding – for a limited number of opportunities. The conclusion of this line of thought is that growth – represented as GDP – as a measure of well-being is too restrictive, since it does not take into consideration those factors which occur outside of the economic market. The costs of pollution and the need to offset these against economic production are well documented (Pigou, 1920; Coase, 1960; Turner et al, 1994; Mather and Chapman, 1995; Begg et al, 1997); however, less obvious are the social costs of inefficient consumption patterns (Klein, 2001) associated with economic growth that can also be detrimental to subjective well-being.

GDP as a measure of social well-being is therefore limited (or even 'hopeless' (Layard, 2003)) since it does not take into account the difference between negative and positive outcomes of economic activity (Clarke and Islam, 2002). And although Clarke and Islam (2002) argue that GDP could only become a

—

measure of societies' well-being where it is adjusted to take account of the other subsystems of society – namely the social, environmental, political and spiritual domains – this of itself would be limited, since not all aspects of well-being lend themselves to association with a monetary value.

Despite awareness of the multifactoral nature of inequalities in society there has still been a tendency for research to focus on the economic aspects of material disadvantage rather than the psychological or social impact of changing circumstances, whereby well-being has become politicised in terms of economic growth. However, some areas of research are addressing this bias and are working towards valuing quality of life and well-being as opposed to focusing on economic progress alone and its associated negative consequences. Well-being is synonymous not only with the possession of resources necessary for the satisfaction of individual needs, wants, desires and participation in activities enabling personal development and self-actualisation, but also takes account of satisfactory comparison between oneself and others (Shin and Johnson, 1978).

Where measures are derived from market activity, this fails to capture the full breadth of well-being experience, since pleasure can be derived from things that are not exchanged within an economic arena. Good health, social interaction, non-polluted air/water are all aspects of life that can enhance well-being, but they tend to be forgotten where income and purchasing power are deemed to raise standards of living by which well-being can be inferred. The criticism of utilitarian economics has given recognition to these limitations and the idea of 'social costs' has been developed and incorporated into welfare economics, leading to an increased need for a whole variety of social factors to be measured (Carley, 1981).

Factors other than individuals' self-reported levels of happiness or satisfaction need to be considered if we are to fully understand individual well-being states. Such factors are seeping into the policy arena, where steps are being taken to account for the relatively static state of national well-being despite increases in national (economic) prosperity. During the late 1980s the King of Bhutan proclaimed that the ultimate purpose of his government was to promote the happiness of the people, declaring that 'Gross National Happiness was more important than Gross National Product', and gave happiness precedence over economic prosperity (Thinley, 1999).

But such national interest is not only limited to societies following the Buddhist spiritual philosophy. Economists and policy advisers in the UK are also turning the tide on the 'myth of economic progress', arguing for the development of an alternative to GDP as a measure of national progress (NEF, 2004). The think-tank the New Economics Foundation argues for the development of a new 'Measure of Domestic Progress (MDP)' to replace traditional measures of GDP, which reflects progress towards sustainable development including economic progress, environmental costs, resource depletion and social factors. It suggests that life satisfaction is a valid measure of human welfare, arguing that qualitative measures of subjective well-being are a 'useful and valid way of assessing some aspects of social progress' (NEF, 2004, p 5). Within the London School of Economics, Bentham's philosophy provides ample justification for the use of happiness measures since 'happiness matters because it is what people want' (Layard, 2003, p 11). Layard argues that 'people concerned with policy can (and should) revert to the task of maximising the sum of human subjective well-being based on a steadily improving social science' (Layard, 2003, p 3). Happiness depends on much more than consumption or purchasing power, and a philosophy of life should be pursued that encourages security and production of relationships, and discourages self-defeating work and the search for status (Layard, 2003, 2004, 2005; Offer, 2006; Jordan, 2007). Within the British government the Cabinet Office has raised the issue of the 'paradoxical effects of income', whereby years of economic growth have not led to equal growth in life satisfaction (Donovan et al, 2002). However, as Donovan et al (2002) acknowledge, this is an area of 'young literature' and there remain many unanswered questions about what factors are associated with life satisfaction and how they interact with each other.

Despite such progress, the pre-occupation with happiness and satisfaction represents a limitation of the economic approach, which prevents it embracing a wider and perhaps more desirable notion of well-being – namely, contentment. A measurement that accounts for how inequality provokes a sense of injustice and exclusion at all levels of the wealth spectrum needs to incorporate the notion that perceptions of circumstances, and satisfaction with them, are related not just to the observable environment but to experiences and opportunities compared with other social groups.

The politicisation of risk and well-being

As alluded to in the previous section, positive well-being is increasingly seen as an important political goal – in some sense an entitlement of citizenship. Within the policy arena this has been pursued through a 'disease prevention' paradigm evidenced in the public health movements of the early part of the twentieth century and later in the lifestyle/behaviour approach to prevention. Understandings of health have moved from a focus purely on ill health to comparing degrees of healthiness, embracing as it does the notion of positive health as it relates to the wider concept of well-being (Cameron et al, 2006).

The idea that well-being is an individual – as well as national – responsibility emerged within the political sphere of the nineteenth century amid concerns (which prompted debate) over the extent to which state provision could – or could not – secure welfare. As the means of production (and economic responsibility) transferred from the family unit to the owners of industry, the population became the concern of political scrutiny in the name of economic progress. Following the war and economic depression early in the twentieth century came a need to exert political control and intervention in the existing laissez-faire regime. Individuals became the concern of the state as governments sought information (through collection of statistics) on the economic welfare of their nations (Carley, 1981), and because of concerns about the demands being made on limited (government) resources.

The earliest concerns of 'well-being' emerged in respect to public health, particularly through the work of the Poor Law Commission (1832) and the economic strain of the poor, which established the connection between poverty and ill health (Baggott, 1991). By the nineteenth century a greater understanding was developing of the relationship between people's environment and the state of their health. Reports such as those of Chadwick in 1842, Booth (1902–03) and Rowntree (1902) established the link between physical environment and disease, paving the way for the Public Health Acts (1848, 1872, 1875) and subsequent public policy in relation to sanitation, food quality, housing, mother and child welfare, and workplace health and safety (Baggott, 1991; Jones, 1994). The initial focus was on public health, but this began to embrace the wider aspects of the conditions in which people functioned, whereby the underpinnings of a healthy existence lie within the home, work and community.

Through a focus on public health, research began to show that health was as much about the different living conditions – cultural, environmental, work and social (Dahlgren and Whitehead, 1991) – to which people were exposed as it was about their physiology. As interest spread into these different areas of life, so the means by which society was observed increased. Not only was there a continued interest in those who were ill, but new concerns developed over those who had the potential to become ill. New surveillance methods developed in the late nineteenth and early twentieth century led to a reduction of the binary separation that existed in the eighteenth century between the 'abnormal and observed' and 'normal and unobserved', as public health concerned itself not only with mapping ill people within their locality but also with identifying the potentially ill (Armstrong, 1983). Understandings of health began to move from a notion of disease resulting from infection to the idea that health – in its broadest terms – was about lifestyle, to some extent being 'everybody's business' (DHSS, 1976). Health, then, 'was no longer seen as a private state of the body known only to doctor and patient but as something social and relative' (Williams (1973), cited in Armstrong, 1983, p 10).

The key advancement in theory here was '*social and relative*' – that a healthy existence was related not only to a medical configuration but had a social element, was about a quality of life dependent upon where people were placed in the social hierarchy. Where research was showing that the inequalities that existed in society were aligned to inequalities in health (Acheson, 1998; Townsend and Davidson, 1988), the connection between poverty and ill health was re-established but, as discussed in the preceding section, this was now set within developing understandings of the relative nature of poverty.

In searching for explanations in health inequalities, research has turned its attention towards the psycho-social effects of the different social and economic conditions in which people live (Wilkinson, 1996). However, whereas there was an initial focus on the effect this had on the poorest members of society, what

Richard Wilkinson has shown is that health is not just about affluence and poverty or individual behaviour and risk factors, but that what matter are the effects of social relativities; what become important are the social meanings associated with societal position. Absolute material standards, then, are not the main obstacles to better health, but it is the impact of the experience of inequality that undermines psychological well-being.

It has been shown that – through an understanding of the economics of well-being – poverty has become conceptualised as a relative rather than absolute state. The focus on necessities shows a change in attitudes towards needs, and that the detrimental effects of poverty relate as much to the inability to participate in society as they do to a lack of material possessions. So where early concerns were about promoting the good health of a nation, this has developed into a wider consideration of the extent to which inequality could also be damaging to well-being. As such, the politics of good health – and now well-being – is a condition of being able to participate fully in society, something that should be promoted.

So one aspect of the political focus of well-being is – or should be – concerned with the ability to interact and function in society, a fundamental right of citizenship. However, this draws in another strand of the politicisation of well-being, where political systems determine what aspects of society we should be functioning in – and to some extent control the availability of resources needed for participation. So well-being becomes a function of social control (political power) as much as it does the pursuit of the good life. Where governments have adopted methods to secure participation in society, the dissemination of wealth and welfare has given rise to new forms of power and the 'governmentality' of society (Foucault, 1991). This is the process through which the population has become the concern of political scrutiny, leading to the emergence of a new politics of behaviour that focuses on the moral and ethical conduct of individuals (Flint, 2004).

The potential for good health – through disease prevention – it was recognised, lay not only within the individual but extended to the community, where there were risk factors associated with the physical environment, social interactions and lifestyles (Armstrong, 1995). So, although political intervention was in the name of good health, it occurred through a moral lens. Public health legislation was as much about behavioural changes as about improving physical and environmental aspects. Within this context, the underlying theme of health promotion was the extent to which individuals were exposed to, or put themselves at, risk.

Where political concerns developed a focus on morals and character that placed the emphasis of good health on the individual at the beginning of the nineteenth century, this ideology remanifested itself and came to dominate government policy by the mid-1980s. Increased costs of public services and the economic crises of the 1970s meant the government's attention became focused on looking for economies in public spending (Baggott, 1991; Glennerster and Hills, 1998). The answer was deemed to lie in the system for providing public services, with a move away from state to private ownership. The subsequent neo-liberal promotion of market forces, it has been suggested, led to a 'political economy of insecurity' (Smart, 2003, p 32), where the risks associated with capitalist economic activity become redistributed 'away from the state and the economy and towards the individual' (Beck, 2000). This gave rise to the era of 'victim blaming culture', whereby the consequences of poor individual behaviour were deemed to manifest themselves in unemployment, poor education, poor health and so on. Individuals' economic, material and subjective well-being was therefore associated with personal lifestyle factors (Mills, 1993) that put people 'at risk' of experiencing deprivation. By this understanding, prosperity was the responsibility of the individual and deprivation a consequence of inappropriate behaviour.

Through this moral discourse the political lens focused less on well-being and was more concerned with risk. As individuals were increasingly required to take responsibility for their own welfare there grew a need to make financial or material investments to insure against future risks (Nettleton, 1997). Individuals were deemed 'at risk' of a downward trajectory and so they must make personal effort (and investment) in order to sustain stability or defer the start of a downward turn.

But the identification of risk factors (and their eradication) does not automatically lead to an improved quality of life: the situation here is much more complex. Few things in life are purely healthy or unhealthy and many of the risk factors that were being identified affected most aspects of everyday living (BMA, 1987; Feinstein, 1988), and their eradication was no guarantee of enhanced well-being. As Skolbekken observed in 1995, 'research in recent years has made us aware of more risk factors than ever before in history. This does not automatically make us healthier and happier human beings. In fact, this knowledge may in some instances lead to a duller way of life, restraining people from a quality of life that is open to them' (p 302). It was further posited that advancements in techniques of observing and monitoring the population also gave rise to the identification of 'fake' risks, with assumptions being made about the association of multiple factors with an illness or disease (Skolbekken, 1995). Being 'at risk' became a code for negative well-being, firstly through an association with demographic disadvantage (Blum et al, 2002) and secondly where 'risky behaviour' was associated with moral panics and the growth of a sector detached from mainstream society – termed as the 'underclass' (Murray, 1994; Mitchell et al, 2000).

Although initially individuals were deemed responsible for their behaviour and for putting themselves at risk, this ideology gave way to a belief that responsibility lay not only with the individual but with government and society as well, and recognition that the 'causes of decline are multiple, compounding, and often far reaching, affecting social lives and becoming a barrier to improvement' (SEU, 1998). The association of health and well-being with risk, however, led to the incorrect use of resources to enhance well-being, as a result of the wrong risk factors or risk groups being identified and targeted for preventative intervention (Skolbekken, 1995, Mitchell et al, 2000). The fragmentation and limitations of government initiatives were also identified as a cause of decline (SEU, 1998), leading to certain groups or areas being deemed at risk. This opened up the possibility that being at risk was as much about the existence of inequalities resulting from societal forces as it was about individual behaviour.

The development of new means of surveillance expanded the time/space dimension of social experience and the consequences for health in its broadest term. As with economic understandings of well-being, realisation increased that measures needed to be broader in scope, embracing as they did individuals' actual conditions and subjective understandings. The notion of risk developed in the health arena has seeped into the economic one as individuals have become exposed to a plethora of options to purchase a 'healthy lifestyle' and subsume a 'healthy image'. Herein lies the potential for new risks associated with the choices made in consuming 'health promoting' goods and services, whereby making the wrong choices could be detrimental to overall well-being.

Choosing well-being?

The politics and economics of health promotion thus began to merge where the individual was encouraged to choose those aspects of life that would promote living standards and the ability to function in society. While on the one hand this suggests a positive move towards individual freedom of choice (the individual as 'consumer' has not only the ability but the right to choose their well-being), on the other hand it exposes a fine balance between self-actualisation and political and economic manipulation.

The ever-increasing surveillance of society led to the creation of new disciplines in the late nineteenth century within which the individual could be more closely observed. The creation of psychology, in particular, led to a general increase in the interest of mental well-being (Beiser, 1974). The creation of psychotherapy led to a therapeutic movement and the 'whole person, the self as a living, experiencing, feeling subject … [came] into focus' (Rose, 1990, p 214). The therapeutic movement aimed 'to improve greater self awareness: encouraging the individual towards valuing one's self and one's feelings; to develop problem-solving skills, leading to a willingness to take risks' (Rose, 1990, p 242).

The individual then took centre stage in the pursuit of self-fulfilment. However, the method by which the observation of society was extended ultimately served to increase the recording of personal information and observation of behaviour (Armstrong, 1983, p 54) and this in turn closed the lens of observation evermore around the individual. The self-help philosophy of the therapeutic movement began to ripple out into other areas of political and economic control, encompassing general medical practice, counselling, social work, human resources and ultimately the mass media (Rose, 1990), exposing the potential for cognitive and behavioural manipulation.

This is particularly evident in the adoption of psychological understandings of human behaviour within the realm of economics and the increasing emphasis on the role of the consumer in society. The Protestant work ethic provided an initial moral obligation at the beginning of the twentieth century for the accumulation of capital and wealth within the emerging capitalist system (Weber, 1976), but the limitations placed on the consumption of wealth were soon out of step with the developments and reality of a capitalist economic life (Smart, 2003). New means of motivating people to continue to both work *and* consume were needed. Through the adoption of psychoanalytic principles[3] – the manipulation of human's innate need to seek pleasure – it was realised that people's needs could be 'artificially enhanced' (Etzioni, 1998) and industrialised society brought 'the consumer' to the foreground. The individual was no longer shaped for the needs of mass industrial labour but 'first and foremost by the need to play the role of consumer' (Bauman, 1998, p 24). By the early twentieth century the pursuit of wealth had been 'stripped of its religious and ethical meaning' and any 'residual sense of duty' was no longer to be found in work but in consumption (Weber (1976), cited in Smart, 2003, pp 21–2).

Within the 'consumer society' well-being is presumed to be achieved through the consumption of a healthy lifestyle, and self-identity becomes fused with product identity (Shaw and Aldridge, 2003). The commercialisation of health has led to an emphasis on social values pertaining to health and well-being through the promotion of body maintenance, not only in respect of health but also in terms of clothing, food and cosmetics. The outer body has become the focus of attention whereby the attributes valued in the free market – competence, self-control and self-discipline – become assigned to the individual through the products consumed in respect of maintaining bodily shape and physical appearance. Identities are no longer stable entities of 'who we are', born out of historical and institutional settings (Hall and du Gay, 1996), but increasingly created and re-created (Bauman, 1998) through a desire of who we might become (Hall and du Gay, 1996) based on our consumption activity.

Although enshrined in the pretence of the rights of individuals to look and feel their best (after all, 'you are worth it'), the distinction between the actual and imagined life-enhancing functionality of objects becomes blurred. As Barron and Mellor (2003), Baudrillard (1998) and Gardner and Sheppard (1989) suggest, the consumption of signs and symbols has become more important than the material goods themselves, as individuals establish an identity in an otherwise transient existence. Under traditional systems and beliefs an order in life was established according to lineage, gender, social status, and religious beliefs (Baumeister, 1986). With the loss of such restraints in modern society there is little foundation on which to build an identity. The Protestant work ethics of trust, loyalty and moral commitment have been replaced by a modern work ethic of mobility and flexibility that is in sharp contrast with traditional means of determining the self through social networks established in the community (Sennett, 1998) and the home (Beck and Beck-Gernsheim, 1995). The decision-making process of 'who to be' in the consumer society therefore gives rise to stress in relation to the difficulty of making a responsible choice, with no firm point of reference.

Where the decision maker previously sought legitimation for action via divine consultation, there is no 'oracle' for making life decisions (which affect well-being) in a post-traditional era.

In a consumer society new points of reference need to be sought on which to make or justify decisions. While 'logos' become identities (Klein, 2001), self-help books, documentaries, chat shows or radio phone-ins serve to perpetuate the philosophy of individual responsibility for sorting out one's life (Giddens, 1991; Beck and Beck-Gernsheim, 1995) and ultimately one's sense of well-being. But this is encased within the choices that are created and made available through economic and political means.

Whereas social control was sought through surveillance (Armstrong, 1983) and the governmentality (Foucault, 1991) of society at the beginning of the twentieth century, by the end of the century such social control exists in the form of the consumer's freedom of choice (Marcuse, 1968). The continued need to consume arises out of 'self-illusory hedonism' advocated by 'the controlled and organised production of novelty' (Campbell, 1997, p 38). Needs are contrived by extended powers (Marcuse, 1968) with a self-interest, such that consumers must continually be exposed to new temptations (Bauman, 1998) and 'kept in a suspended state, never quite satisfied with what they have, and perpetually anticipating their next purchase in the belief it will make them happier, forgetting that many previous such purchases have failed to live up to promised expectations' (Smart, 2003, p 67). As such, any happiness or satisfaction born of consumption is short lived, since only 'imagined' and not 'real' needs are being fulfilled (Campbell, 1997). The negative outcome of economic growth may therefore be the harmful effects of 'too much wealth' (such as consumerism and materialism), which, paradoxically, can be detrimental to life satisfaction (La Barbara and Gurhan, 1997).

With increased freedom of choice comes an inherent risk of making the wrong choice from the plethora that is available, and the 'fear of failing to act' being a risk in itself (Sennett, 1998, p 84). The creation of a 'risk culture' through the process of modernity (Giddens, 1991) may also be seen as an impingement on well-being. The process of modernity has led to the 'certainties from external control and general moral laws' associated with traditional cultures (Beck and Beck-Gernsheim, 1995) being replaced by 'a multitude of abstract systems' of 'superficial knowledge' (Giddens, 1991). Personal identities are no longer determined by traditional gender roles (Beck and Beck-Gernsheim, 1995), but instead are being subject to the process of 'reflexivity' as self-identity is negotiated and renegotiated, based on an individual's knowledge of a given situation (Giddens, 1991). Although a release from traditional beliefs and systems brings with it a new kind of freedom, such freedom means taking on responsibilities and making decisions. The existence of freedom of choice extolled in a free market economy places the notion of risk with the incorrect choices individuals make, without acknowledging the limitations that restrict not only what choices are available, but the choices people are able to make (Marcuse, 1968; Offer, 2006).

—

In a consumer society, the individual takes centre stage and subjective well-being becomes assigned to the individual through their consumption of the right goods and lifestyle. The signs and symbols that consumers are buying have replaced the 'must have' component that was once subsumed within the material goods themselves, as the identity of the product becomes merged with the identity of the individual. The move away from traditional roles, responsibilities and life trajectories, while presenting new freedoms, has become a race against time as we become consumer chameleons, changing our identities to blend into, or indeed stand out from, the changing background that is society. The plethora of signs, symbols, products and options that have emerged leave consumers in a quandary as they are faced with a stifling choice of possible identities of who to be (Coleson, 1973) or who to become (Hall and du Gay, 1996).

In the (political) market economy the availability – or freedom – of choice is ranked highly, and associated with positive outcomes. However, 'choice' in itself can create problems with adverse consequences. On the one hand, excessive and continual choice may be deemed overwhelming, creating a space of fear and concern over making the right selection. Economic theory assumes that if some choice is good, more is better, but this fails to acknowledge that, for some, increased choice results in paralysis rather than liberation, with consequential misery rather than satisfaction (Schwartz, 2004). On the other hand, where the excess of modern society clashes with a breaking down of social or self-control, individuals are faced with 'myopic choices' – their consumption now having detrimental consequences in the future (Offer, 2006). With affluence, Offer (2006) suggests, comes a 'relentless flow of new and cheaper opportunities' but the means of regulation (at societal or individual levels) lag behind. Consuming without constraint today may lead to individual or social problems in the future in the form of addiction, obesity, marital infidelity, crime and so on.

In these examples it is the ability to choose that is considered to be the underlying problem; however, the fallacy of choice can also undermine well-being. Lawlor (2004), for example, argues that – within the UK – the problem is not an abundance of choice, but too little choice in the things that really matter. Choice has become an illusory word, when most often what people can do is express an opinion, but the actual choice (or decision) is made within a culture of political institutions. Although too much choice may be associated with stress, the expectation of choice where in reality there is none may be equally detrimental to well-being.

So on the one hand increased choice does not – as the marketing would have us believe – necessarily bring about prolonged happiness or satisfaction, but, through the dilemmas of (inappropriate) selection, becomes detrimental to well-being. On the other hand, where the adoption of the market system in public services is deemed enabling, this too will impact on well-being where individuals' time and effort becomes wasteful consumption, where choice is promised but not realised.

These dilemmas suggest that understanding well-being is a complex issue, determined not only by the resources that individuals have at their disposal, but by the living conditions and societal forces that they are exposed to and the decisions they take, whether these relate to everyday shopping or life-changing events. Although such conditions and choices are deemed to be within the realm of individual decision making there are societal forces in play – the political and economic manipulation – that determine the capacity for individuals to achieve self-fulfilment. It is to these psycho-social underpinnings – the existence of these external forces and how the living conditions of individuals manifest themselves in positive or negative emotions – that the next section turns.

Psycho-social underpinnings

As outlined at the beginning of this chapter, the study of subjective well-being is being fuelled by a positive psychology movement. However, this was not always the case. Initial concerns of psychological well-being focused on the individual – particularly those who deviated away from an acceptable 'normal' level and experienced poor mental health. Psychological approaches were concerned with the role of personality and 'ill-being' whereby explanations for behaviour were sought through a psychopathological approach. The link between life events and mental health problems was dominated by the role of personality traits in individuals' varying ability to cope under stressful circumstances.

Since the beginning of the twentieth century the link between environmental stimulus, emotional arousal and changes in physiological process has been known through the study of extreme emotions such as hunger, fear and rage (Cannon, 1929). Although attention was given to the detrimental effects of sudden and rapid cultural change such as industrialisation or urbanisation (Ahmed and Coelho, 1979), through the work of Adolf Meyer an understanding developed that even the 'most normal and necessary life events could potentially lead to the development of a pathological condition' (Meyer (1951), cited in Dohrenwend and Dohrenwend, 1974, p 3), and 'life charts' (Lief, 1948) were subsequently developed. These sought to identify the causal process of psychological ill health and its relationship to everyday events – the social and biographical disruptions considered to be of significant importance in people's lives (for example death, marriage, problems with work, changes to social or work environment or eating habits, mortgage debt, vacations). The principal theory of such an approach was that it implied that change per se was stressful in that it demanded adaptation of existing routines.

Although it was acknowledged that these lists included events that could be perceived as both negative and positive, it was argued that any changes in life routines or established patterns required some form of adaptive or coping behaviour (Holmes and Masuda, 1974) which Mechanic (1974), in developing Seyle's (1956) theory, argues is costly to the organism by wearing on the biological system. Therefore life events become stressful due to their 'ability to change an individual's usual activities' and not because of their 'desirability or undesirability' (Gerston et al, 1974, p 159).

In line with this theory, measures were devised that established the link between everyday life events and mental health problems, as well as individuals' varying ability to cope under stressful circumstances. Subsequently there developed a particular interest in the impact that change and life events had on individuals' mental health status. However, it emerged that not all individuals responded to similar events in the same way. Explanations for these variations have been accounted for through differences in personality. For example, those who are less satisfied with their circumstances are deemed to have a propensity to play the 'sick role' as a means of coping, suggesting that '(s)ome persons . . . may develop a career of such responses, managing their lives through a vocabulary of illness' (Mechanic, 1974, p 95). By contrast, people who are less introspective, are task oriented and accept their environment rather than struggle against it (Kessel and Shepherd, 1965), have a tendency to 'experience greater personal comfort and less psychophysiological symptomology' (Mechanic, 1974, p 95).

Similarly, the extent to which people see themselves as being in control of the forces that importantly affect their lives may influence their response to life events. People who experience persistent role strain perceive this as 'evidence of their own failure and proof of their inability to alter the unwanted circumstances of their lives' (Pearlin et al, 1981, p 340), whereas a perceived sense of control and competence gives rise to dispositional optimism and feelings of positive well-being (Schwarzer, 1994; Smith et al, 1991; Triemstra et al, 1998). Such behaviour can be explained in respect of 'locus of control', whereby people are located along a dimension of personal control. Based on social learning theory, internal locus of control develops through early socialisation which rewards good behaviour and punishes bad, whereby the individual learns to site control within their own behaviour and effort. By contrast, external locus of control develops where rewards and punishment have been indiscriminate, thus control becomes located outside the individual and is associated with luck, chance, fate or interventions by powerful others (Rotter, 1966; Phares, 1991). Identifying a person's locus of control as internal or external was deemed important in developing an individual's sense of well-being because 'the belief that one's own efforts can produce changes is an important ingredient in getting people to better their lives' (Rotter and Hochreich, 1975, p 165).

These variations in personality – measured by personality scales – have been used in advancing the understanding of positive subjective well-being. Personality measures have been used in conjunction with happiness scales to show that extroverts are more likely to be happier than introverts (Argyle and Lu, 1990) or that extroversion and internal control are associated with increased subjective well-being (Argyle, 1987). Using these scales, subjective well-being is inferred from an individual's personality type, leading to conclusions that some people may be born with a positive well-being disposition. Indeed, the consistency of average subjective well-being over time would suggest that this may be applicable to the majority of the population.

This line of thought provides the basis for the Homeostatis Theory (Cummins and Nistico, 2002), which suggests that subjective well-being is controlled and maintained by a set of psychological devices that function under personality (analogous to the homeostatic maintenance of blood pressure or temperature). This theory suggests that individuals generally have a positive bias towards their self-image and self-view which provides a buffer to the experience of personal misfortune (Cummins et al, 2003). However, separate research shows that 'happy personalities' are mainly born out of environmental factors, in particular the socialisation process and child/parent relationships (Sroufe et al, 1983) and even supporters of the Homeostatis Theory acknowledge that sufficiently adverse environments can defeat the homeostatic system (Cummins et al, 2003).

The extent to which life events have a positive or negative impact on individuals may therefore be as much about the wider conditions in which the event is experienced as about the particular event itself. Researches using life scales as their instrument of measurement have thus been considered as misleading in that they focus on events in isolation, without taking into consideration the context in which they occur. There is the potential to 'ignore the more extended life circumstances of which the event may be a part' (Pearlin, 1989, p 244), leading to overemphasis of the importance of a particular event in respect of its stressful outcome. The interpretation of the relationship of events with health is therefore 'susceptible to exaggerating the importance of eventful change and to minimizing – or overlooking altogether – the problematic continuities of people's lives' (Pearlin, 1989, p 244).

Differences in the experience of stress, then, may be a reflection of other aspects of their lives, including the resistance resources (Antonovsky, 1974) that individuals have available in the event of a life crisis. For example, simply knowing that the resources of others are available, even if not called upon, increases an individual's strength and tension-resolving ability (Antonovsky, 1974). Several studies show that social support is consistently the most significant factor in reported satisfaction with life and well-being (Campbell et al, 1976; Veenhoven, 1984; Ville et al, 2001). The extent to which coping mechanisms can reduce the effect of stressful life events, however, is dependent upon the other resources or events affecting the individual at the same time, that is, a single event needs to be put in context, and the point in the change process at which coping resources become available and are utilised also is important (Pearlin et al, 1981).

Coping mechanisms may exist at a societal level, for example: whether the change is something that is expected as part of life-cycle transitions (Pearlin and Lieberman, 1979); whether the change or life event is accepted within a societal context; and how present circumstances compare to those of others in society (Pearlin et al, 1981). By addressing the societal aspects of coping it has been shown that coping strategies have emerged as 'institutionalised' rather than 'individual' solutions, whereby people with shared characteristics adopt similar defensive mechanisms (Pearlin and Schooler, 1978). Social structures, therefore, have the potential to be the source of, and defence from, stress. However, while coping mechanisms may be available through social structural conditions, they may not be equally available to all groups in society, with a failure to cope – as with the exposure to risk – being due to a failure of social systems and not to individual shortcomings (Pearlin and Schooler, 1978).

The suggestion that dissatisfaction is rooted in society is embedded within the psycho-social theory of well-being, that society provides the conditions that make up an individual's existence and that such conditions are not evenly distributed throughout society. It is this inequality that some people react to as being unjust, leading to a sense of deprivation and subsequent negative emotional outcomes (Wilkinson, 1996), what Elstad (1998) refers to as the 'psycho-social injuries of inequality structures' (p 40). According to this theory, stressful responses are not individual but collective – embedded in the extent to which people see themselves as being in control of the forces that importantly affect their lives. This 'self-efficacy' approach is rooted in the structural features of society – its systems of material inequalities – and in the supportiveness of the social environment (Elstad, 1998).

The research into psychological well-being gives rise to the notion that psychological functioning is more than an internal phenomenon but is a consequence of individuals' reactions to their external environments. Developments in economic and political theories of well-being have also shown that household or individual resources have consequences for individuals' engagement in society. Research therefore should encompass more than just the immediate focus of the area under investigation, and embrace the wider concepts within which the individual lives and functions. Measuring this social context – through social indicators – has become an important technique in the development of models of social life and social well-being.

The social context

Economic studies that seek to understand variations in well-being have been criticised due to their limitations and normative assumptions based on measures restricted to a living standard determined by income level. However, a greater awareness of the psycho-social consequences of poverty has given rise to a recognition that consideration needs to be given not only to the individual but also to the wider contextual issues that determine the conditions and resources deemed appropriate for participation in the society within which they live. These theoretical advancements have also brought about a change in methodological approaches to the study of subjective well-being.

The development of the social sciences throughout the nineteenth and twentieth centuries saw the emergence of methodological tools that sought to capture the different aspects of individual existence within a social context. One such method – the social survey – pioneered by Booth (1902–03) and Rowntree

(1902) presented new ways of measuring and 'mapping' well-being. They gave rise to many modern surveys and were the precursor to the detailed geographic mapping of societal experience in Britain's towns and cities (Smith and Noble, 2000). Since these early beginnings there has been an increasing development and sophistication of large-scale social surveys, for example the General Household Survey in 1971, the Labour Force Survey that started in 1984, the Family Resources Survey established in 1992, and the British Household Panel Survey, which commenced in 1991.

By the 1970s, social surveys were being compiled and conducted which sought to get a better understanding of national and international social well-being through the development and measurement of 'social indicators'. The social indicators movement emerged during the mid-1960s as a 'reaction against what was perceived as an overemphasis on measures of economic performance as indicative of social well-being' (Carley, 1981). Social indicators sought to measure not only external circumstances such as crime, housing and the environment but also individuals' perceptions of their surroundings, namely their satisfaction levels. As no definitive measure of subjective well-being existed, social indicators were developed as 'surrogate' or proxy measures of observable traits of social phenomena through which a value could be assigned to unobservable traits of those phenomena (Carley, 1981), thereby operationalising abstract concepts such as 'subjective well-being' or 'quality of life'.

These subjective well-being measures were first developed in the vein of the Rogerian (Carl Rogers) phenomenological approach. For example, the semantic differential scale is a technique originally developed by Osgood and colleagues (1957). It seeks to assess the meanings people attach to events or objects and measures people's reactions or feelings to stimulus words and concepts. The method uses two contrasting adjectives at either end of a scale and measures directionality of reaction (for example, boring vs interesting) as well as intensity (for example, neutral (0) through to extreme (3)) (see Heise, 1970). Campbell and colleagues (1976) adapted this technique and asked respondents to rate their life as a whole according to adjectives that represented bipolar extremes (for example, miserable vs enjoyable, useless vs worthwhile). Individual item scores were combined to give an overall 'global sense of subjective well-being' or the 'index of subjective well-being' (Campbell et al, 1976, p 49). The index was used to measure the relationship between subjective well-being and the importance of satisfaction with different aspects of individuals' lives.

Andrews and Withey (1976) also sought to identify people's satisfaction levels within eleven general 'regions' of concern. These were analysed in nine major subgroups based on gender, age, race and social status. Having tested the relationship between different methods of questioning people's satisfaction, they concluded that asking people directly 'How do you feel about life as a whole?' was the greatest predictor of subjective well-being (Andrews and Withey, 1976, p 107).

Although discussed earlier in this chapter in respect of economic developments in measuring well-being, the work of Townsend (1979), Mack and Lansley (1985), Gordon and Pantazis (1998) and Gordon et al (2000) also contributed to the development of social indicators in Great Britain. The focus of these surveys was the measurement and definition of poverty. However, this was extended to include an element of subjective well-being by raising an awareness of the subjective definition and experience of poverty. Townsend's survey not only included objective circumstances, for example having a job or a house, but explored the qualitative aspects associated with them in terms of satisfaction levels; additional, previously unmeasured resources such as fringe benefits or job security; access to open spaces, shopping or health facilities. Mack and Lansley (1985) (and later Gordon and Pantazis (1998) and Gordon et al (2000)) identified publicly perceived necessities (see Table 2.1) and differentiated between those people who did not have those 'necessities' because they chose not to and those who lacked the financial resources to purchase them.

The social indicators movement has also developed at the international level. The OECD (1976) used both objective measurements of individual and family circumstance and satisfaction levels, in order to develop internationally comparable social indicators of well-being. Its concept of well-being not only included 'what is valid in life' but also sought to identify 'the standard above which there is much well-being and below which there is little or no well-being', as shown by aggregate levels of national economic status (OECD, 1976, p 13).

At international levels, however, social indicators tend to be used as a means for evaluating government policy through social outcomes, identifying geographic areas of population subgroups experiencing social exclusion and deprivation rather than promoting subjective well-being. However, the EU and the World Bank are now addressing those issues that promote quality of life through social cohesion, social capital and social quality. This has led to the introduction of dimensions such as 'human development'[4] and 'environmental sustainability'[5] as well as embracing economic security, social inclusion, social cohesion and autonomy or empowerment when considering national and individual subjective well-being.

The development and use of social indicators is, however, subject to criticism. Caution is expressed over the extent to which measured phenomena can be used as a causal explanation of the unobserved, and the less than systematic way in which they have been developed has led some to question 'what social indicators are and what they are suppose to do' (Carley, 1981, p 13). Despite their limitations, a particularly important element that the 'social indicators movement' has brought to the understanding of subjective well-being is the acceptance that reported well-being is not static, but that 'actual levels of well-being within its component parts may differ between ... different points in time' (OECD, 1976, p 14). It is through understanding the 'forces behind fluctuations of well-being that we can perhaps gain some control or influence over them' (The Commission on Critical Choices, 1976, p 108). Just as single measures of subjective well-being do not provide a valid measurement of the phenomenon (this argument is developed in Chapter 3), so too are single time references limited in their understanding of the causal connections of circumstances and subjective well-being. In order to 'determine directionality of links which connect certain factors with well-being' longitudinal (causal modelling) studies must be developed (Ville et al, 2001).

Despite the shortcomings of earlier research, modern social surveys – along with other social research methods – have enhanced the research of social issues. The advancement of research techniques enables the tapping of subtle and complex issues such as perceptions, attitudes and feelings (Oppenheim, 1992; Putnam, 2000). Longitudinal studies – as with 'surveillance techniques' generally – advance social science methodology's ability to understand and describe social processes and social change – the emphasis moves away from identifying a single 'norm' instead focusing on a 'normal variability' (Armstrong, 1983). In particular, the establishment of the panel survey method enables comparison of the observed changes in individuals set within the context of themselves, as opposed to other subjects arguably providing the perfect control (Lewis, 1933).

Panel surveys provide the opportunity to establish more sophisticated behavioural models, in particular models of lagged effect (Rose, 2000). Analysing relationships between variables may often discover a correlation; however, causality is more difficult to determine, events may not always happen in sequence, and where there is a delay in the effect of one event on another cross-sectional studies will fail to make this connection. Longitudinal panel surveys, however, in enabling observations of the same individuals over time, allow such causal mechanisms and processes to be recorded and analysed (Dale et al, 1988).

While the main emphasis on the development of social indicators has been to gain a greater understanding of the experiences of poverty – with the aim of addressing the social costs of economic advancement – this has enabled a broader understanding of well-being. Through combining economic, psychological and sociological aspects, this has given rise to an emphasis on outcomes, as shown through self-reported subjective circumstances, leading to an understanding of poverty as a deprivation of well-being. The social indicators movement has been influential at both national and international levels and indicators are increasingly becoming more refined and detailed in nature, including changes in household and family formation, employment and working conditions, environmental pollution and transportation, standards of living, social and political integration and the impact of information and communication technology, as well as subjective assessments of satisfaction or overall happiness.

From deprivation to positive subjective well-being

In summary, this brief historical overview has shown that conceptualisations of well-being have been dominated by psychological theory and definitions of negative subjective well-being within a capitalist framework, whereby economic improvement has been theorised as providing its alleviation. Such theories have come under criticism due to their normative assumptions, and a somewhat blinkered approach that limits their capacity to address the notion of positive emotions and the social underpinnings of well-being. The adoption of sociological theorising has, however, led to a wider exploration of the concept of well-being as individuals' social and environmental circumstances are also analysed with respect to understanding their influence on a person's psychological state. The 'individual' has therefore emerged as the focal point, and theories of well-being have developed along different cultural, socio-economic, and socio-psychological themes.

These developments show that, using Maslow's motivation theory as a basic principle, conceptualisations of well-being have developed to take account not only of individuals' desires and needs but also of the resources they have available to fulfil those needs. This has led to definitions that address two key aspects: contextual elements and subjective assessment. The contextual element refers to an individual's social and physical environment. The subjective element refers to an individual's feelings, a value judgement about levels of satisfaction or dissatisfaction with their own lives or with societal structures. Contextual elements on the one hand provide a comparative basis for *identifying* differences in the level of reported well-being, while on the other hand subjective assessment provides a means of *understanding* differences in reported levels of well-being. Only by comparing actual circumstances with perceptions of them is it possible to understand what is of importance in life and how it contributes to national levels of well-being.

The research into change, life events, stress and coping implies that subjective assessment is important in respect of experienced life events and their impact on subjective well-being. Meanings, aspirations, adaptation, trust and locus of control are all subjective elements used as explanations for variations in the ways in which people cope with different stressors. Satisfaction therefore acts as a function of life changes whereby aspirations become adjusted to reality, and the impact of change on subjective well-being is relative to the meanings individuals attach to those changes. Studies of quality of life now consider attributes as well as domain satisfaction, with individuals' subjective assessment of their circumstances being considered a greater predictor of well-being than their actual conditions. This is not to say that either measure in isolation is sufficient in understanding subjective well-being. Actual conditions are essential determinants in understanding the kind of life people lead; however, subjective elements need to be measured in order to understand how satisfying, fulfilling or frustrating those lives are. Both measures are needed in order to understand subjective well-being and 'both should be the slogan of well-being researchers' (Kahn and Juster, 2002, p 641).

Economic, psychological and sociological studies of well-being have been used as the basis for this research, which will develop a multi-disciplinary model that seeks to address not only individual circumstances and behaviour but also societal influences in resource availability and accessibility as they relate to self-reported well-being. New methods and merging theories continue to pave the way to a greater understanding of factors associated with positive subjective well-being. The research reported in the next two chapters adds to this growing area of knowledge by developing a social model combining the singular disciplinary approaches. The data selected for this research has the strength of being an extensive panel survey that includes economic and material indicators of all kinds alongside subjective attitudinal data. Both kinds of indicators have limitations as well as strengths, but they are the best we have, and in combination it is worth exploring them.

Notes

1. See, for example, OECD (2001) *Society at a Glance: OECD Social Indicators*, OECD, Paris; EuReporting, which is a European-wide project with the long-term objective to create a science-based European System of Social Reporting and Welfare Measurement will analyse development, quality of life and changes in social structure at the European Level − www.social-science-gesis.de/en/social_monitoring/ social_indicators/EU_Reporting/eusi.htm.

2. For links to surveys, see: http://wvs.isr.umich.edu/index.html.

3. Edward Bernays used the 'pleasure principle' theory (developed by his uncle, Sigmund Freud) to convince people to purchase items merely for their own pleasure, rather than because they needed them. He used Freud's idea that people are basically irrational, and that by creating an emotional attachment to products people would consume them through an innate need for gratification (that is, where products would enhance the self-image) (reference made during 'Century of the Self', BBC2, Autumn 2001).

4. The United Nations Development Programme has developed a Human Development Index, which seeks to collect regional and national data on economic, political, social and cultural factors. Human Development Reports are produced annually: http://hdr.undp.org/reports/default.cfm.

5. The Treaty of Amsterdam provides for environmental protection requirements to be integrated into Community policies and activities of all European Union member states. The ultimate goal is sustainable development, that is, 'development that meets the needs of the present without compromising the ability of future generations to meet their own needs' − in other words, ensuring that today's growth does not jeopardise the growth possibilities of future generations (extracted from: www.europa.eu.int/scadplus/leg/en/lvb/l28100.htm − accessed 18 January 2005).

THREE

Achieving high subjective well-being

> A lifetime of happiness! No man alive could bear it: it would be hell on earth.
>
> (George Bernard Shaw,
> *Man and Superman* (1903), Act I)

There is currently a revitalised interest in the study of happiness and positive mood; arguably this is a period when the 'concept of Gross National Happiness is coming of age' (Stehlik, 1999, p 52). Academics, professionals and politicians are all working towards a new generation of measurements of social progress that value quality of life and subjective well-being and that recognise that these are not simply a measure of affluence. However, the study of well-being is in its infancy (Donovan et al, 2002) and there is still an element of mystery surrounding which factors are associated with life satisfaction and how they interact with each other.

This chapter unveils some of that mystery and presents a new analysis of the factors associated with experiences of positive well-being in both the short and the long term (reported in Chapter 4). This chapter builds a model of subjective well-being using the most comprehensive data available on UK trends. A positive subjective well-being scale, specially developed for this research, is discussed before presenting an overview of the wide range of factors shaping individual experiences of subjective well-being.

The empirical findings are based on secondary analysis of the first nine waves (1991–99) of the Economic and Social Research Council Research Centre on Micro-Social Change, British Household Panel Survey (BHPS). The BHPS was designed as a nationally representative sample in 1991 of around 5,500 households containing approximately 10,000 individuals who are re-interviewed each year. The survey follows members of the original household if they move to new households as well as adding people to the sample as they join existing households or reach the age of 16. This is an attempt to ensure that family and household history is not lost and there is no reduction in the number of interviewees. Changes to sample composition are, however, inevitable – for the period studied the average yearly response rate is 88%, so that just 65% of individuals interviewed in 1991 were interviewed in 1999. Corrective measures are taken to address the issue of bias that will arise through attrition, as the make-up of the sample no longer represents that found in the population nationally. The BHPS contains two sets of weights that address the issues of bias at individual wave level as well as over time. Both cross-sectional and longitudinal weightings have been used where appropriate in the course of this analysis.

The main advantage of using a panel study is that it facilitates both cross-sectional and longitudinal analysis. A snapshot of individuals' circumstances can be analysed, and their fortunes can be followed over time. The BHPS generates data on the nature and duration of a variety of aspects of individuals' lives and thus enables the exploration of how conditions, life events and individual behaviour are linked with each other.

In this chapter, statistical results are presented on national distributions of well-being, and regression analyses of factors associated with high levels of subjective well-being are reported. The new analyses included in this chapter show how experiences of high subjective well-being for men and women vary across a range of demographic, socio-economic, social, health, spatial and domain satisfaction factors.

The BHPS data indicate that generally most people report having high levels of well-being, and that this remained the case throughout the 1990s. However, analysis of high and low subjective well-being shows that these two states are not necessarily the mirror image of each other. Each has different predictors, so it cannot be assumed that low subjective well-being can be turned into high subjective well-being simply be altering the factors associated with a lower well-being score. In order to enhance the well-being of a nation, positive subjective well-being needs to be measured and analysed in its own right. To this end the remainder of the chapter provides information on factors specifically associated with the experience of *high* subjective well-being.

Measuring subjective well-being

If one thing emerges from a review of literature on well-being, it is its complexity: well-being is multifaceted, multidimensional and pertains to individuals as well as society. The complex and contested character of subjective well-being is reflected in the debates on how best to measure it.

In the literature, measures of happiness and life satisfaction have been used as indicators of subjective well-being, and both measures are included in the BHPS. Although these represent outcome measures of quality of life experience, they have their limitations. Happiness is arguably a less reliable measure of subjective well-being than life satisfaction, since it implies a short-term mood, whereas life satisfaction represents a more complex cognitive assessment of quality of life over time and has been shown to be the best predictor of subjective well-being (see Chapter 2).

However, single measures of subjective state have been criticised. Ryff and Keyes's (1995) research found that life satisfaction had a weak association with purpose in life, personal growth and autonomy, which are also important elements in determining subjective well-being. There may also be a tendency for bias – evaluations of global subjective well-being may reflect transient moods influenced by temporal recollection, or a tendency to give socially desirable responses (Schwarz and Strack, 1999). Similarly Oppenheim (1992) argues that perceptions (such as those which determined subjective well-being) are best measured 'through a range of questions that ... seek to address different aspects of the non-factual topic', namely, the use of multiple questions or scaling (Oppenheim, 1992, p 150).

Another theory is that well-being operates on a spatial scale, whereby the impact that events have on satisfaction levels diminishes as evaluations move from a personal to a societal level (Cummins et al, 2003, p 165). As such, singular global measures are an ineffective means of capturing the components that influence well-being and questions are needed that increase the distance from the self and capture external forces of change (Cummins et al, 2003). This line of thought is also expressed by Diener et al (2003) and Nettle (2005), who suggest that there is a hierarchy of components that influence well-being at both a temporal (momentary to more considered judgements) and a spatial (personal fulfilment to global assessment) level.

This complex nature of subjective well-being suggests that it is best measured through obtaining information on a range of areas of experience. Single measures fail to provide the detailed information of quality of life experience that would help explain its rise and fall. Over time, studies have adopted techniques that combine questions on different aspects of well-being to form an index measure. For example, Campbell et al's (1976) American study, which comprised a multiple semantic differential measurement technique;[1] Hills and Argyle's (2002) British study, whose measure taps different aspects of emotional and psychological functioning; or Cummins et al's (2003) Australian study, which combined satisfaction levels in 10 domains at the personal and national level.

Although there is an increasing number of measurement tools which seek to understand subjective well-being from many different conceptual standpoints, they are not all appropriate to the particular aims of this book. Many measures have been devised within specific fields of research and are therefore limited to the discipline from which they have derived. For example, in respect of health outcomes Spitzen et al's (1981) 'Quality of Life Index' is designed to measure quality of life in cancer patients before and after treatment; for socio-economic resources Townsend (1979) devised a measurement of deprivation based on access to perceived necessities; and Gordon et al (2000) devised a measure of well-being based on notions of social exclusion. Such measures focus on well-being as it relates to an absence of disease or poverty as opposed to factors directly related to positive subjective well-being. Other measures – as discussed in Chapter 2 – have developed within the discipline of psychology. Early measures, originally devised to tap into different emotional states, have more recently been developed in the vein of positive psychology, where new measures of happiness, satisfaction and quality of life are merging to provide more holistic subjective well-being measures.

So, arguably there are innumerable measurement scales that could have been selected. However, in the study reported here subjective well-being is conceptualised as a state of mind arising from a socio-psychological assessment of everyday circumstances. This is most effectively captured in the General Health

Questionnaire (GHQ) (Goldberg, 1972). The GHQ was originally designed to identify the changing aspects of mild psychological distress and was applicable to the whole population (unlike previous measures, which have tended to focus on the extreme ends of psychological experience within society). It focuses on the inability to carry out one's normal 'healthy' functions, as well as detecting the appearance of new phenomena of a distressing nature (Goldberg and Hillier, 1979). The full questionnaire addresses five themes: general; psychic depression vs somatic depression; agitation vs apathy; anxiety at night vs anxiety during daytime; and personal neglect vs irritability. Short-form GHQs (SF36, SF20 and SF12) are commonly used, based on questions selected from just the general theme, or from across all themes.

Since its introduction in the 1970s the GHQ has become one of the most widely used measures of quality of life (Hemingway et al, 1997). It has been validated cross-culturally among adult populations (Goldberg et al, 1997) as well as among specific groups, for example, in the community (Carver et al, 1999; Walters et al, 2001), in primary care settings (Lim and Fisher, 1999; Dempster and Donnelly, 2001) and in prison populations (Smith and Borland, 1999). The GHQ12, in particular, is the most widely used screening instrument because of its brevity, which makes it attractive to administer and complete (Goldberg et al, 1997) (Table 3.1).

The GHQ12 was designed to measure minor psychiatric morbidity and has been well validated in this respect (Grundy and Sloggett, 2003, p 938) – indeed it has been reported to be one of 'the best instruments to measure psychological distress of its kind' (Goodchild and Duncan-Jones, 1985, p 59). So its inclusion in a measure of positive well-being may be open to question. However, this measurement tool addresses different aspects of stress and ability to cope with everyday life events and, as can be seen in Table 3.1, includes questions that tap into negative emotional states as well as more positive feelings. For example, negative outcomes may result in feeling under strain, unhappy or depressed, or not being

Table 3.1: General health questionnaire

Have you recently:
- Been able to concentrate on what you are doing?
- Lost much sleep over worry?
- Felt that you are playing a useful part in things?
- Felt capable of making decisions about things?
- Felt constantly under strain?
- Felt that you couldn't overcome your difficulties?
- Been able to enjoy your normal day-to-day activities?
- Been able to face up to your problems?
- Been feeling unhappy and depressed?
- Been losing confidence in yourself?
- Been thinking of yourself as a worthless person?
- Been feeling reasonably happy, all things considered?

Source: Goldberg, 1972, Appendix 6, pp 139–40.

able to overcome difficulties, while more positive outcomes are reflected through being useful, capable of making decisions or feeling happy.

These questions elicit responses that measure a person's state of well-being compared to how they usually feel. Recording 'better than usual' is not, therefore, necessarily indicative of a good state, just not as poor as usual. While this raises doubts about the reliability of such measures in capturing a consistent state of well-being, as will be explained below and in Chapter 4, the focus of this research is to identify *changes* in individual subjective well-being, in particular an improved sense of well-being. As such, a response set that implies things are getting better provides a reasonable indication of enhanced feelings and is an appropriate measure for this study.

Notwithstanding these limitations, of the measures available in the BHPS, the GHQ12 is deemed the most representative measure of subjective well-being as defined for this research. Well-being will be operationalised through a summation of scores from these 12 questions which seek to address people's self-esteem, happiness and ability to cope with life in general, running along a scale from 0 (least distressed) to 36 (most distressed).[2]

The literature review showed that there has been a propensity to study subjective well-being in its negative state. As noted above, the GHQ is no exception. The summed GHQ12 scores in the BHPS use a negative scale, where an increased score equates to increased psychological distress. However, the aim of this research is to analyse the factors influencing positive subjective well-being; therefore, as an heuristic aid a measure was developed that reflects a positive rather than a negative scale. In order to create a positive scale for this research the polarity of the summed scores has been reversed, whereby low subjective well-being is represented by a score of 0 and high subjective well-being by a score of 36. This may not be the best measure of positive well-being, but it is a means of making the best use of the measure contained in the BHPS. The reversal of scores means that answers securing the highest score (of 3) against each individual question are arguably an indicator of a much improved state of well-being. So, for example, a score of 3 would arise, when asked 'Have you recently felt capable of making decisions about things?', from a response of 'More so than usual'. By contrast, answers that have the lowest score (0) are indicative of a deterioration in well-being; for example, when asked 'Have you recently being losing confidence in yourself?' a score of zero would represent a response of 'Much more than usual'. While this measure is deemed a fair representation of subjective well-being and is used for this research, it is acknowledged that positive subjective well-being is a rapidly growing area of research interest and new insights are emerging. There is scope to develop new scales of well-being – elements of which will be revealed throughout the analysis and discussion in the following chapters.

National distribution of subjective well-being

This section will provide a description of the base-line data on subjective well-being at the national level. It will provide cross-section estimates of positive subjective well-being based on median well-being scores using the positive measure described above.

National and international reports show that, generally, within the population there is a normal distribution of subjective well-being, with most people being fairly happy or satisfied (Inglehart, 1990; Blanchflower and Oswald, 2002). Using the positive subjective well-being measure, this research has found that subjective well-being is negatively skewed,[3] with most people scoring towards the higher level of the scale. Seventy-five per cent of the population score 22 or more on a scale running from 0 (low subjective well-being) to 36 (high subjective well-being) each year between 1991 and 1999 (Figure 3.1).

Average subjective well-being remains constant throughout this period (at 25), and this is indicative of subjective well-being expressed by different groups. Individuals in the top 20% of the population consistently report high scores of 29 or above, while those in the bottom 20% consistently score 21 or below.

Figure 3.1: Subjective well-being (%) in Great Britain 1991–99

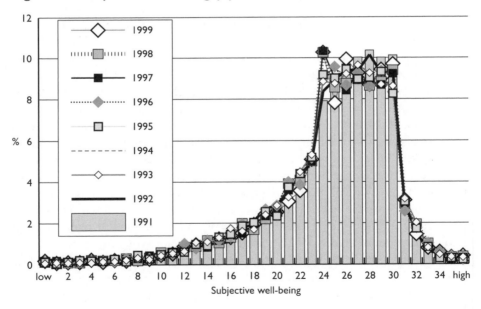

Variations in average subjective well-being

To explore further the underpinnings of well-being this section looks in detail at variations of well-being across some of the social divisions in society – based on demographic, economic and spatial variables. Table 3.2 documents demographic

Table 3.2: Demographic variations in subjective well-being 1991–99 (median scores)

	1991	1992	1993	1994	1995	1996	1997	1998	1999	n = min-max*
Gender										
Male	27	26	27	27	26	26	26	27	27	3.331–4.337
Female	26	25	25	25	25	25	25	25	25	3.847–4.766
Age										
25-34	26	26	26	26	26	26	26	26	26	1.416–1.845
35-44	26	26	26	26	25	26	26	26	26	1.473–1.700
45-54	26	26	25	25	25	25	25	25	26	1.402–1.544
55-64	27	26	26	26	26	26	26	26	26	1.069–1.228
65-74	26	26	26	26	26	26	26	26	26	1.018–1.141
75+	25	25	25	25	25	25	25	25	25	705–884
Marital status										
Never married	27	26	26	26	26	26	26	26	26	811–1.560
Married	26	26	26	26	26	27	26	26	26	4.692–5.594
Cohabiting	26	26	27	26	26	26	26	26	26	525–635
Widowed	25	25	25	25	25	25	25	25	25	743–828
Divorced	25	25	25	25	25	24	25	25	25	386–457
Separated	24	24	23	24	24	23	24	24	22	128–172
Household type										
Single non-elderly	26	26	26	26	25	25	25	26	25	467–574
Single elderly	25	25	25	25	25	25	25	25	25	778–845
Couple: no children	27	26	26	26	26	26	26	26	26	2.553–2.751
Couple: dependent children	26	26	26	26	26	26	26	26	26	1.896–2.744
Couple: non-dependent children	26	26	26	26	26	26	26	26	26	896–1.326
Lone parent: dependent children	24	25	25	25	24	23	24	25	24	244–294
Lone parent: non-dependent children	25	25	25	24	25	25	25	25	25	285–397
Ethnicity										
White	25	25	25	25	25	25	25	25	25	7.150–8.814
Ethnic minority	25	24	24	24	24	24	24	24	24	177–260

* For the sake of clarity annual base numbers have not been reported, but the maximum and minimum number of respondents across the period 1991–99 have been recorded.

variations in respect of gender, age, marital status, household type and ethnicity. Table 3.3 reports economic variations in respect of social class, housing tenure, education, employment and household income. Spatial variations are reported in Table 3.4 in respect of region and area of residency.

The variables used for this stage of the analysis were selected for comparability with measures of well-being used across the economic and psychological literature. The extent to which they impinge on well-being varies. At the aggregate level it can be seen that, although there is some variation in the experience of subject well-being between different groups in society, within groups there is little variation, with average subjective well-being scores falling in the range of 25–27 each year between 1991 and 1999.

Of the measures used here, there are clear differences between the factors associated with low and high well-being. The most detrimental factor for well-being relates to economic status, with those who are classified as long-term sick/disabled consistently reporting the lowest levels of subjective well-being with an average score of 22. Other factors that impinge on low well-being are: ethnicity; being separated or a lone parent; or where employment status is classed as 'engaged in family care'. Each of these groups at some point has an average score of 24 or less between 1991 and 1999.

Factors important for high well-being, however, relate to gender and social class. The groups that have consistently averaged scores of 26/27 include males, social classes I and III (manual), and those identified as being students or on government training schemes.

Spatial distributions of subjective well-being vary little in Great Britain (Table 3.4), at least on the scales available in this analysis. Dividing the country into areas representative of government offices of the regions shows that all regions average a subjective well-being score of 25–26. Spatial divisions based on local authority area classification (ONS, 2001) show average scores varying between 25 and 27 in all groups, although scores tend to be lower in the London suburbs and mining and manufacturing areas.

While some patterns are emerging from the analysis of mean well-being scores, they are limited in terms of what we can understand about differences across the well-being spectrum, given the small variation in scores. Further analysis was thus undertaken, segregating the well-being scores in order to elicit information on factors that underpin experiences at the extreme ends of the scale – namely, those of very low and very high subjective well-being.

Variations in high and low subjective well-being

In the last section, variations in subjective well-being were highlighted in respect of socio-economic group differences. Another way of examining the variations in the experience of subjective well-being is to look at the tendency for different socio-economic groups to be represented among those experiencing high subjective well-being and low subjective well-being in the population. Although

Table 3.3: Economic variations in subjective well-being 1991–99

	1991	1992	1993	1994	1995	1996	1997	1998	1999	n = min-max
Income[a] quintiles after housing costs										
Top 20%	27	26	26	26	26	26	26	26	26	1,556–2,096
4	26	26	26	26	26	26	26	26	26	1,478–1,842
3	26	26	26	26	26	26	26	26	26	1,476–1,753
2	26	26	25	25	25	25	25	25	25	1,478–1,783
Bottom 20%	25	25	25	25	25	25	25	25	25	1,399–1,664
Social class										
I	27	26	27	26	26	27	27	27	26	265–307
II	27	26	26	26	26	26	26	26	26	1,445–1,569
III non-manual	26	26	26	26	26	26	25	26	25	920–1,332
III manual	27	27	27	27	26	27	27	26	27	856–1,221
IV	27	26	26	26	26	26	26	27	27	563–779
V	26	26	26	26	26	25	26	26	26	187–250
Housing tenure										
Own outright	27	26	26	26	26	26	26	26	26	2,057–2,257
Mortgage	26	26	26	26	26	26	26	26	26	3,342–4,335
LA/HA rented	25	25	25	25	25	25	25	25	25	1,358–1,968
Private rented	26	26	26	26	26	26	26	26	25	428–668
Education status										
Higher degree	27	26	26	26	26	26	26	26	26	2,233–2,729
A Levels	27	26	26	26	26	26	26	25	26	629–881
CSE/O Levels	26	26	26	26	26	26	26	26	26	1,246–1,801
Lower qualifications	26	26	25	25	25	25	25	26	26	695–982
None of these	26	25	25	25	25	25	25	25	25	2,092–3,191
Employment status										
Employed	27	26	26	26	26	26	26	26	26	4,283–5,447
Unemployed	25	25	25	25	25	25	25	25	26	155–466
Retired	26	26	26	26	26	26	26	26	26	1,650–2,051
Family care	25	25	25	25	25	24	24	25	25	542–1,066
Student/government training	27	27	27	27	27	27	27	27	27	49–227
Long-term sick/disabled	22	23	22	22	22	22	22	22	22	256–306

[a] Household income has been equivalised using the McClements Scale to take account of the number and type of people in a household (McClements, 1978), and has been deflated to 1991 prices.
LA = Local authority.
HA = Housing association.

Table 3.4: Spatial distribution of subjective well-being 1991–99 (median scores)

	1991	1992	1993	1994	1995	1996	1997	1998	1999	n=min-max
Government regions										
London	26	26	25	26	26	25	26	26	26	801–1,152
Rest of S East	26	26	26	26	26	26	26	26	26	1,467–1,712
S West	26	26	26	26	26	26	26	26	26	673–786
E Anglia	26	26	26	26	26	26	26	26	26	305–339
E Midlands	26	26	26	26	26	26	26	26	26	594–667
W Midlands	26	26	26	26	26	26	26	26	26	945–1,203
N West	26	26	26	26	26	25	26	26	26	521–634
Yorks + Humber	26	26	26	26	25	25	26	26	26	694–872
N East	26	26	26	25	25	25	25	25	25	450–562
Wales	26	25	25	25	25	25	25	26	25	405–448
Scotland	26	26	26	26	26	26	26	26	26	584–728
LA area classification										
Centres + services	26	26	26	26	26	25	25	26	26	1,370–1,718
London suburbs	26	25	25	25	25	25	25	26	26	304–390
London centre	26	26	26	26	26	25	26	27	26	96–175
London cosmopolitan	26	26	26	26	26	25	26	27	26	166–278
Prospering UK	26	26	26	26	26	26	26	26	26	2,489–2,946
Coastal + countryside	26	26	26	26	26	26	26	26	26	538–633
Mining + manufacturing	26	26	25	25	25	25	25	25	26	1,443–1,745

various measures could be used to represent the extremes of well-being, for the purposes of this research those whose scores put them in the top 20% of the positive subjective well-being measure (scores of 29 or more) are categorised as 'high subjective well-being', and those whose scores put them in the bottom 20% (scores of 21 or less) are categorised as 'low subjective well-being'.

The analysis so far has shown that the greatest variations in average subjective well-being exist in respect of marital status, household type, employment status and social class, and these variables – together with age and gender – are selected by way of example for this next part of the analysis. Variations in high and low subjective well-being in respect of selected demographic variables are shown in Table 3.5 and economic variables are shown in Table 3.6. These tables are quite complex and therefore the numbers of cases within each sub-group have not been included, as they have already been reported in Tables 3.2, 3.3 and 3.4 above.

Table 3.5: Demographic variations in high and low subjective well-being 1991–99 (%)

	1991	1992	1993	1994	1995	1996	1997	1998	1999
Gender									
Males									
Low	15	17	16	16	17	18	16	16	16
High	31	29	30	29	29	30	30	30	32
Females									
Low	20	23	24	24	25	25	24	24	23
High	22	21	20	20	20	19	20	21	21
Age									
25–34									
Low	17	21	19	20	21	22	20	20	17
High	27	25	27	27	26	25	27	29	29
35–44									
Low	19	23	21	20	23	23	21	23	21
High	24	20	21	21	22	22	22	23	24
45–54									
Low	18	22	23	23	24	24	23	23	21
High	25	23	23	21	20	21	21	23	24
55–64									
Low	16	17	18	20	18	20	20	20	20
High	29	27	28	28	26	25	25	26	26
65–74									
Low	17	16	17	16	17	18	15	17	16
High	26	26	25	24	27	27	29	28	30
75+									
Low	22	21	18	24	19	23	21	20	23
High	23	24	25	19	25	23	22	22	23
Marital status									
Never married									
Low	15	18	19	18	18	21	19	20	18
High	31	28	29	29	28	27	29	26	30
Married									
Low	16	19	19	19	20	20	19	19	18
High	27	25	24	24	25	25	24	26	26

(continued)

Table 3.5: Demographic variations in high and low subjective well-being 1991–99 (%) (continued)

	1991	1992	1993	1994	1995	1996	1997	1998	1999
Marital status (continued)									
Cohabiting									
Low	20	20	15	15	17	21	19	21	18
High	29	27	27	26	24	26	26	27	28
Widowed									
Low	23	24	25	26	25	26	22	23	25
High	19	20	19	20	18	20	21	19	21
Divorced									
Low	26	28	29	33	28	31	27	30	26
High	19	20	22	20	21	22	24	23	26
Separated									
Low	29	38	35	30	39	47	39	40	46
High	13	16	17	15	19	17	25	22	18
Household type									
Single non-elderly									
Low	22	25	21	25	23	29	28	25	23
High	25	25	27	26	24	23	26	25	25
Single elderly									
Low	21	22	24	24	25	24	20	23	22
High	20	21	20	20	18	22	24	22	24
Couple: no children									
Low	15	17	17	17	19	19	19	18	18
High	29	27	27	27	26	28	26	21	29
Couple: dependent children									
Low	18	21	20	19	21	21	20	20	18
High	25	23	24	22	23	22	23	25	24
Couple: non-dependent children									
Low	16	18	20	21	18	18	19	18	17
High	28	26	27	28	27	25	26	29	27
Lone parent: dependent children									
Low	30	33	28	31	31	38	32	29	30
High	14	21	17	19	20	15	21	18	20
Lone parent: non-dependent children									
Low	19	26	26	29	25	24	21	28	28
High	24	18	19	16	18	21	23	16	21

**Table 3.6: Economic variations in high and low subjective well-being
1991–99 (%)**

	1991	1992	1993	1994	1995	1996	1997	1998	1999
Social class									
I									
Low	14	21	13	21	21	14	15	19	17
High	30	25	26	22	29	33	29	28	26
II									
Low	13	19	16	17	20	21	19	20	17
High	27	25	27	26	24	24	24	25	27
III non-manual									
Low	15	17	20	20	21	21	21	22	19
High	26	23	23	24	22	24	24	25	21
III manual									
Low	12	16	13	13	16	13	13	15	14
High	33	29	34	31	29	29	28	30	32
IV									
Low	14	16	17	18	16	20	18	15	15
High	30	28	25	28	28	27	28	31	31
V									
Low	14	13	18	19	18	21	21	16	14
High	26	25	25	20	26	25	27	26	33
Employment status									
Employed									
Low	14	17	16	17	18	19	18	18	16
High	29	26	27	26	26	26	26	27	27
Unemployed									
Low	34	32	30	26	27	33	29	31	31
High	26	26	24	24	25	26	26	27	27
Retired									
Low	17	18	20	19	20	20	19	19	20
High	26	26	24	24	25	26	26	27	27
Family care									
Low	24	29	27	27	27	31	26	25	25
High	20	18	16	16	15	16	18	20	21
Student/government training									
Low	16	12	15	13	17	17	18	26	18
High	36	39	36	30	28	33	35	28	33
Long-term sick/disabled									
Low	48	44	47	50	46	49	49	46	48
High	9	9	11	11	12	10	9	12	10

These tables contain a vast amount of information, much of it lending further support to findings at the aggregate level. However, a focus on the polar extremes provides further insights. In particular there are two key points worth elaborating. Firstly, the relationship between economic activity and well-being is complex; secondly, the longitudinal nature of the data reveals that there are not only variations between groups but, intriguingly, variations within groups over time, suggesting that the same circumstances have different effects at different points in time. This may be a reflection of cohort effects – the different political, social and economic conditions that mean the consequences of being in a particular group at the beginning of the 1990s is not the same as being in that group at the end of the decade. Finally, the data challenge the economic idea, suggesting that well-being is contingent upon aspects of social participation rather than income.

Addressing the first point, the greatest variation in subjective well-being can be seen in respect of employment status (or rather a lack of it), with low subjective well-being being most prominent among those on long-term sickness/disability (44–50%), while being employed is associated with high well-being (26–29%). Such findings are consistent with other studies reporting the positive effects of employment status or the negative impact associated with long-term health conditions or disabilities (Shields and Wooden, 2003). Students or those on government training schemes are also consistently among those with the highest levels of subjective well-being (28–39%), so in line with Shields and Wooden (2003) this research suggests that it is the learning aspects of employment that seem to be conducive to positive well-being. A key finding to emerge from this part of the analysis, however, concerns a lack of economic activity, so contrary to general findings among the literature (Feather, 1990), the experiences of unemployed people appear complex, as this category stands out as being among those most likely to experience high well-being (24–27%) as well as most likely to experience low well-being (26–34%). This suggests that there are other factors which mediate the impact of negative experience following loss of employment – a point which is discussed more fully in Chapter 5.

Secondly, while differences between groups are clearly visible, and may be accounted for in cross-sectional analysis, the longitudinal nature of this study intriguingly reveals that, far from being static, there is a temporal nature to well-being experience within groups. For example, differences according to social gradient are once again evident, but there is no clear relationship between economic prosperity and subjective well-being. Far from being a linear association – as more generally found among research on health outcomes (Marmot, 2005) – it is the middle of the social hierarchy, social class III manual (29–43%), who elicit the highest well-being scores. Looking at the proportions over time further reveals that the elite of society (social class I), while not always securing the greatest proportion with high well-being (dropping to 22% in 1994), has also been representative of those with the lowest levels of well-being (ranging from 14–21%). At the other end the social hierarchy, up to a third of social class V has secured some of the highest well-being scores (reaching 33% in 1999). Although social standing has been shown to directly affect health and longevity (Marmot, 2005), such findings question the extent to which this holds true for experiences of well-being over time, and achieving positive well-being would appear to be a more complex process involving mechanisms other than advancements through personal economic progress.

Finally, this brief exploration of the data suggests that while economic variables have limited success in predicting well-being, well-being may be contingent on levels of social support and societal integration. Here marital status is used as an indicator of social relationships and social support, while economic activity is used as an indication of integration within a capitalist society. Looking at average proportions across the nine years, it can be seen that lack of social support or ability to function in the labour market is clearly linked to low well-being. Being separated or divorced suggests some breakdown in social relationships, while being unemployed or long-term sick/disabled can precipitate a lack of participation in a major part of social life and may account for the propensity for these groups to be over-represented among those at the lower end of the well-being scale (ranging from 29% to 47%). Another key finding to note here is the extent to which caring responsibilities may also impinge upon social participation and well-being. On average, a third of lone parents with dependent children (31%) and those who have family caring responsibilities (27%) also fall within the bottom end of the well-being scale. However, having established that being unemployed increases the chances of experiencing low subjective well-being, it should also be noted that unemployed people are no less likely to experience high subjective well-being (25–27%) than employed people (26–27%).

Understanding subjective well-being is far from straightforward. While social support is important in respect of subjective well-being, this may be found from within or outside the family and cannot always be inferred through marital status. Not all marital relationships are indicative of social support (for example, see the classic study of Dobash and Dobash, 1979), while being 'single never married' does not necessarily imply being deprived of any social relationships. The lack of a social relationship or the absence of a particular social activity does not, then, appear to provide an explanation in the variation of subjective well-being. Social participation or integration may occur through means other than engagement in the labour market, for example participation in community or leisure activities. An analysis of subjective well-being would therefore benefit from the inclusion of measures of social participation in different domains of life, as well as an assessment of individuals' perceived levels of social support, and social integration. The inconsistencies between the measures used so far suggest that other factors are affecting individuals' subjective well-being – factors that may be captured in reported experience rather than some 'objective' categorisation. Thus it is to the emotional – subjective – aspects that this research turns.

Subjective measures and variations in national subjective well-being

The measures discussed so far have, in a sense, been structural: categories that express people's measurable location within a social hierarchy. Although some patterns emerge, the variations experienced by some groups over time would suggest that such conditions on their own appear to be insufficient in explaining variations in subjective well-being. As discussed in the literature review, experience of circumstances may be a better indicator of subjective well-being. This was the finding of Campbell et al (1976), who concluded that individuals' subjective assessment of their circumstances was a greater predictor of well-being than their actual objective conditions, while Andrews and Withey (1976) quite confidently state that asking individuals how satisfied they were with their life as a whole was the greatest predictor of subjective well-being.

An indication of the relationship of subjective assessments on reported subjective well-being can be seen in the following example using a measure of satisfaction with life overall on a scale of 1 (not at all satisfied) to 7 (completely satisfied). The data are somewhat limited compared to the previous sections, as questions relating to life satisfaction are only included in the BHPS from 1996 – nevertheless even with this short-time series a clear pattern is evident.

Comparison of median well-being scores to a global satisfaction measure shows a positive relationship between being satisfied and high subjective well-being. Being completely satisfied with life overall elicited higher subjective well-being scores than any other measure reported in this chapter (on average 27/28), while individuals who were not at all satisfied had the lowest average subjective well-being scores (12 to 14) (Figure 3.2). This relationship is also borne out when high and low subjective well-being are analysed separately. This positive association suggests that subjective assessment is important in understanding well-being and

Figure 3.2: Subjective well-being by satisfaction with life overall 1996–99

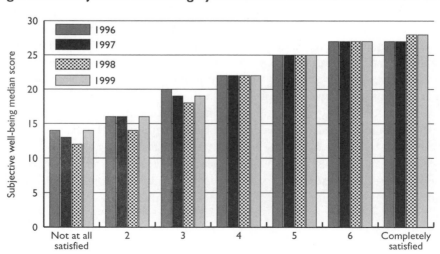

should form part of any analysis of well-being states alongside other measures of life circumstances.

The findings thus far have shown the characteristics of those who are most likely to experience high and low subjective well-being, but such analysis is limited because it does not assess the relative importance of different factors on the experience of subjective well-being or whether, in fact, some measures have repeated elements – that they are measuring the same thing. For example, those in social class III manual are extremely likely to be male, and both these factors have been identified as being among the greatest influences for experiencing high subjective well-being. Being separated or divorced could also imply living in a lone-parent household: these three categories have been shown to increase the likelihood of experiencing low subjective well-being. In each example these groups of factors could contain repeated elements of measurement. In order to identify which factors have the greatest influence, modelling techniques need to be applied that will enable the differentiation of the importance of each factor by controlling for others. This initial exploratory analysis would therefore suggest that while some factors have been shown to be important in understanding subjective well-being, further and more complex analysis needs to be carried out in order to develop a causal model for the attainment and maintenance of positive subjective well-being.

This preliminary analysis is useful in highlighting variations that exist in subjective well-being at an aggregate level. However, this level of analysis has its limitations. In order to gain a better understanding of the key factors that underpin well-being experience, analysis needs to be done at a more local (individual) level. The literature review showed that 'change' and 'adaptation' are important factors of happiness, satisfaction (Meyer, 1951; Hinkle, 1974; Scitovsky, 1976) and, ultimately, subjective well-being, since they influence both perception of circumstances and relative standing through the process of comparison (Scitovsky, 1976; Oswald, 1983; Wilkinson, 1996). Analysis using median scores has shown that there is little variation of subjective well-being within specific groups in society; however, analysis using proportions at the extreme ends of the scale has highlighted the changing nature of the experience of subjective well-being. These changes could be explained by either the movement of individuals between different groups in society or a difference in opinion of an individual's assessment of their circumstances as those circumstances remain unchanged but take on different meanings relative to the changing political and social context over time.

While the analysis so far gives some indication of the influence of change, accustomation or adaptation on subjective well-being, this is merely speculation and we cannot say with certainty what processes have taken place. In order to understand and analyse the factors that lead to changes in subjective well-being experiences, new measures need to be developed that express well-being at the individual level and that enable analysis of individual trajectories. But this process presents new methodological problems.

Measuring individual subjective well-being status

Measuring well-being scores of individuals and setting them within a spatial and temporal context – in this case across nine years – potentially presents a vast amount of data. In order to make the data manageable it needs to be reduced. Although this means losing some of the richness of the data, it is necessary in order to conduct meaningful statistical analysis, and reducing the amount of data presented makes them more readable, which in turn makes it easier to detect patterns (de Vaus, 2002).

There are no simple solutions to this particular problem. In this analysis the kind of reduction selected is by categorisation of the key variable of subjective well-being and considering the way its composition changes over time. The main challenge for this research is how to define the categories of subjective well-being.

As Bryman and Cramer (1994) discuss, one of the main sources of concern with collapsing data is that the 'choice of cut-off points is bound to be arbitrary and will have a direct impact on the results obtained' (p 178). They suggest that it may be better to either 'use more than one method of grouping or to employ a fairly systematic procedure like quartiles as a means of collapsing cases' (p 178). When deciding on cut-off points there are three main issues that need to be addressed: firstly, to ensure that the scores are grouped in such a way as to make them a valid categorisation of the experiences of subjective well-being within the population; secondly, to ensure there are sufficient numbers of respondents within each group to make the findings representative (and generalisable) to the population; and thirdly, to use a suitably scientific approach to ensure that the methodology is reliable. To this end several methods were tested to group the data in time periods and categorise different levels of subjective well-being experience (for a fuller explanation of the methodology refer to Searle, 2005).

For this analysis annual subjective well-being scores were initially summed across three equal periods of three years: 1991–93, 1994–96, and 1997–99. The next stage was to reduce the individual scores into manageable groups. The methods tested were not exhaustive but they are reasonably comprehensive in addressing the three main issues of validity, reliability and generalisability. The method that proved most suitable in operationalising positive subjective well-being was based on a mixture of subjective assessment of a valid measure of high subjective well-being and statistical division to make the method reliable. For this research, therefore, high subjective well-being is represented by those whose cumulative three-year score is 85 or above (20%); those whose three-year cumulative score is 65 or less represent low subjective well-being (20%); and for the purpose of clarity the remainder are labelled as 'moderate' subjective well-being (60%).

Using this positive measure, factors are selected from those available that best engage with the known predictors of well-being. These are summarised in Table 3.7. Their relationship to subjective well-being is analysed using logistic regression – a more appropriate method than linear regression for analyses using categorical variables. Linear regression may have provided information on a gradation of

Table 3.7: Independent variables by themes

Theme	Variables
Demographic	Age Gender Ethnicity Household type
Socio-economic	Household income after housing costs (quintiles) Self-perceived financial situation Employment status Employment commitment (full- or part-time) Employment security (permanent or temporary) Social class Housing tenure Educational qualification
Social	Marital status Childcare responsibilities Social support Times of day worked Number of hours in paid work Number of hours on housework Participation in local groups Political interest Religious activity
Spatial	Region Local authority area classification Neighbourhood problems Neighbourhood resources
Health	Registered disabled Number of health problems Self-reported health status Health functioning (health limits daily activity) Leisure activity Smoking behaviour
Domain satisfaction	Satisfaction with: Health Income Accommodation Spouse/partner Work Social life Amount/use of leisure time Life overall

'higher' well-being; however, this research was specifically interested in analysing 'high' subjective well-being compared to those who did not have high subjective well-being, and a dichotomous dependent variable was created to reflect these two distinct categories. Linear regression would also not have been appropriate for analysing the circumstances of those with high subjective well-being over the long term or those whose well-being had changed from low to high, compared to those whose well-being did not fall into these specific categories (see Chapter 4).

Distributions of subjective well-being at the aggregate level showed that there are differences between the experiences of men and women in terms of subjective well-being (Table 3.5). So, in line with Arber (1991) and Fujita et al (1991), the statistical analysis is modelled separately for men and women.

In her work on health inequalities Arber (1991) argues that we need to move beyond the 'legacy of Parson's functionalist conception of gender roles' to understanding men's and women's health separately in relation to both structural and role analysis (p 425). Her own research, for example, found that health inequalities among men were mainly associated with employment status, occupational class and, to a lesser extent, with housing tenure, whereas for women the picture was more complex, involving, in addition to the three factors found for men, those of marital status and parental role. Research by Fujita and colleagues (1991) on psychological well-being has also highlighted gender differences and shown that women tend to experience stronger emotions (both negative and positive) than men and that they also tend to dwell on the causes of negative emotion, while men generally distract themselves when they have experienced a similar unhappy event. This, they conclude, provides an explanation for why women are generally found to be happier than men, but also experience greater psychological distress.

Analysing the influence of roles and structures is important not only for understanding both men's and women's health, but understanding the differences between them. Men and women attach different meanings to the roles they hold in society as well as to the social position they occupy. Therefore, in order to understand these effects fully, gender should form the basis for separate analysis, rather than controlling for gender within a single model. Based on this evidence and the findings from the earlier stages of analysis, gender is analysed separately during the next stages of the research – with a view to capturing more fully the main influencing factors on subjective well-being for both men and women.

The analysis – based on separate gendered models – draws on circumstances at three different time points: 1993, 1996 and 1999, or where appropriate on the majority state (that is, two out of three years for each period) (see Appendix Table A1 for details). It is conducted in two phases. First, by creating individual models for each of the themed groups: demographic, socio-economic, social, health, spatial and domain satisfaction – that is, self-reported levels of satisfaction with different aspects of life experience such as marriage, home, leisure or work. In the second phase only those variables that were found to be statistically significant during the first phase were used to create consolidated models for each of the three-year periods 1991–93, 1994–96 and 1997–99.

In the second phase, analysis is conducted using three separate models (Table 3.8). The first model contains all the variables. The second model does not include variables that ask about satisfaction levels with accommodation, spouse, or life overall and so on (grouped under the theme of domain satisfaction). This is to test the importance of subjective measures – in particular life satisfaction – which are generally seen as the greatest predictors of subjective well-being (Andrews and

—

Table 3.8: Regression models (variables and process)

Themed models	Model 1	Model 2	Model 3
		Include variables if statistically significant	
Demographic*	Yes	Yes	Yes
Socio-economic	Yes	Yes	Yes – except 'self-reported financial situation'
Social	Yes	Yes	Yes
Spatial	Yes	Yes	Yes
Health	Yes	Yes	Yes – except 'self-reported health status'
Domain satisfaction	Yes	No	No

*Age and ethnicity were used as control variables in all models.

Withey, 1976; Campbell et al, 1976). In the third model the domain satisfaction variables are excluded, as well as financial status and self-reported health status. This is because these variables represent an evaluation – a subjective assessment – of many different aspect of individuals' health or economic circumstances. In addition, self-reported health status could include a subjective assessment of the psychological elements that are also included in the individual measures that are combined to make the measure of subjective well-being, potentially creating a tautology and masking the effect of other variables if analysed in their separate terms.

The results presented here are in a summary form – Figures 3.3, 3.4 and 3.5 for women and Figures 3.6, 3.7 and 3.8 for men (full results are presented in the Appendix, Tables B1.1, B2.1 and B3.1 for women and Tables B1.2, B2.2 and B3.2 for men). In order to avoid repetition, and as an aid to interpretation, only results at the extremes have been presented. The figures below represent those factors that significantly increase or decrease the odds of subjective well-being being high – rather than being moderate or low – when all the variables in the model have been taken into consideration (that is, they have been controlled for). Throughout the analysis, age and ethnicity[4] have been used as control variables. In some instances, although variables are included in the model, the variations between categories are not always significant and therefore 'no model' is recorded.

The variables included in the figures – and the subsequent discussion – are presented in order of their relative importance in the model. The relative importance of each variable is determined by the change in log-likelihood ratio (ΔLLR), which shows the strength of the influence that the variable has in explaining the overall variation in the odds of reporting high subjective well-being. For example, in Figure 3.3 the figure on the left shows that the variable that is most likely to increase the odds of having high well-being is self-reported health status, followed by self-reported financial situation, age and social support. Where the odds of having high well-being are reduced (the figure on the right) the most influential variable is self-reported health status, followed by age and health functioning.

The adjusted odds – the relative impact on the odds of being in one category rather than another after the influence of all of the other variables in the model has been allowed – are shown in parentheses within each variable box. The odds are calculated based on a reference category, which in most cases is the average for the group (where the reference category is different this will be explained in the descriptions of the figures). For example, in Figure 3.3, compared to a group average those in excellent health are three times more likely (2.9) to have high well-being, whereas those in poor health are only half (0.5) as likely to report high well-being.

Figure 3.3: Factors associated with high subjective well-being 1991–93 (females)[+]

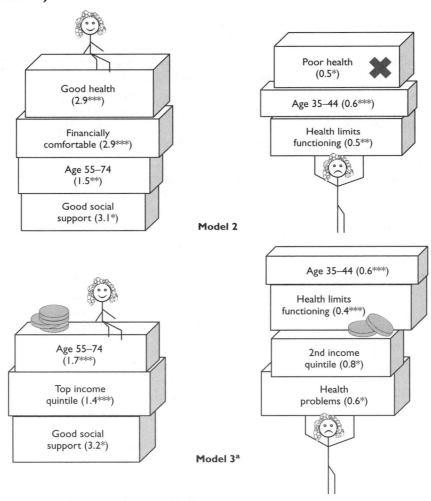

†Model 1 is not applicable because data is not available on domain satisfaction variables during 1991–93.
a Excluding financial situation and self-reported health status.
Adjusted odds are significant at: * p < 0.05, ** p < 0.01, *** p < 0.001.

Figure 3.4: Factors associated with high subjective well-being 1994–96 (females)

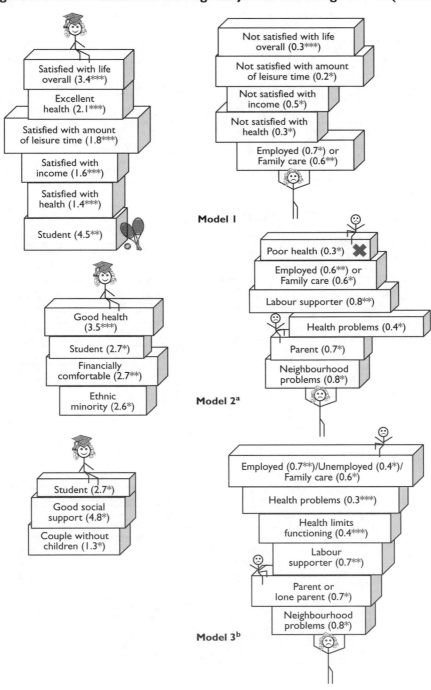

Model 1

Model 2[a]

Model 3[b]

[a] Excluding domain satisfaction variables.
[b] Excluding domain satisfaction variables, financial situation and self-reported health status.
Adjusted odds are significant at: * p < 0.05, ** p < 0.01, *** p < 0.001.

Figure 3.5: Factors associated with high subjective well-being 1997–99 (females)

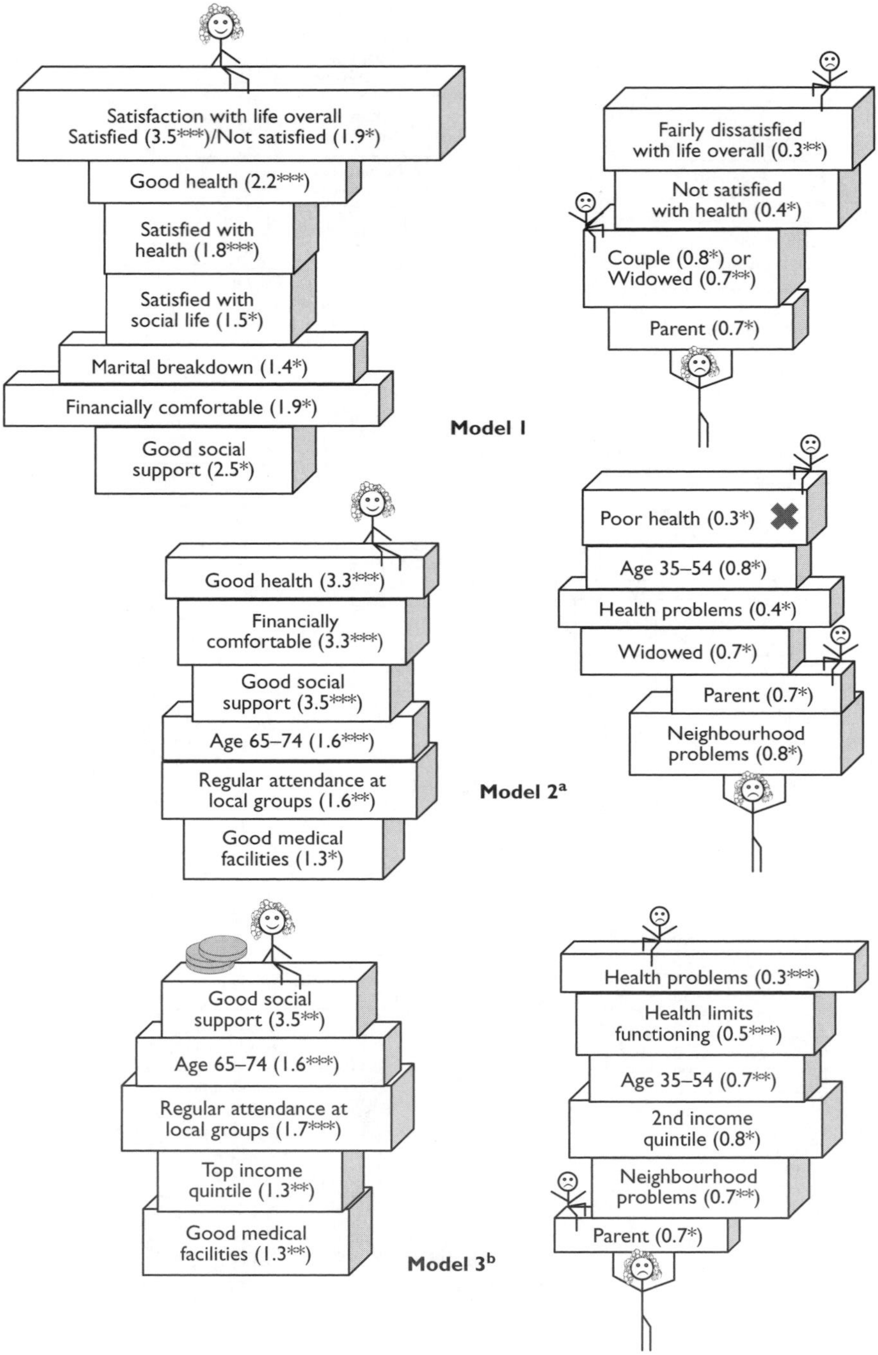

Model 1

Satisfaction with life overall
Satisfied (3.5***)/Not satisfied (1.9*)

Good health (2.2***)

Satisfied with health (1.8***)

Satisfied with social life (1.5*)

Marital breakdown (1.4*)

Financially comfortable (1.9*)

Good social support (2.5*)

Fairly dissatisfied with life overall (0.3**)

Not satisfied with health (0.4*)

Couple (0.8*) or Widowed (0.7**)

Parent (0.7*)

Model 2ª

Good health (3.3***)

Financially comfortable (3.3***)

Good social support (3.5***)

Age 65–74 (1.6***)

Regular attendance at local groups (1.6**)

Good medical facilities (1.3*)

Poor health (0.3*) ✖

Age 35–54 (0.8*)

Health problems (0.4*)

Widowed (0.7*)

Parent (0.7*)

Neighbourhood problems (0.8*)

Model 3ᵇ

Good social support (3.5**)

Age 65–74 (1.6***)

Regular attendance at local groups (1.7***)

Top income quintile (1.3**)

Good medical facilities (1.3**)

Health problems (0.3***)

Health limits functioning (0.5***)

Age 35–54 (0.7**)

2nd income quintile (0.8*)

Neighbourhood problems (0.7**)

Parent (0.7*)

ª Excluding domain satisfaction variables.
ᵇ Excluding domain satisfaction variables, financial situation and self-reported health status.
Adjusted odds are significant at: * p < 0.05, ** p < 0.01, *** p < 0.001.

Figure 3.6: Factors associated with high subjective well-being 1991–93 (males)⁺

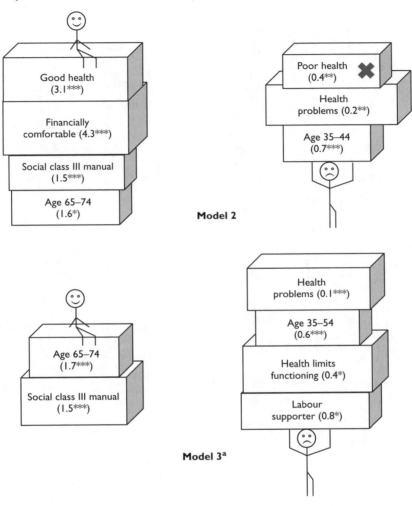

Model 2

Model 3ᵃ

⁺ Model 1 is not applicable because data is not available on domain satisfaction variables during 1991–93.
ᵃ Excluding financial situation and self-reported health status.
Adjusted odds are significant at: * p < 0.05, ** p < 0.01, *** p < 0.001.

Figure 3.7: Factors associated with high subjective well-being 1994–96 (males)

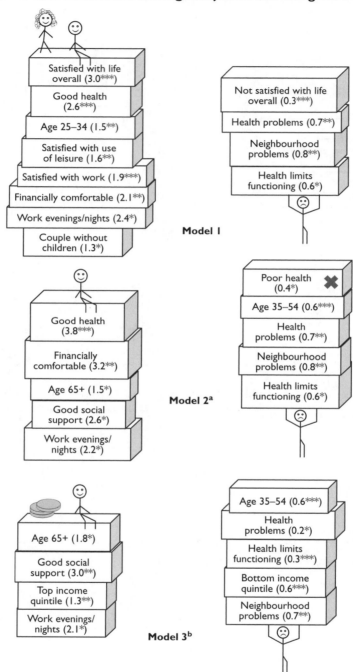

Model 1

Model 2ᵃ

Model 3ᵇ

ᵃ Excluding domain satisfaction variables.
ᵇ Excluding domain satisfaction variables, financial situation and self-reported health status.
Adjusted odds are significant at: * p < 0.05, ** p < 0.01, *** p < 0.001.

Figure 3.8: Factors associated with high subjective well-being 1997–99 (males)

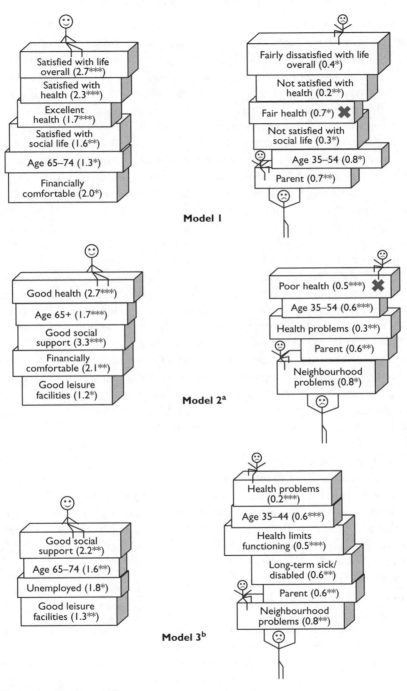

Model 1

Model 2ᵃ

Model 3ᵇ

ᵃ Excluding domain satisfaction variables.
ᵇ Excluding domain satisfaction variables, financial situation and self-reported health status.
Adjusted odds are significant at: * p < 0.05, ** p < 0.01, *** p < 0.001.

Satisfaction

The results clearly show that subjective measures of individuals' circumstances, in the main, appear to have a greater influence on the odds of experiencing high subjective well-being. In particular, these results show that domain satisfaction variables – life satisfaction emerging during the latter periods – were the most important aspects of explaining variations in subjective well-being among both men and women. The odds of having high subjective well-being increased with higher reported levels of satisfaction. For example, compared to an average for this category, among women the odds of experiencing high rather than moderate or low subjective well-being in 1994–96 rose from 0.3 for those with low levels of life satisfaction to 3.4 among those who were completely satisfied, and this pattern was generally true across other areas of satisfaction for both genders.

This evidence would support psychological and sociological theory that the meanings that individuals attach to specific events have the potential to affect feelings of subjective well-being as well as – if not more than – the actual objective circumstances themselves. While these findings would generally support Andrews and Withey (1976), it is interesting to note that dissatisfaction with life does not necessarily impede positive mood. Women who report being completely dissatisfied with their life overall, for example, are twice as likely to have high well-being (1.9; p<0.05), casting further doubt on the extent to which satisfaction with life overall fully represents individual well-being.

Another interesting finding is that satisfaction with different life domains, intriguingly, varies over a period of time. Among women, satisfaction with health, amount of leisure time and income were important during 1994–96, while during 1997–99 satisfaction with health and social life were important. Satisfaction with use of leisure time and with work were important to men during 1994–96, and health and social life during 1997–99. These findings are consistent with the changes observed by Gordon et al (2000), which suggest a shift in values away from material and eonomic-related needs towards the social aspects of life. Such findings also lend new insights into how well-being could be measured, suggesting a need to look deeper than a global measurement of well-being; individuals' assessment of their overall quality of life may involve a more complex cognitive assessment than can be captured by a single, overarching question relating to satisfaction.

Health

Health emerged as an important factor at this stage of the analysis. Much of the previous research on well-being has its origins in health – in particular, concerns with public health and the economic consequences of experiencing ill health (Baggott, 1991, and see Chapter 2). Where health inequality and inequalities in society have become aligned (Mitchell et al, 2000), this has given rise to a theory that health status is more a reflection of perceived material state and social standing (Wilkinson, 1996; Marmot, 2005) than of actual conditions.

There is no doubt that for a significant proportion of the population health is important. Using data from the 1998 wave of the BHPS, 95% of the population rated health at 7 or above on a scale of 1 'Not at all important' to 10 'Very important' – with 78% falling into the top point of this scale. Where health is deemed important it is reasonable to assume that, a priori, any deterioration of health will have a negative impact on subjective well-being. Within this research, indicators were used that addressed the influences of both physical and psychological aspects of health on subjective well-being. This is not, of course, to imply that the health measures used may fit neatly into two such distinct categories. The recording or registering of health 'problems' in itself suggests a recognition that a health issue has become a psychological burden, therefore there may be some overlap between what is defined as a medical health issue and how acknowledgement of having a medically defined problem can itself have negative consequences for subjective well-being. Throughout this research these different aspects of experiencing health-related problems have been analysed in respect of registered disability, number of health problems, functioning ability and self-reported health status. Links to health are also made through health-related behaviour (smoking and physical exercise) and the health implications for employment status as they relate to disability or long-term sickness.

When the domain satisfaction variables are removed from the regression model (Model 2) then self-reported health status becomes the most important variable for women and men, with the odds of having high well-being greater among those reporting excellent health (for example 3.5 for women and 3.8 for men in 1994–96) and lower among those with poor health (0.4 and 0.5 respectively). When self-reported health status is removed from the analysis (Model 3) health problems and health functioning become important, with lower odds associated with a deterioration in health. For example, compared to those with no health problems, the odds of having high subjective well-being fall from 0.8 to 0.1 as the number of health problems increases from one to four; similarly, where health limits daily functioning the odds drop to a low of 0.3 ($p < 0.05$) as compared to those whose health does not limit their daily activities.

Although health has previously been at the centre of research into well-being, studies that focus on positive subjective well-being have found little relationship between health status and overall life satisfaction, suggesting that changes in physical health may not necessarily reduce a general sense of subjective well-being until such time as they become a practical and psychological burden. This view is supported by Maslow's (1954) theory, which suggests the importance of basic needs (such as health) may be underestimated where individuals are satisfied, only to re-emerge where dissatisfaction occurs. While studies report that good physical health is associated with happier people, who live longer (Veenhoven, 1984), good health generally is taken for granted (Campbell et al, 1976) and only emerges as an important factor in reported well-being when its deterioration interferes with daily functioning, particularly in old age (Campbell et al, 1976; Argyle, 1987; Smith et al, 2002). The strong positive relationship between high subjective well-being and satisfaction with health, or self-reported health status, and the negative association of deterioration in health and ability to function reported here would, however, suggest that health does not become a function of well-being upon its decline, but may be an important underpinning of positive well-being experience. This evidence suggests that the active promotion of health could potentially provide a means of raising well-being states.

Wealth

Another factor that is important to well-being is wealth. The dominance of economic theory suggests that income should be considered as a key feature of personal well-being, particularly where increased wealth is equated to increases in national (and individual) well-being. However, studies have shown that although satisfaction does increase with recent improvements in financial circumstances, over the long term, variations in levels of satisfaction and finances are not significant (Inglehart, 1990). Comparative studies have also reported that the relationship between income levels and satisfaction is very weak (Argyle, 1987). Significant increases in wealth, such as winning the football pools or national lottery, are also no guarantee of increased satisfaction with life; the increase in reported happiness associated with increased wealth can be offset by the hostility or envy of friends, being pestered by requests for money, or rejected if the 'winner' moves to a 'better class of neighbourhood' (Arglye, 1987, p 97). Comparative, longitudinal analysis has also shown that although, overall, rich people tend to be happier than poor people, in advanced societies people have not grown happier as they have grown richer (Layard, 2003).

The BHPS indicates a positive relationship between actual income and high subjective well-being; on average the odds double from 0.7 among those in the lower quintiles to 1.4 among the top quintiles. However, this does not emerge as an important influence until domain satisfaction and perceived financial situation are removed from the analysis. The results in Model 3 show that although household income is important to female subjective well-being during 1991–93 (ΔLLR 27.0), by 1997–99 it has become less important (ΔLLR 9.9), and is only important in explaining male subjective well-being during 1994–96 (ΔLLR 17.5). Variations in well-being are not, then, easily accounted for in objective terms of material affluence, so, in line with Wilkinson (1996), attention turns to individuals' assessment of their financial circumstances.

Interestingly, here, perceptions of wealth do appear to have a greater bearing on well-being. When domain satisfaction factors are removed from the analysis (Model 2), perceived financial situation is the second most important variable in explaining variations in women's high subjective well-being during 1991–93 (ΔLLR 52.8) and 1997–99 (ΔLLR 47.3) and men's high subjective well-being during 1991–93 (ΔLLR 69.8) and 1994–96 (ΔLLR 45.1), with those who are financially comfortable being up to four times more likely to report positive well-being. This evidence would support theories of the role of internal mechanisms, such that what matters is how we compare our wealth to that of those around us (Wilkinson, 1996; Blanchflower and Oswald, 2002), suggesting that subjective wealth may be a better predictor of well-being than objective income.

Social support and relationships

Another area considered important for this research is that of social support. The importance of social support and integration into collective life was recognised as early as Durkheim's 1897 study, which found that the greater the integration in society, the greater the immunity of individuals to suicide (Durkheim, 1952). More recently, 'social capital' has been coined as a term relating to the social ties and trustworthiness that exist within communities (Putnam, 2000), while the collective value of relationships is deemed a productive resource that underpins well-being (Jordan, 2007). National and international studies have consistently reported the importance of social relationships on satisfaction and happiness levels (see, for example, Campbell et al, 1976; Veenhoven, 1984; Argyle, 1987; Shields and Wooden, 2003). In part this is due to the effect it has on buffering the negative impacts of difficult experiences and related stress outcomes (Veenhoven, 1984; Stark, 1987; Triemstra et al, 1998).

The BHPS supports these earlier findings. In the sample population, social relationships were valued during the 1990s. For example, drawing on two questions included in the 1998 BHPS that aim to find out how much people value others, 70% of people think a good marriage or partnership is very important, while 65% of people report having good friends as very important. Furthermore, the availability of good social support has been shown to have a positive impact on experiences of subjective well-being – potentially being up to five times more protective of high well-being as compared to poor social support (Figure 3.7).

In addition to personal social support, people may gain a sense of subjective well-being through feeling engaged with their local community or with society in general. Social relationships and social interaction have also been shown to be an important factor in relation to satisfaction with leisure and employment (Argyle, 1987; Hills and Argyle, 1998). The effects of social relationships therefore provide an important link between different aspects of subjective well-being, including family, work, leisure and community.

Social integration can be measured in the BHPS with reference to questions on participation in local groups, political interest and religious activity. Religious activity has previously been associated with higher levels of satisfaction (Gurin et al, 1960; Hadaway, 1978; Inglehart, 1990). In this research, however, it did not exert a significant independent effect on experiences of high subjective well-being when other variables were controlled for. Political interest and participation in local groups, on the other hand, did. Supporting Labour is associated with significantly lower odds compared to a group average (0.8; p<0.05) for both genders (while bivariate results show that Conservative supporters had significantly higher odds (1.2–1.4; p<0.05 – Appendix, Table B1.2). During 1997–99 women who participated in local groups on a regular basis were between 1.6 and 1.7 times more likely to experience high subjective well-being (p<0.01) as compared to women who never or almost never participated. The availability of group support and feelings of belongingness potentially provide important means of understanding and enhancing individual well-being. However, the differences between political party supporters would suggest that there are other, more complex, factors associated with group identity and that the existence of social capital may not always be equated to positive outcomes.

Age

Another factor of importance in this study is the variation of subjective well-being experiences across the life course. Age has an independent influence on male well-being when all the variables in the model are controlled for, and emerges as the most important variable once the domain satisfaction, self-reported financial situation and health status variables are removed from the analysis (Model 3). The relationship between age and well-being is U-shaped, with the dip occurring in middle age. Those between the ages of 34 and 54 generally are less likely to report high well-being as compared to the group average (0.6; p<0.001), whereas those close to or at retirement age (55+) are at least one and a half times more likely to report positive well-being (1.4–1.8; p<0.05). Previous research reports contradictory findings in respect of age, ranging from no significant association (Inglehart, 1990; Dirksen, 2000; Cummins et al, 2003) to reporting an increase in life satisfaction across the life course (Blanchflower and Oswald, 2002; Campbell et al, 1976; Inglehart, 1990). This new analysis, however, supports a general consensus that dissatisfaction is greatest during the early 40s (Shields and Wooden, 2003) or middle age (Theodossiou, 1998).

Social roles

The characteristics of individuals that may impinge on well-being not only include those that are ascribed (such as age or gender), but also their achieved identity through the social roles they either adopt or have imposed upon them by society. These roles provide the normative framework for social behaviour, set within the context of the rights and responsibilities an individual may have (Taylor et al, 1997). Such roles will be subject to change throughout the life course and the time at which they change may have a positive or negative effect on subjective well-being (Moen et al, 1995).

This research shows that having or losing social roles is important in explaining variations in high subjective well-being among men and women. Parenthood has a negative association, whether this is experienced as a couple relationship or lone (female) parent (0.6–0.7; p<0.001). Living in a couple household without children, on the other hand, is associated with higher odds of reporting high levels of well-being (1.3; p<0.05). Among women also, the loss of a partner through widowhood has a negative effect (0.7; p<0.01), although losing a partner through divorce or separation is associated with higher odds of positive well-being (1.4; p<0.05).

Social relationships are important to an understanding of well-being, but these findings suggest that the extent to which life events – which create or change relationships – impact on psychological health will depend upon how they are perceived by the individual and that the family unit may not always be a safe, secure environment. The acquiring of social roles may bring with it additional responsibilities – especially towards children – and may be a cause of stress and concern that impinge on well-being regardless of the level of other support available within the immediate family unit. Bereavement, understandably, has negative outcomes; however, the loss of a partner through marital dissolution may, for a time at least, be a period of positive reflection, a chance for a fresh start, a chance to regain a sense of control, in the light of unsettling differences.

Place and well-being

As discussed at the beginning of this chapter, measures of well-being need not only to address the individual, but to be set within the context of the social and physical setting. Physical location and environment have previously been identified as being important in determining the 'shape of stressors to which we are exposed, as well as the resources available to deal with them' (McCulloch, 2000, p 3), but despite this, the extent to which neighbourhood effects impact on subjective well-being remains a much understudied area (Shields and Wooden, 2003). This in part may be due to the difficulties associated with spatial analysis, reflected in the limited findings among this and previous research. For example, a focus on area differences based on poverty and affluence tends not to provide any significant insights into variations in satisfaction (Inglehart, 1990). Within the evidence presented here, spatial analysis based on area or region of residency does not have a significant effect when other variables are controlled for.

It may be difficult to unpack the influential elements of neighbourhood on well-being where areas are grouped according to geographic divisions or prevailing socio-economic conditions. Addressing individuals' own experiences of their neighbourhood – its problems as well as its resources – may provide a more insightful understanding of how neighbourhood effects impact on well-being. The physical environment presents itself not only as a source of stress – real or perceived – but mediates individuals' ability to cope with such stress through the resources it provides (Campbell et al, 1976; McCulloch, 2000).

Here again, though, studies have found limited association between place and well-being. Satisfaction with community, neighbourhood and housing – including availability of amenities and differences of perceived vulnerability – generally accounts for only a small proportion of life satisfaction overall (Campbell et al,

1976). But this new analysis shows that, on the one hand, having problems in a neighbourhood – such as noise, pollution, vandalism or crime – perhaps not surprisingly, significantly reduces the odds of having high subjective well-being (0.8; $p<0.05$) (Figures 3.3 to 3.5 and 3.6 to 3.8); and that, on the other hand, the availability of good neighbourhood resources significantly increases the odds – although gender differences are evident.

Those who perceive facilities as 'good' – compared to those who report them as 'poor' – are generally more likely to experience high subjective well-being (on average 1.3; $p<0.05$). This relates particularly to the standard of local leisure resources for men (Figure 3.8), and standard of medical facilities for women (Figure 3.5). Such findings, although interesting in themselves, serve to reinforce other areas of research into well-being. As discussed earlier, separate studies have suggested that pursuit of leisure activities is associated with the positive benefits of social interaction (Argyle, 1987), improved self-concept (Marsh et al, 1986) and deep levels of satisfaction (Csikszentmihalyi, 1975). This may account for why the perceived standard of leisure services was the only neighbourhood resource to have an influence on experiences of high subjective well-being for men. Among women the importance associated with health – and possibly linked with a caring role – is reinforced by the inclusion of satisfaction with medical facilities.

As will be shown in the results reported in the next chapter, none of the spatial variables – including perceptions of neighbourhood problems or resources – has a significant influence on long-term well-being. Although these findings may be in line with previous research that generally reports little – if any – influence of neighbourhood effects, it is more widely recognised that 'context' is a problematic variable to measure. It is difficult to unpack the neighbourhood aspects that are often contained in quantitative models from those aspects that make up an individual's socio-economic status (MacIntyre et al, 2002), and a mix of methods is required to appreciate the effects (Smith and Easterlow, 2005).

The lack of significance of place in this research may be due to methodological limitations. First, although attempts were made to cross-analyse regional data with area classification, this resulted in low or missing cases within many categories and inhibited further analysis. Oakes (2004) has referred to this as the 'residual confounding' problem familiar to neighbourhood effects research. Second is the extent to which the other variables included in the models are mediators or confounders of neighbourhood effects, such that attributes of the neighbourhood, including medical facilities, schools, labour or housing markets, may determine individuals' health, education, occupation, social class and housing tenure, which show independent influences on well-being – a problem familiar to neighbourhood effects research (MacIntyre et al, 2002; Diez Roux, 2004).

While it is acknowledged that the geographic units of analysis are often too large to have any real explanatory power, there may also be a problem attached to the different spatial boundaries people recognise as being important (Lupton, 2003). The neighbourhood effects on subjective well-being may therefore benefit from a more focused approach that not only reduces the number of areas to be studied and increases the sample size within each area but also acknowledges the social spaces that individuals themselves recognise as 'neighbourhood' according to the particular activity that takes place in that space. A round-up of research by Parkes et al (2002) and findings from work by Shields and Wooden (2003) further complicates the picture where satisfaction is perhaps less about a neighbourhood's external attributes or objective features and more about the internal workings of those who reside in them, whereby satisfaction is based on degree of attachment, social interactions and expectations.

Although findings on neighbourhood effects are inconclusive, there does seem to be a pattern emerging and, where significant differences are found, these tend to stem from individual experiences of neighbourhood rather than from more traditional observed measures of its material characteristics, arguably making satisfaction with neighbourhood a shorthand measure for neighbourhood effects. As with the study of well-being generally, the types of measures selected for spatial analysis may also benefit from a combined approach – addressing subjective experience and observed aspects.

Gender differences

The above factors have explained the similarities in understanding variations in the subjective well-being of both men and women. However, this research also shows that there are significant gender differences. Three differences are worth emphasising here: social stratification, employment and ethnicity.

Social structure has previously been identified as being important to male well-being (Arber, 1991), and this is borne out here. Although perhaps somewhat counter-intuitively (a point I will return to later), this is not a linear relationship. Men in social class III manual, for example, are one and a half times more likely to experience high subjective well-being as compared to a mean for all social classes (Figure 3.6).

Different aspects of employment also emerge as being important to men and women. The social aspects of employment – times of day worked – are pertinent to male well-being where, compared to men who are not working, those working evenings or nights are twice as likely (2.4, $p<0.05$) to experience high subjective well-being (Figure 3.7). Among women, lack of employment is a key factor. Absence from the labour market due to family care commitments (0.6; $p<0.05$) or being unemployed (0.4; $p<0.05$) has a negative association with subjective well-being, although it is interesting to note that women who are employed also have lower odds (0.7; $p<0.01$) (Figure 3.4). Not all absence from the labour market, however, is negatively correlated to female well-being, as is shown by those who are students being nearly three times more likely to report high subjective well-being (2.7; $p<0.05$) (Figure 3.4). By contrast, absence from the labour market for men (as previously noted) had somewhat contradictory outcomes. Employment status only became important to male subjective well-being during the last period studied (1997–99) and produced some surprising results. The experience of being on long-term sickness or disabled perhaps not unexpectedly is associated with lower odds (0.6; $p<0.01$); however, intriguingly, unemployed males have higher odds of reporting high subjective well-being (1.8; $p<0.05$) as compared to the group average (Figure 3.7), a result that generally seems counter-intuitive.[5]

Such findings expose the limitations to an understanding of well-being in previous research that does not account for the variability in well-being across the full spectrum of well-being scores. The results from the BHPS may be a reflection of the resilience of unemployed men or, as other research has shown, an indication of positive evaluation – where present circumstances are considered in a more favourable light than previous experience. Research, for example, has found that unemployment may result in psychological benefits where it has been preceded by a period of insecurity (Arnetz et al, 1988), boredom or stress (Little, 1976; Fineman, 1983), or indeed that there may be mediating effects associated with living in a neighbourhood of high unemployment (Shields and Wooden, 2003). The employment factors underpinning well-being may be a reflection of more complex experiences and relationships than can be fully explored through statistical analysis alone. This is an area of well-being research that may benefit from more in-depth qualitative insights into the experiences of employment and unemployment.

A final difference to emerge from this stage of the analysis relates to ethnicity. In general it has been shown that women tend to experience stronger emotions than men; in particular they are more self-critical and prone to psychological distress (Back, 1971). However, the findings from the BHPS suggest that there may be more complex relationships than a simple gender division. On the one hand, females from ethnic minority groups are more than twice as likely to report high well-being as compared to white women (2.6; $p<0.05$) (Figure 3.4), while on the other hand men from ethnic minorities are half as likely to report high subjective well-being than white men – although here the findings were not statistically significant (see Appendix, Table B1.2).

Cultural aspects will impact on well-being – or indeed any – research in many ways. In order to explore these differences further, key methodological implications need to be addressed. Previous research reports contradictory findings in respect of ethnicity and subjective well-being, which may be accounted for in respect of the method of measurement adopted. Nazroo's (1997a) research of a national survey focusing on ethnicity in Britain, for example, found that ethnic minorities generally have a lower risk of psycho-social health problems as compared to a white British group, although more detailed analysis (Nazroo, 1997b) shows that levels of psychological well-being are higher, similar or lower than for whites across different ethnic groups – in part accounted for by the 'differences in performance of the mental health assessments used' (Nazroo, 1997b, p 84). Research by Shields and Price (2003) also reported that the psychological well-being of people from ethnic minorities is higher, lower or the same when compared to white people in the UK, depending upon which measurement is used.

There are two possible implications for such differences: either psychological well-being is a personal issue that is not influenced by cultural differences; or existing measures of subjective well-being do not capture the cultural aspects that influence subjective well-being among different ethnic groups. Although the subtleties of such variations cannot be explored within this data, due to limitations of the sample make-up, the open-ended findings from this and previous research suggest that this is an area that may benefit from further research.

The evidence from the BHPS suggests that the nature of well-being is to some extent tied up with the cultural (political and social) construction of gender, addressing the expectations and meanings attached to the roles of lover, care-giver and breadwinner. But the findings here are a reminder that men and women in themselves are not homogenous groups and some of the differences found may be subject to cultural variations which in turn influence perceptions and expectations of what it is to be a man or woman at a given point in time.

Exploring well-being

This chapter has reported the findings from research that seeks to explore trends in the underpinnings of well-being within the same individuals over time. While differences have emerged in respect of both ascribed and acquired roles and responsibilities, it is individuals' assessments of their circumstances which appear to have the greatest influences on reported well-being, as opposed to their actual circumstances. Even here, though, different aspects emerge as being important at different times of individuals' lives, as well as different times in a period of British political and social history, with clear variations along gendered divisions.

This initial exploratory analysis has gone some way to describing and explaining variations in experiences of low and high well-being over time. However, the research would benefit from adopting a longitudinal approach, identifying the circumstances under which experiences of positive well-being are maintained. There is also benefit in moving towards a causal explanation of well-being by adopting a pathways approach, looking at changes in well-being – specifically, improved well-being – and changes in circumstances. These aspects are dealt with in the next chapter.

Notes

1. Described in Chapter 2.

2. It is acknowledged that the summing methodology is open to criticism, due to the assumptions made about the relative importance of individual answers at an ordinal level; however, the summing of scores is a recognised method in the use of the GHQ (Goldberg and Williams, 1991) and will be adopted for the research reported here.

3. Statistically speaking, a curve is described as 'skewed' when one of its tails is longer than the other. A 'negative skew' is when the tail is longer along the lower (or towards the

negative) frequencies. A 'positive skew' indicates that the tail is longer along the higher (or positive) frequencies.

4. Although data is available on different ethnic origins, within the dataset on average 96% of the sample were 'white', with the remaining 4% being black–Caribbean, black–African, Indian, Pakistani, Bangladeshi, Chinese or of other ethnic origin. The latter groups have therefore been collapsed and ethnicity is analysed in respect of 'ethnic minority' compared to 'white'.

5. This finding highlights one of the issues of statistical analysis, where results may be an artefact of measurement. Although being unemployed is a valid category, the number of cases that fit this description has reduced over time – falling from 279 (8%) in 1993 to 88 (3%) in 1999 – so the analysis presented here may not be generalisable.

FOUR

Advancing the study of subjective well-being[1]

> If you're in a bad situation, don't worry it'll change. If you're in a good situation, don't worry it'll change.
>
> (John A. Simone, Sr)

Times change. Life in Britain in the 1980s is not the same as that experienced in the 1990s, nor indeed in the new millennium. Politics shift, economies unwind, cultures reform. Well-being today may not be what it was half a century ago – the mix of factors affecting well-being is likely to vary over time. This chapter is about the temporal dynamics of well-being.

One of the problems of previous well-being research (identified in Chapter 2) has been the lack of longitudinal analysis. Previous research has been limited by its treatment of subjective well-being as a static phenomenon (Kahn and Juster, 2002), with studies seeking to measure subjective well-being through a single survey. Advances in the collection of social information at national and international levels mean that longitudinal analysis of subjective well-being is being addressed through repeat panel surveys or an accumulation of cross-sectional studies. However, much of this analysis is at the national level and fails to address the factors affecting individuals and their subjective well-being. By using panel data, this study is able to analyse subjective well-being of the same individuals over time. It can thus move towards a greater understanding of the factors that are associated with positive subjective well-being over the life course and through history.

The purpose of this chapter, then, is to provide new knowledge in well-being studies by looking at changes in circumstances in order to assess the importance of prolonged exposure (or lack of exposure) to different life situations as well as identify conditions that can maintain or promote positive subjective well-being. Several different methods could be used to analyse changes over time. For the purposes of this research it is approached in two different ways: firstly, by a longitudinal analysis using data for each year between 1991 and 1999; secondly, by identifying changes in circumstances between two time periods; 1993–96 and 1996–99.

Taking the first of these methodologies, the key aim is to identify factors associated with maintaining high subjective well-being from 1991 to 1999. Where possible, variables have been coded according to the majority circumstance (that is, six out of nine years). However, where data were not available, selective years were chosen, for example comparing individuals' circumstances in 1993, 1996 and 1999.[2] To complement this methodology, the subjective well-being variable is also reclassified, by combining individuals' subjective well-being status for each of the three periods 1991–93, 1994–96 and 1997–99.

Three main categories of subjective well-being are assigned to the typology according to whether an individual's subjective well-being remains consistently high, moderate or low over the three periods (a stable well-being state); whether they have two out of the three years with the same level of subjective well-being (coded as mostly high, moderate or low); or whether they have a different level of subjective well-being in each of the three years (coded as 'mixed'). Using this method to create a typology of subjective well-being shows that 47% of the population's subjective well-being remains stable at the high (9%), moderate (32%) or low level (6%). Half (51%) of the population's subjective well-being is mostly consistent at the high (11%), moderate (30%) or low level (10%), while the remaining 2% have subjective well-being levels that are complex in nature and fluctuate between all three levels.

It was intended that this measure be used to assess the relationship between subjective well-being and change (or stability) in circumstances over the long term. But this method of analysis has its limitations. While it was envisaged that change in circumstances over time would be analysed, the complexity of individuals' lives means that in many circumstances the combinations of experiences across nine years are too complex to be grouped into meaningful categories. In most instances the categorisation involved some 'stable' element and a single category of 'mixed' experience as being indicative of all changes in status. Although this method sought to retain as much of the data as possible in the analysis, this inevitably loses some explanatory power. The second method, then, is selected with a view to addressing some of these difficulties.

One of the key aims of this research is to understand the extent to which changing circumstances influence (or not) experiences in subjective well-being. In order to tease out the complexities of changing circumstances, in the second method the amount of data analysed is reduced, with a view to increasing its analytical potential. This limits the number of changes to be coded and enables a greater variation in circumstances to be examined, with a view to increasing its explanatory power.

For the second method, data are selected from 1993, 1996 and 1999 *only*, and change in circumstance between 1993 and 1996, and between 1996 and 1999 are coded. Variables have been recoded as far as possible to show variation in individuals' circumstances between these two time periods. However, in certain circumstances data is not available in these years, and other years of data are selected (see Appendix, Table A1 for details). To complement this method, the dependent variable (subjective well-being) is also recoded to reflect change in experience between the two periods. A dichotomous variable is created that distinguishes between those whose subjective well-being has improved to the highest level (a move from low or moderate well-being in 1993 to high in 1996; or a move from low or moderate well-being in 1996 to high in 1999) and those whose well-being has not improved in this way. Although this significantly reduces the size of the sample (8% and 10% respectively), it is envisaged that it will maximise the explanatory power of the results.

As with the cross-sectional analysis, logistic regression is carried out in two stages, with the final analysis being conducted using three different models (as described in Chapter 3). Figures 4.1 and 4.2 show a summary of the results of the regression to predict the adjusted odds of maintaining high subjective well-being (full results are given in the Appendix, Table C1.1 for women and C1.2 for men). The results from the regression analysis to predict the adjusted odds of enhancing subjective well-being are presented in Figures 4.3 and 4.4 for women and Figures 4.5 and 4.6 for men (full results are presented in the Appendix, Tables D1.1 and D2.1 for women and D2.1 and D2.2 for men).

Temporal perspectives

The results from this stage of the analysis reinforce some of the findings from the cross-sectional analysis. However, the longitudinal nature – in particular the charting of changing circumstances – highlights some interesting new insights. Across both methods described above, four notable findings are worth elaborating. Firstly, satisfaction with life does not mirror feelings of well-being across time; secondly, health is a key component of long-term well-being; thirdly, well-being fluctuates across different stages of the life-course; fourthly, the link between economic factors and well-being is not as straightforward as economic theory would imply.

Satisfaction

The longitudinal analysis, while supporting the importance of satisfaction with life domains in understanding well-being, does raise some intriguing findings that question the dominance of life satisfaction as a well-being measure. The analysis shows – perhaps not surprisingly – that where individuals' satisfaction levels change, where they become more satisfied, this is associated with improvements in subjective well-being (increasing by up to four times). Subjective measures of individuals' circumstances – the meanings that people attach to life events – do have an influence on experiences of well-being. While satisfaction with parts of life is connected with achieving and maintaining positive well-being, there would also appear to be a cumulative effect where increases in satisfaction go hand-in-hand with increases in the combined feelings of self-worth, control and being useful (although directionality is not determined here).

However, this research shows that, over the long term, variations between levels of satisfaction are not always significant – most notably for satisfaction with life overall. This is reinforced where the evidence shows satisfaction with life overall is not always *the* most important factor for well-being. While this research found that satisfaction with life overall was the most important variable in understanding

Figure 4.1: Factors associated with stable high subjective well-being 1991–99 (females)

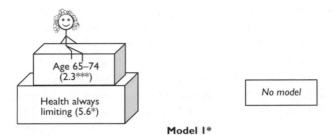

No model

Model 1*

*Satisfaction with life overall was the most important variable followed by satisfaction with use of leisure time, and although those who were satisfied had higher odds this was not significantly different from a group average. Self-reported health status was the next most important variable, but again the differences between categories were not significant.

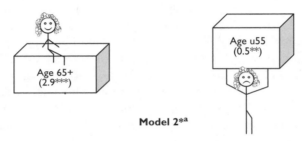

Model 2*ᵃ

*Self-reported health status was the most important variable but the differences between categories were not significant. After age, financial situation and social support were important, although again there was no significant variation between categories.

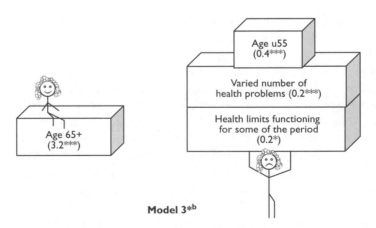

Model 3*ᵇ

*Social support was also important but there was no significant variation between categories.

ᵃ Excluding domain satisfaction variables.
ᵇ Excluding domain satisfaction, financial situation and self-reported health status variables.
Adjusted odds are significant at: * p < 0.05, ** p < 0.01, *** p < 0.001.

Figure 4.2: Factors associated with stable high subjective well-being 1991–99 (males)

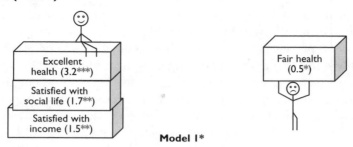

Model 1*

*Employment status, satisfaction with life overall, social support and financial situation were also important but there was no significant variation between categories.

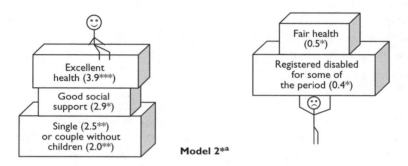

Model 2*ᵃ

*Employment status, financial situation and social class were also important, but there was no significant variation between categories.

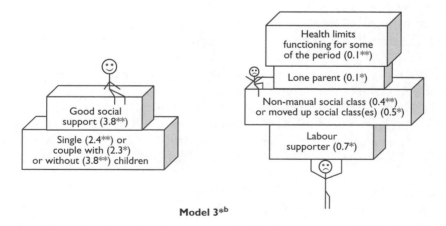

Model 3*ᵇ

*Marital status was also included in the model but there was no significant variation between categories.

ᵃ Excluding domain satisfaction variables.
ᵇ Excluding domain satisfaction, financial situation and self-reported health status variables.
Adjusted odds are significant at: * p < 0.05, ** p < 0.01, *** p < 0.001.

variations in well-being over the short term (see Chapter 3), satisfaction with life overall is not the best predictor of *long-term*, or *changes* in, subjective well-being. Using gendered models showed that different aspects of life were important to men and women – for men, satisfaction with health, social life, income and work; for women, in contrast, key factors rested with health and the use of leisure time.

Although the research reported here supports the findings of previous studies that emphasise the role of global satisfaction as a function of well-being, it has also provided evidence that well-being is a complex phenomenon operating at various levels through space and time. For example, different life domains are significant at different times and their effects vary between men and women. Likewise, levels of satisfaction matter at some times, and at other times other factors are associated with enhanced subjective well-being, such as health, employment status and social support. Although a single global measure may be sufficient to capture the elements of subjective well-being in the short term, the evidence presented here implies that more subtle measures might be required to monitor changes in well-being status, and that other aspects of well-being need to be accounted for. One such aspect is health.

Health

Health is an important factor for the long-term analysis of well-being – whether this is expressed as satisfaction with health, self-reported health status or health functioning. In particular, there is a positive association with improved or good health and a negative association with poor health. The loss of health functioning or increase in the number of health problems both have a negative association with improvements in subjective well-being, providing further support to the emerging properties of health deterioration. So, on the one hand, self-reported health status or satisfaction with health has a greater bearing than satisfaction with life overall. For example, men reporting excellent health are three times more likely to report high well-being (3.2; $p<0.001$) (Figure 4.2, Model 1); and a more positive evaluation of health status – reporting increased levels of satisfaction with health – is an important factor in respect of improved levels of well-being for both women (4.0; $p<0.01$) (Figure 4.4, Model 1) and men (2.1; $p<0.05$) (Figure 4.6, Model 1). On the other hand, experiencing problems with health functioning (including being registered disabled) for a period of time, or sustained health problems over the longer term, has a negative association, with odds falling as low as 0.1 ($p<0.05$) (Figure 4.2).[3]

These findings emphasise the debilitating effect of depleted health in both psychological and physical terms, but being in good health brings with it positive feelings. In contrast to previous theories, this research shows that health is not taken for granted and that being in good health is associated with achieving and maintaining high subjective well-being. Analysis of changes in circumstances shows that, where people perceive their health as having improved, where it has stopped limiting their daily activities or where their satisfaction with their health has increased, this is more likely to be associated with improvements in their subjective well-being.

From a hierarchical perspective we see here the importance of a basic need such as health, which may be taken for granted until it is impaired, impacting on well-being only when it is a source of functional limitation or dissatisfaction. As mentioned previously, the importance afforded to health would imply that any loss of health functioning would be detrimental to feelings of well-being. The negative consequences of health limitations have also been reflected in the analysis of economic status that shows that being on long-term sickness or disabled is associated with low odds of having high subjective well-being. The reduced odds of being in older age may also be linked to the loss of health functioning (see Chapter 3). However, a key finding of this research is that it contradicts previous studies that have focused on positive subjective well-being and that found little relationship between health status and overall life satisfaction (Argyle, 1987; Campbell et al, 1976). So, having previously identified the importance of health for well-being over the short term, the new analysis confirms it as a major component in prolonged experiences of positive subjective well-being.

A tautology, however, may exist here, since it could be that an individual's perceived health status or functioning ability includes a cognitive assessment of

Figure 4.3: Factors associated with improved subjective well-being 1993–96 (females)[+]

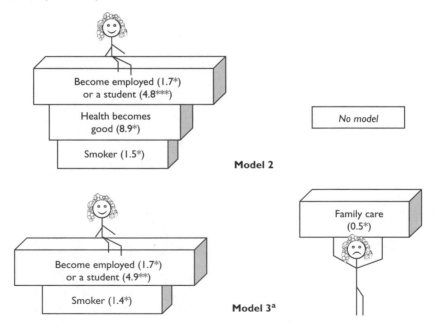

+Model 1 is not applicable because data is not available on domain satisfaction variables for 1993.
a Excluding financial situation and self-reported health status.
Adjusted odds are significant at: * p < 0.05, ** p < 0.01, *** p < 0.001.

Figure 4.4: Factors associated with improved subjective well-being 1996–99 (females)

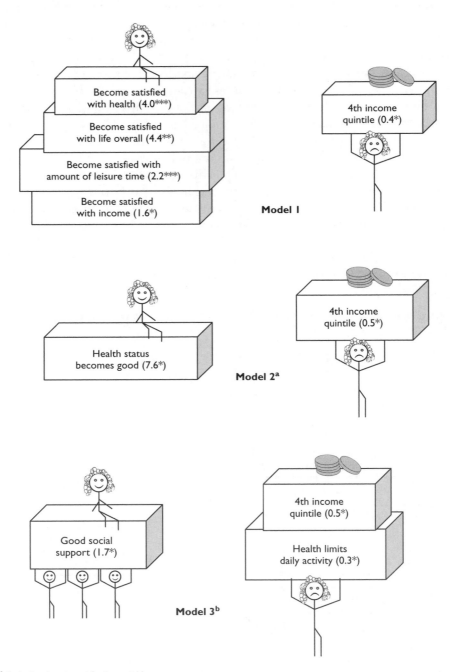

Figure 4.5: Factors associated with improved subjective well-being 1993–96 (males)[+]

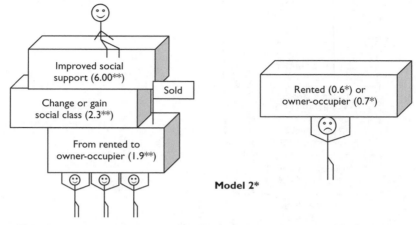

Model 2*

*Self-reported health status was also included in the model, with the odds of subjective well-being becoming high, increasing with improved health status; however, the odds did not significantly vary from people with poor health.

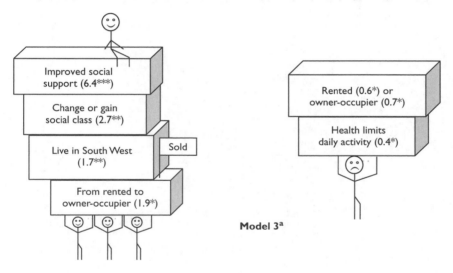

Model 3[a]

[+]Model I is not applicable because data is not available on domain satisfaction variables for 1993.
[a] Excluding financial situation and self-reported health status.
Adjusted odds are significant at: * $p < 0.05$, ** $p < 0.01$, *** $p < 0.001$.

the psychological elements that are also included in the individual measures that are combined to make the measure of subjective well-being. As Blaxter (1987) suggests, people's attitudes towards health vary from an understanding of a 'healthy person' as someone who is physically fit and active, to perceiving their own healthiness in terms of psychological fulfilment and ability to cope. That is not to say that subjective health elements are not relevant; however, it does suggest that health represents more than its physical components.

Figure 4.6: Factors associated with improved subjective well-being 1996–99 (males)

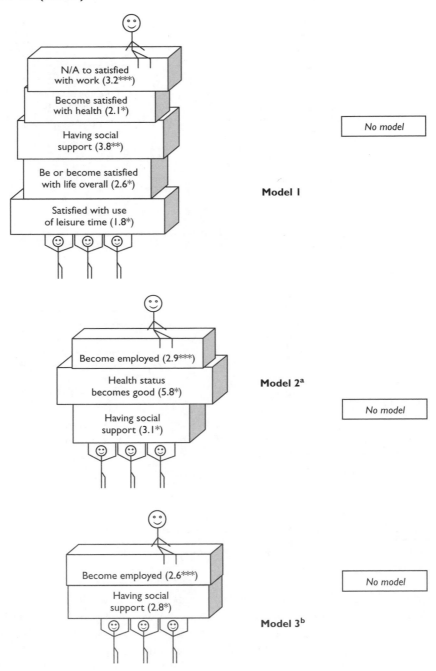

a Excluding domain satisfaction variables.
b Excluding domain satisfaction, financial situation and self-reported health status.
Adjusted odds are significant at: * p < 0.05, ** p < 0.01, *** p < 0.001.

As discussed previously (Chapter 3) the recording or registering of health 'problems' in itself suggests a recognition that a health issue has become a psychological burden and there may therefore be some overlap between acknowledgement of health problems and subjective well-being but, importantly, overall the findings suggest that the value of health is not underestimated and being in good health or experiencing improvements in health status corresponds directly with improvements in subjective well-being.

The health aspects of subjective well-being, however, may be more complicated. Longitudinal analysis shows that improvements in well-being – among women at least – are related to behaviour that would normally be associated with a reduction in health-related status. Compared to non-smokers, for example, women who smoke are one and a half times ($p<0.05$) more likely to have improved well-being (Figure 4.3). Such findings are in line with studies that have highlighted the relationship between anxiety, or negative effect, and onset or maintenance of smoking behaviour as a form of relief (for a review of studies refer to Kassel et al, 2003). Among the women in this study, then, smoking may be a mechanism for dealing with daily problems, a stress–coping (Wills and Shiffman, 1985) or self–medicating (Khantzian, 1997) approach to regulating mood through expectations that smoking will alleviate negative affect (Copeland et al, 1995).

The evidence suggests that the psychological underpinnings of health need to be accounted for, particularly where unhealthy behaviour (in this research smoking, but it could easily relate to alcohol or substance abuse) becomes a form of stress relief. In short, the analysis points to a more holistic approach embracing the social and emotional context of health. Health promotion may benefit through adopting some of the techniques used in happiness research, for example recording activities and feelings before and after particular (un)healthy behaviour. This may help develop a better understanding of the potential conflict of the perceived psychological benefits of behaviours that have a positive influence on subjective well-being, but a damaging effect on health.

While this supports the move towards a health service geared towards prevention rather than cure, a more effective strategy is the development of a society rooted in an ethic of care. Well–being – and the factors that underpin it – is as much a function of the social and political systems within which people's lives are experienced as it is about individual behaviour. Enhancing health – along with well–being – is a social, and not just an individual, responsibility.

Age and the life course

A third key finding from the longitudinal analysis reflects changes of well-being status across the life span. Age – and its associated life-course factors – is important if subjective well-being is to be improved or maintained. In Chapter 3 we discovered a U-shaped relationship between age and subjective well-being, representing a fall during middle age and a rise as people approach or experience the early years of retirement. The longitudinal perspective reinforces this association, although only significantly so for women – the odds being lower among under 55s (on average 0.5; p<0.05) and higher among those aged 55 and over (ranging from 2.2–3.2; p<0.01) (Figure 4.1).

This may be accounted for where age represents a combination of several other important life circumstances. The dip in middle age could be explained by financial and family commitments or the multiple social roles that individuals undertake during this stage of the life course. Factors that have been shown to have a negative impact on subjective well-being include parenthood (Argyle, 1987; Shields and Wooden; 2003), the insecurities of mortgaged home ownership (Nettleton and Burrows, 1998) and the psychological stress associated with being of working age through experiencing unemployment (Blanchflower and Oswald, 2002; Inglehart, 1990), job insecurity (Ferrie et al, 2005) or the stress associated with full-time work (Argyle, 1987; Pahl, 1995; Ferrie, 2001; Rodriguez et al, 2001). These are compared to the positive effect of retirement – represented by those aged 55 and over – which is increasingly viewed as a 'period of enjoyment, creative experience and a reward for a lifetime of labour' (Costa, 1998, p 27).

Where the differences in age may be accounted for by the different roles and responsibilities of individuals across the life course, the negative association may be further compounded in line with research that suggests that combining partner, parent and worker roles can lead to 'role strains' and inter-role conflicts and can be the cause of stress (Pearlin et al, 1981; Sun, 1993). These findings suggest that prolonged exposure to multiple roles is detrimental to subjective well-being, and the fact that this impacts negatively on women further suggests that the labour divide remained a gendered issue during the 1990s.

Wealth, well-being and status

Finally, this stage of the analysis also points to the less than straightforward relationship between well-being and economic circumstances. Analysing change in well-being and changing circumstances shows the complex relationship between economic factors and subjective well-being – that they do not necessarily operate through a linear, progressive, accumulating effect. Affluence – measured in monetary terms – does not necessarily enhance well-being. Women in the fourth quintile, for example, had significantly lower odds of their subjective well-being improving (0.4; p<0.05) (Figure 4.4).

Perhaps the most striking finding from the longitudinal analysis, however, can be drawn from the absence of income as a factor from the models that look at predictors of maintaining high levels of well-being. Income may operate within a relative framework, subsumed into subjective aspects (satisfaction with income, or self-reported financial circumstances), where perceptions of income are more pertinent to well-being than take-home pay. Where there is a link between higher income and high well-being in the short term (Chapter 3), the new analysis shows that at some point they become uncoupled and are not important for predicting improvements in well-being or for maintaining high levels of well-being. This

—

finding has important implications for how we measure well-being and how the role of finance fits into the equation.

This evidence again raises doubts over the use of monetary-based measures as a proxy for well-being. It brings into critical focus the assumptions underpinning the economic idea and questions the extent to which economic progress provides the key to understanding – indeed enhancing – subjective well-being states. This is further reinforced by another key finding from the longitudinal analysis: a factor important to men's stable high subjective well-being is social structure, although here the results are somewhat counter-intuitive to the economic model for enhancing well-being states. Being in a non-manual social class over the long term is significantly associated with lower odds of maintaining high subjective well-being (0.4; $p<0.01$); so too is moving up the social hierarchy (0.5; $p<0.05$) (Figure 4.2, Model 3). Such findings suggest that a higher social position is no guarantee of increased subjective well-being. This supports the theory that there are social limitations to economic growth and that relative social standing may impinge more on psychological evaluation – the experience – than absolute conditions, a point I shall return to in more detail in the next chapter.

What can we learn about improving well-being?

This longitudinal analysis, while reflecting the findings of cross-sectional studies, has raised some new insights, particularly in respect of the complex interrelationship between gender, age and social roles and the extent to which economic progress can bring about prolonged positive feelings. This section will draw upon these issues and develop some of the broader themes to emerge from analysing the temporal predictors of subjective well-being states. It will consider the impact of social integration and how social relationships – other than those associated with economic inclusion and traditional measures of family life – are mediators of subjective well-being.

Having established the complex relationship between wealth, social standing and well-being, it is feasible to consider that there are other factors pertaining to the economic predictors of well-being that are related to inclusion in society. Firstly, some improvements in economic conditions – participation in or attainment of resources deemed normal or acceptable in society – may be important in respect of promoting well-being. This will be explored in respect of economic and other forms of integration, namely employment, home ownership, education and leisure. Secondly, integration may occur within different social settings and the level at which integration occurs – individual and societal – may be important for understanding variations in subjective well-being. This will be considered by drawing upon family and other relationships and the social support they provide; and engaging with national politics.

Firstly, the findings show that entry into employment or changes in employment status can be positively associated with improvements in subjective well-being. Compared to those who were already employed, the odds of well-being improving were 1.7 (p<0.05) times higher among women who became employed (Figure 4.3) and 2.6–2.9 (p<0.001) times higher among men who became employed (Figure 4.6). Reducing social class status into two categories – manual and non-manual – the results show that joining either of these groups (either by gaining a social class identity through entry into the labour market or changing between a manual and a non-manual classified job) increases the odds of improving well-being by up to a third (2.7; p<0.01) (Figure 4.5). So, while there is a raft of literature showing the positive aspects of employment as compared to being unemployed (Jin et al, 1995), what the findings reported here show is that gaining employment has a positive effect over and above that associated with employment status generally.

The relationship between improvements in subjective well-being and such socio-economic conditions, however, may not just be attributed to monetary gains. Engagement in the labour market is an indication of social integration, and work has been positively related to happiness levels where it is a source of social respect and is perceived as rewarding (Veenhoven, 1984). Argyle (1987) also found that the most important factors associated with satisfaction with employment related to the social relationships and social interaction that occurred in the workplace.

Employment status is a key factor for understanding well-being, resulting from valuing both the material and emotional rewards. However, the type of 'employment' engaged in is equally important in accounting for variations in levels of positive mood. For example, women who are engaged in family care have lower odds (0.5; p<0.05) of well-being. While this may be a reflection of the 'burden' felt by those with caring responsibilities, these lower levels of well-being could also be indicative of the injustice felt from being excluded from other forms of social interaction.

Another means of integration into society may be achieved through acquiring the resources deemed acceptable or 'normal'. In the UK the majority of households are owner-occupiers (DCLG, 2006b). Becoming a home owner, then, may be deemed a desired state, something that will enhance a sense of integration and well-being. The results would certainly support this notion where – among men – moving from renting to owner-occupation doubles the odds of improving well-being (1.9; p<0.05) (Figure 4.5).

Becoming an owner-occupier may be an indication of increased income; however, home ownership may represent more than a monetary asset. Research has shown that there are not only health effects associated with owner-occupation (MacIntyre et al, 1998, 2003), but that the concept of 'home' draws upon emotional factors (Searle et al, 2007). Home ownership is bound up in notions of self and identity and also provides a source of social integration with the association of a physical and permanent location in society (Saunders, 1990), or ontological security. Ontological security refers to the existence of 'basic trust' – the existence of confidence in the self and trust in the world – a 'protective cocoon' or non-reality that enables people to get on with their daily lives. Giddens (1991) argues that we need a sense of ontological security in order to 'carry the individual through transitions, crises and circumstances of high risk' (p 38). The home becomes associated with ontological security where it is seen to provide a secure base – an environment where people feel in control, free to be themselves – that puts them at ease in a world perceived as threatening or beyond control (Saunders, 1990). The emotional aspects of home ownership therefore may be as important to understanding well-being as those traditionally associated with its financial status.

The ability to participate and become integrated in society may also be linked to knowledge – which is also a key component of some measures of well-being (for example the Human Development Index (UNDP, 2006)). Promoting subjective well-being may then be linked with education and the motivation towards self-fulfilment (Maslow, 1954). The results show that women who have become students have an increased probability of subjective well-being becoming high (4.8–4.9; p<0.01) (Figure 4.3), while the possession of educational qualifications also increases the odds of enhancing subjective well-being when compared to people with none.[4]

As discussed in Chapters 1 and 2, studies of well-being have tended to focus on the economically related components. However, this analysis is more in sympathy with a growing literature that looks towards the non-economic activities that may impinge on a sense of well-being. Social participation or integration – and related improvements in well-being – may occur through means other than engagement in the labour market, and this leads to a fourth area of interest, leisure activities.

Leisure activities are of particular interest in this respect 'because there selection is a matter of individual choice and they are more under personal control than other sources of satisfaction' (Hills and Argyle, 1998, p 523). This research shows that increased satisfaction with amount of leisure time for women (2.2; p<0.001) (Figure 4.4), and use of leisure time for men (1.8; p<0.05) (Figure 4.6) is associated with improved subjective well-being. This is in line with studies that show that leisure activities can be a source of different positive effects such as excitement, joy, absorption, altruism and enhanced self-esteem (Hills and Argyle, 1998). It has also been aligned to improvements in self-concept (Marsh et al, 1986) that have been associated with increased feelings of subjective well-being. Community-based activities have been shown to provide supportive environments that reduce social isolation and develop social networks (Milligan et al, 2004), while engagement in some activities has been linked to subjective well-being, by providing a source of identity, particularly for people who are unemployed, retired, housewives or dissatisfied with their work (Argyle, 1987).

These findings show that social support and social integration are important elements in improving and maintaining subjective well-being and, while this may be found through participation in the labour market, there are other sources of support and means of feeling integrated in society that should also be included in the analysis of well-being. The ability to participate in and be a part of society through employment, education, home ownership or pursuit of leisure activities suggests that the ability to have 'the resources and amenities necessary to participate in the societies to which people belong' (Townsend, 1979) is just as important to understanding improvements in subjective well-being as it is in understanding or measuring deprivation.

Social integration, through different means, is then generally associated with improvements in subjective well-being, and for some time has been shown to be important in buffering negative well-being (Durkheim, 1952). This may be due to the mediating effect of the social relationships and social support that are components of integration in society, whether this is through work, home or leisure. This is in line with the idea that emotional support and feelings of 'belonging' within society are basic human needs (Maslow, 1954). Social engagement provides a source of identity, feelings of belonging and a sense of purpose that give meanings to our actions (Putnam, 2000; Jordan, 2007) and can be a buffer to stress (Veenhoven, 1984; Stark, 1987; Triemstra et al, 1998), negative well-being (Durkheim, 1952), or social exclusion (for example see Burchardt et al, 1999; Gordon et al, 2000). Comparative research further shows that participation in a cohesive family and the availability of group support in the community can function as buffers against influences that cause disease or disability (WHO, 1979). Similarly, factors providing a protective function (for young people) deemed 'at risk' include caring parents and other adults, collective self-efficacy and neighbourhood engagement (Blum et al, 2002). Social relationships, then, have consistently been found to be an important element of life satisfaction and happiness, and for some should form the basis for public policy 'for the sake of the well-being of citizens' (Jordan, 2007, p 77).

This leads to the second theme to be considered here – that there are contextual aspects to social integration that operate across a spectrum from an individual to a societal level. The positive influence of social relationships – within an individual context – are well reported at national and international levels, and the new analysis confirms that social relationships are important in explaining variations in experiences of well-being over time. These variations may be indicative of the social support found within marital or couple relationships. For example, for men the presence of a partner (notably, though, an absence of children) has a positive impact on long-term well-being (up to four times the average for all household types); by comparison, lone-parent households have lower odds (0.1; p<0.05) (Figure 4.2).

Where it has been shown that social support is an important factor in understanding high subjective well-being (Chapter 3), further analysis shows that it is also significant in terms of promoting subjective well-being. Improvements in social support are positively associated with improvements in well-being for both genders, although generally for men any form of social support is better than none or poor support. The odds of well-being enhancing are between 2.4 and 6.0 times higher among men where support has improved and 1.7 and 4.9 times where support is good (p<0.001), compared to those with none/poor or reduced support (Figures 4.5 and 4.6). Among women, only those with good support have higher odds (1.7; p<0.05) (Figure 4.4; Model 3). Previous research suggests that the availability of social support can be a valuable 'resistance resource' in the event of life changes: even if not called upon, simply knowing that the resources of other people are available can enhance coping and stress-resolving ability (Antonovosky, 1974).

While social relationships within households may be indicative of the availability of social support, lacking such support does not necessarily reduce the odds of maintaining positive well-being over time. Social relationships can occur within the wider family, neighbourhood or community settings (Argyle, 1987). The higher odds of maintaining high subjective well-being found among single men (2.4; p<0.01) may be accounted for by the availability of social support outside of a spouse/partner relationship. This is a theory supported by Roseneil's (2004) study of the construction of care and support networks among the most individualised in society (those not living with a partner), which found that friendship operated as a key value among single people and that there was a higher degree of reliance on friends than on biological kin or sexual partners for the provision of care and support in everyday life.

As previously discussed, marital status may be considered an indicator of an individual's social relationships, while economic activity might be one indicator of social integration through an individual's ability to participate in society. Breakdown in social relationships (for example through separation, divorce or lone-parenthood) and lack of participation in the labour market (for example through unemployment, or experiencing exclusion through long-term sickness, impairment or family care) would, at face value, provide some explanation for the lower levels of subjective well-being among these groups in society. However, the findings reported here also show that not all forms of social integration necessarily promote a sense of well-being.

It has been established that social integration is generally associated with enhancing subjective well-being. However, not all societal engagement has positive outcomes. The norms and networks that service some groups can obstruct others. Depending on how and why social ties are made, those who are inside (socially included) may benefit from social capital, while those who are outside (socially excluded) will not (Putnam, 2000). This theory may apply to the distinct cleavages of subjective well-being that operate at a societal level, based on political ideology. Long-term political interest (which has been used here as an indicator of social integration) may have negative consequences. The results show that men who support Labour are significantly less likely to have high subjective well-being over the long term as compared to a group average (0.7; p<0.05) (Figure 4.2). These results, together with findings of the positive relationship between subjective well-being and Conservative supporters (reported in Chapter 3), raise interesting questions about the characteristics of these two disparate groups. Despite a change of government during the mid-1990s (a landslide that led to the Labour party replacing the Conservatives), this does not seem to have had an impact on the subjective well-being of these two parties' long-term supporters. This suggests that there are underlying characteristics of Labour supporters that manifest themselves as negative outcomes, and vice versa for Conservative supporters.

These were the findings of research by Johnston et al (2004), which showed that Labour supporters were more likely to be male, younger, better educated, in lower levels of the class system, on low incomes and living in local authority rented housing, whereas Conservative supporters were more likely to be in the older age group, less well qualified, owner-occupiers, with higher incomes and have two or more cars per household. Labour supporters were generally more pessimistic about their future financial circumstances than Conservative supporters and they were also more likely to be concentrated in disadvantaged neighbourhoods as compared to Conservatives, who were more likely to be located in the most advantaged neighbourhoods.

Such findings correlate to factors found throughout this research (and support previous evidence) of measures associated with increased odds of high subjective well-being (for example older age, higher incomes, owner-occupation and good neighbourhood resources) or lower odds (for example lower incomes, rented accommodation, living in poorer areas or experiencing neighbourhood problems). However, the differences in gender, education and social class of Labour and Conservative supporters would not account for the differences in subjective well-being based on the findings presented here. Firstly, men consistently report higher levels of well-being than women. Secondly, on the one hand, sustained or improved levels of well-being have been shown to be associated with having educational qualifications or returning to education and being in the lower social classes, while, on the other hand, remaining in the higher social classes is associated with reduced odds of reporting high well-being over the long term.

Given such discrepancies, it may be that the more important finding from Johnston et al's (2004) work is that based on subjective measures, in particular perceptions of financial situation that may be characterised by Conservative optimism and Labour pessimism. Where government seeks to improve the subjective well-being of a nation it needs to understand this underlying philosophy associated with political support, and it can only do this where it recognises the importance of subjective experience as well as actual conditions in measures of subjective well-being.

The lack of a social relationship, or the absence of a particular social activity, of itself does not, then, appear to provide an explanation in the variation of subjective well-being. Social relationships are forged through interaction in different aspects of society and the research reported here shows that engagement at the community or societal level has important consequences for subjective well-being. The independent effect that community participation and leisure time has on high subjective well-being, together with the positive well-being experienced by those who lack an intimate social relationship, suggests that forms of social relationships, and participation other than economic inclusion or traditional measures of family life, may act as mediators of subjective well-being.

The changing nature of well-being

Definitions of psychological well-being initially concentrated on the impact of stressful experiences; in particular, life-event theory suggested that all change is stressful in that it demands adaptation to existing routines. This chapter has argued that life events and change are not necessarily a source of stress. The evidence shows that while some changes in circumstances may inhibit improvements in subjective well-being, changes in satisfaction levels, employment status, housing tenure, education, social support and health are positively associated with enhancing well-being.

Previous means of measuring the psychological impact of changing circumstances have been subject to criticism. By their methodology, life-event scales have developed a bias in emphasising the overall 'negative' effect that change could have through its relationship to the onset of disease. Such an approach has been criticised as a valid tool for measuring well-being on several grounds, including the assumptions that such scales make that events lead to stress because the individual is intolerant of change (Pearlin et al, 1981); their assumptions about the levels of stress experienced throughout the life course (Kellan, 1974); and their bias towards measuring 'anxiety', which was 'likely to be the first result of any change' whereas '(t)he appearance of other forms of disturbed behaviour ... may depend on the quality of the life event and not the fact that it introduces change per se' (Gerston et al, 1974, p 161).

By focusing on the negative physical effects of life events, such research fails to identify the effect that positive life events can have on subjective well-being. In fact, evidence suggests that most people report feeling good most of the time (for example, Campbell et al, 1976; Inglehart, 1990; Cummins et al, 2003). It has also been suggested that positive events do not add stress and may in fact help to alleviate it, 'acting as breathers from stress, sustainers of coping effort, and restorers ... facilitating recovery from harm or loss' (Lazarus et al, 1980, pp 208–11). As Reich and Zautra suggest: 'positive events enhance one's sense of control over the events in one's life ... they allow an enhancement of one's mood, generate optimism about upcoming events, enhance judgements of the positivity of other events, and raise self-esteem, among other possible outcomes' (Reich and Zautra, 1988, p 169). Indeed the experience of a 'life event' may provide the opportunity for personal growth, a chance to 'discover the self' (Rose, 1990, p 245). To paraphrase Nietzsche, 'that which does not kill us makes us strong'.

Definitions of psychological well-being tended to concentrate on the stressful impact of life events where changes are associated with negative outcomes – found here to be true for events such as exiting the labour market or changes related to deterioration in health. However, many changes in circumstances manifest themselves into positive outcomes providing the opportunity for advancement and self-fulfilment. The availability of improved social support or becoming employed may provide the resistance resources deemed necessary to counteract the negative effects of other stressful experiences (Antonovsky, 1974), while the positive gains associated with returning to education may in part be explained by the opportunity this provides for personal growth, a chance to 'discover the self' (Rose, 1990).

As argued before, stress is not necessarily a component of an event but becomes an emergent property of the meanings associated with particular events and the context in which they occur (Chapter 2). Certain life events may even become accepted as a natural part of the life cycle (Pearlin et al, 1981), buffering any negative response. For example, in Chapter 3 it was shown that widowhood was associated with lower odds in the short term, but that such feelings did not manifest themselves into negative subjective well-being outcomes in the long term. This has been the finding of studies by Parkes (1996) and Bennet et al (2002), who found a positive correlation between number of years bereaved and coping ability, with significant improvements in subjective well-being occurring during the second year after bereavement.

So, where adjustment theories have been used to account for the imbalance of positive feelings relative to increased affluence – that increased income does not lead to sustained improvements in subjective well-being as people become accustomed to their new circumstances (Kahn and Juster, 2002) – such a theory may be applied to the short-term negative impact of losing a partner that, over time, does not manifest itself in long-term negative subjective well-being as individuals adjust to their changing life circumstances.

Economic theory too has been subject to criticism, due to a focus on the negative correlations to well-being. However, the tracking of socio-economic circumstances over time shows that some changes in these conditions are important with regard to the promotion of subjective well-being. Analysis of employment status, social class and satisfaction with work suggests that changes in employment status, in particular the positive association of becoming employed or changes in sector of employment (between manual and non-manual) are important to subjective well-being, while absence from the labour market – unemployment, family care commitments or through long-term sickness or impairment – is negatively associated. The relationship between improvements or maintaining high levels of subjective well-being and increased satisfaction with work or income also suggests that economic factors are important considerations in assessment of individuals' well-being, while material gains, such as becoming an owner–occupier, further support the importance of economic conditions in improving subjective well-being, particularly among males. However, improvements in subjective well-being brought about by improvements in socio-economic conditions may be associated just as much with the social aspects of participation in society or the accumulation of resources customary or approved in the societies to which people belong (Townsend, 1979) as with their monetary gain per se.

The relationship between economic conditions and subjective well-being, however, is not straightforward. Complexities emerge where, on the one hand, social advancement (moving up one or more social classes) did not have a corresponding improvement in well-being, while on the other, maintaining a level of affluence (remaining in the fourth income quintile) was not sufficient to secure improved well-being where a lack of change in economic conditions gave rise to negative well-being. Longitudinal analysis provides further support to arguments that suggest that economic conditions may embrace more than their observed measurements imply and may have social implications for individual identity, perceived position within society and, ultimately, well-being.

Overall, these findings support the argument that economic growth or gain is not a proxy for improved subjective well-being, and that 'progress' needs to be conceptualised in terms of quality of life and public happiness. If success is equated with upward mobility, then economic progress may have detrimental outcomes for subjective well-being, because changes in objective circumstances are not matched by a change in societal position, giving rise to social frustration and negative feelings. However, within capitalist societies economic factors do have some bearing and the operationalisation – and measures – of subjective well-being needs to encompass both observable circumstances and subjective assessments.

A key component of this research has been to address the issue of change as it relates to subjective well-being. A change in circumstance may provide the opportunity for advancement and self-fulfilment; however, short-term change must be backed up by longer-term security and this has implications for policies that seek to enhance national subjective well-being. Life-course factors have important implications for the pressure and stress associated with engagement in or isolation from housing, education, employment, financial and parental commitments and the alleviation from such pressures associated with retirement.

Differences in social roles, working patterns and opportunities for asset accumulation give rise to concerns over inequalities during the working years that become compounded in retirement. Where the evidence shows a continued gendered division of labour throughout the 1990s, this raises particular concerns for women's opportunities. Gender differences have been identified throughout this book, particularly in respect of parental and employment-related roles. Where women are absent from or have fragmented involvement in the labour market this has implications not only for their quality of life but also for how they are to build the resources necessary to sustain themselves in retirement, and a gendered policy response may be called for.

Where analysis of well-being over the short term highlights factors associated with positive well-being, longitudinal analysis opens up the space for possible intervention. Understanding the changes that underpin enhanced well-being provides important clues for where policy can interject and work towards improving national well-being levels. The means by which this could progress – the theoretical components and the practical implications of understanding and enhancing well-being – are the subjects of the two final chapters.

Notes

1. Part of this chapter has previously been published in Searle (2007).

2. A full description of the variables used is given in the Appendix, Table A1.

3. Contrary to this trend, when all the variables were controlled for women (Figure 4.1, Model 1), those whose health had limited their daily activity for the whole period had significantly higher odds (5.6; $p<0.05$) of maintaining high well-being; however, in Model 3 this reduced to 0.5, although the odds were not significant (see Appendix, Table C1.1).

4. Compared to a group average, higher odds were significantly associated with women having O-levels (1.6; $p<0.05$) or higher qualifications (1.9; $p<0.05$) between 1996 and 1999 (Appendix, Table D2.1).

FIVE

Well-being: the state of the art

> The requirements of mere life may have priority in time, but the good life has the priority of importance; it is the end or final purpose in life ... Well-being is the sole ultimate good, the one objective worth pursing for its own sake.
>
> (Aristotle)

Concerns about what constitutes a 'happy' or 'fulfilling' life are not new – indeed this has been a topic of intellectual debate since the times of the early Greek philosophers. This is perhaps not surprising, given that underlying many aspects of everyday practice and experience is the motivation to improve the quality of life for ourselves and those around us. But although individually there may be many different concepts of what constitutes 'well-being', the attention being given to such an ideal in academia and politics signals a growing awareness of the importance of a collective understanding of what 'well-being' is and how it may be achieved.

This chapter provides new insights from the research. It sets out some of the principal issues that have emerged through studying high subjective well-being directly and considers the implications for the direction of future research. Earlier chapters have explored the underpinnings of positive well-being and found them to be complex – and at times counter-intuitive; this chapter explores the parameters of the theoretical and conceptual debates. It suggests that well-being cannot be understood within existing explanatory (predominantly economic) frameworks, and that a multi-disciplinary approach is needed. It then considers one of the key constraints in the advancement of the study of well-being: methodological and data limitations. It does this through two key aspects: firstly, the construction and level of measures of well-being, and secondly, the moral aspects underpinning well-being from a health perspective. Finally, it will consider the social and political underpinnings and suggest ways forward for enhancing the study of well-being.

Beyond economics

Theoretical understandings of well-being have been – and still are – dominated by two key strands of thought: hedonism and eudaemonism (for a review see Waterman, 1993; Ryan and Deci, 2001). The hedonic view concentrates on the pursuit of happiness and has formed the basis for much of the economics-inspired debate on improving welfare and well-being. But how realistic is the pursuit of happiness? To be happy means seeking out experiences that result in hedonic enjoyment and avoiding those things that produce negative emotions. Viewed in this way, happiness may be construed as a means of evading – rather than dealing with – life events. As such, pursuing happiness engages with only half of the spectrum of emotions in human experience. Indeed, it could be argued that happiness is experienced simply as the 'other' to sadness: one desired state that denies the alternate.

The question is: is it not through being able to express remorse, fear and sadness – being aware of these emotions and having the ability to deal with them – that it is possible to pursue a true emotional balance that forms the basis for well-being? Eudaemonic theories would argue that the answer to this question is yes – that there are well-being benefits to both negative and positive emotional disclosure (Butzel and Ryan, 1997). So, on the one hand, not every bad or unhappy experience undermines well-being, and on the other, not everything that seems desirable will result in an enhancement of well-being (Ryan and Deci, 2001). What is important is being challenged and exerting effort (Waterman, 1993). So well-being is – or perhaps should be – about having the motivation to pursue goals that may lead to enhanced mood, while accepting that things may not always work out as planned. The pursuit of happiness may or may not provide moments of elation; the pursuit of well-being is about achieving a state of contentment despite this.

To engage fully in these theoretical and practical understandings of well-being it is important to understand those factors that enhance as much as hinder emotional outcomes. This book is all about the fact that, while much research has focused on the negatives – on ill-being, poverty and exclusion – this has not been matched by a focus on the positives – satisfaction, happiness and well-being. The analysis has shown that what affects positive emotions may not be directly related to what leads to negative feelings. That is why positive subjective well-being is an emotional outcome that should be researched and analysed in its own right; it should not simply be inferred from conclusions born as a by-product of studies of negative emotional states. The absence of a particular factor may be associated with low subjective well-being; however, its presence is not necessarily associated with high subjective well-being.

In the quest to understand poverty and social exclusion we would not look to the lives of the rich and famous (the most socially included through their constant media exposure) and assert that if someone does not have the same material possessions or social networks, then they are in poverty. Equally, it is problematic to assume that enhanced well-being can be achieved by creating the opposite of everything associated with psychological distress. Exposing the dynamics of well-being has revealed that positive and negative well-being states exist in their own right and are not necessarily the mirror image of each other. In order to understand subjective well-being, therefore, an approach needs to be adopted that seeks to address simultaneously the different aspects that influence positive as well as negative feelings.

This book provides information on the factors that underpin higher levels of well-being. This balances the literature traditionally preoccupied with low well-being. Conceptually, it has done this by focusing on two key areas of research: weighing up the relevance of psycho-social and economic theories.

The analysis challenges the economic ideal that success provides the pillar on which well-being stands. In Chapters 3 and 4 it was discovered that actual income is not significantly associated with long-term experience of high subjective well-being. Statistically it only exerts an important influence in the short term, and even here only once measures of satisfaction or perceived financial situation are removed from the equation.

Despite the premise of economic theory, the implications of these findings – as with other critical accounts (Chapter 2) – are that increases in income do not translate into increases in subjective well-being. One explanation for this is the way that people adapt to changes in circumstances, such that the continual struggle for material gains does not lead to increases in happiness or satisfaction as individuals become accustomed to their new circumstances and raise the norm of their expectations. The stability of subjective well-being in relation to improvements in material conditions has been accounted for through a metaphorical 'hedonic treadmill' (Brickman and Campbell, 1971) – a process of accustomisation whereby any gain in material conditions becomes offset as individuals adapt to their new circumstances and any short-term mood does not manifest itself into long-term alteration in levels of well-being (Kahn and Juster, 2002).

Another line of argument – addressing psycho-social concepts – is that a paradox may exist where economic growth has negative social outcomes and that through the process of habituation a higher standard of living is not always associated with higher subjective well-being. As shown in Chapter 4, despite reaching a level of affluence within society (fourth income quintile), for some this is deemed insufficient where failure to move to the next level (the top income quintile) has a dampening effect. This is the idea considered by Campbell et al (1976) and Veenhoven (1984) among others, that the differences in reported well-being are related to subjective comparisons with other people, with previous experiences or with future expectations. Satisfaction with life becomes adjusted in relation to the gap between aspirations and current experience. This may explain why there is no significant difference in the reported satisfaction of different income groups where aspirations adjust to reality and are progressively reduced over time. So, although individuals may be objectively better off they don't *feel* better off, because they still occupy the same position in society.

Within this framework, economic growth, far from enhancing national well-being, can lead to negative outcomes. In line with La Barbara and Gurhan (1997) and Orton and Rowlingson (2007a), the idea is that 'too much wealth' becomes detrimental to subjective well-being. In countries like the UK, for example, economic growth has been associated with wider inequality, opening up the gap between the social groups among whom comparisons are being made. What becomes important, then, is the social meanings attached to actual circumstances, influenced not only by an individual's own experiences and expectations but contextualised through relative comparisons and with the raised expectations of society.

A key finding of the research is the importance of the stratification of society – although perhaps not as expected. As indicated in Chapters 3 and 4, subjective well-being is more likely to be associated with the manual classes than the non-manual classes, and upward mobility has a negative outcome. Economic advancement, then, does not necessarily serve to enhance the well-being of all those who experience it. There are two possible explanations for this: one focused at the individual level, the second addressing the feelings of injustice that operate at a societal level.

The first explanation is based on the level of willingness of individuals to accept their circumstances. The dissatisfaction among the non-manual social classes may be a reflection of their constant striving to improve their circumstances within an individualised society where it has become a 'social must to reach one's full potential' (Beck and Beck-Gernsheim, 1995, p 53). By contrast, people who are more accepting of their circumstances, rather than struggling against them (Kessel and Shepherd, 1965), have a tendency for greater personal comfort and less psychological morbidity (Mechanic, 1974), and this may well reflect the ideology of the manual social classes. While these differences are expressed in respect of individual personality, there are contextual effects at play where the relative natures of satisfaction and grievance arise from the expectations that are embedded in society.

The second explanation then considers the contextual aspects of individual positionality. The terminology of economic progress is very emotive; increased GDP per capita gives the impression that everyone is better off, whereas, in reality – as shown in Chapter 1 – not everyone benefits to the same extent. Economic growth and the expansion of consumerism have not been equally distributed. Through the acquisition of wealth some groups in society secure a disproportionately large share of available resources. This puts them in a position of power where they can influence public attitudes as to what is an acceptable standard of living and, consequently, what constitutes deprivation. But for many lower down the scale, such 'success' comes at a price of rapid change, insecurity, loss of social ties and a frustration born of defensive consumption in the struggle to maintain the same place in society (Frank and Cook, 1995).

Within such a framework it is not unreasonable to speculate that feelings of injustice may arise from perceived differences of position along a socially divided scale of affluence. Where the extent of inequality may be drawn from national statistics, this book provides evidence to support the theory that inequality hurts (Wilkinson, 1996; Orton and Rowlingson, 2007a). For example, as reported in Chapters 3 and 4, the manual classes are more likely to be represented among those whose well-being scores fall into the higher end of the well-being scale. This may be a reflection that the experienced differences between those at the lower and higher end of the manual class structure are less than those between the extremes of the non-manual classes. So, despite the increased wealth, status and consumption arising from being in social class III (non-manual) or social class II there is still a feeling of being positionally isolated from a minority 'powerful elite' (Frank and Cook, 1995) represented by social class I.

This evidence is indicative of the growing inequalities experienced through the 1990s, during which time those in the higher echelons of society saw their wealth grow disproportionately faster than that of those lower down. There is an indication that this wealth gap is not only widening but that Britain is moving back towards levels of inequality experienced more than 40 years ago (Dorling et al, 2007). However, the problem – as Orton and Rowlingson (2007a) note – is not one of poverty but one of riches. The rise in inequality is due not to the poor falling further behind – indeed the proportion of the very poor is in decline (Dorling et al, 2007) – but rests with those who have secured a larger share of society's resources; it is due to the rich getting richer (Orton and Rowlingson, 2007a).

Future research on inequality will need to focus on the accumulation of resources and wealth across the full economic spectrum (Orton and Rowlingson, 2007a) and not just concentrate on those whose incomes fall below the median. Resources and wealth have implications for well-being not just at the present time, but across the life course (a point I will return to in Chapter 6). Any such analysis should therefore be longitudinal in nature, in order to facilitate a better understanding of the pathways from wealth to well-being.

Measuring wealth rather than income is an essential element of subjective well-being research. It facilitates a greater understanding of the kind of life people lead and, more importantly, captures the potential resources they have available to act as buffers to difficult life experiences. However, it remains the case that, in isolation, economic measures are a poor indicator of subjective well-being.

The limited association between economic conditions and high subjective well-being and the importance of subjective and social aspects presented in Chapters 3 and 4 not only supports the change in attitudes witnessed during the 1990s (Chapter 1) but has important implications for the goals that individuals pursue and society endorses. The difficult issue is how to measure what we value in life and, ultimately, what influences our subjective well-being. A measure of well-being may take several years to develop (after all, the measure of poverty has been debated for well over a century) and it is not realistic that a single volume could cover all the possible aspects that may impinge on this most desired of states.

This book provides new insights into subjective well-being. But its conceptualisation is limited by methodological and data constraints. The rest of this chapter will take the debate forward, discussing what the data does and does not show, and how we can progress the study of well-being.

Data matters

Conceptualising

As discussed in Chapter 3, well-being is an entanglement of experiences, a process with no beginning and no end. The subsequent analysis has shown that there are many factors that influence well-being outcomes and that not all of these can be accounted for in any straightforward way. Well-being emerges through a combination of circumstances, experience, subjective evaluations and social conditions. Figure 5.1 aims to capture some of this complexity – acknowledging the limitations of two-dimensional representation – by drawing together three key elements: subjective, temporal and social. Firstly, the subjective element of well-being emerges through a person's evaluation of their circumstances and experiences, which will include both external influences (such as comparison with other people) and internal influences (which includes individuals' aspirations and expectations). This evaluation process feeds into satisfaction levels relevant to the circumstance/experience under consideration.

Secondly, the temporal element is addressed through the inclusion of changes in circumstances that feed back into the evaluation process. Any change in circumstance will lead to a new set of conditions that will not only be evaluated in respect of the external and internal elements as described above, but will also include a reflexive element relative to comparison with previous circumstances and experiences. This will continue as a cyclical, cumulative process as each set of circumstances is drawn into the evaluation process. Finally, there is the social element within which the first two elements are nested. The social element not only forms the context for any subjective assessment (through comparison) but will determine the opportunities and conditions upon which assessments are made. These elements all form part of the process of well-being, a process that is *echoed* across all aspects of life.

In order to capture this process – the extent to which different aspects of our lives inhibit or promote a sense of well-being – it is necessary to devise a series of questions that tap into different emotional responses and feelings.

Measuring

The components of a measure of positive well-being are the source of much debate and increasing interest. There is a tendency within the literature to use a single measure that asks respondents to provide a cognitive assessment of satisfaction with their life as a whole or of their general happiness, all things considered. However, I would argue that, in the case of well-being, the sums of individual experience hold a 'gestaltian' quality – providing a greater insight into well-being states than a single consideration of life as a whole. Personal assessments of life circumstances are undoubtedly important in explaining variations in experiences of high well-being and support the call for a greater emphasis on the use of subjective measures in understanding national well-being (Layard, 2003; NEF, 2004; Defra, 2005).

Figure 5.1: The Echo model: conceptual model to show the temporal relationship between actual circumstances and subjective experiences of aspects of subjective well-being

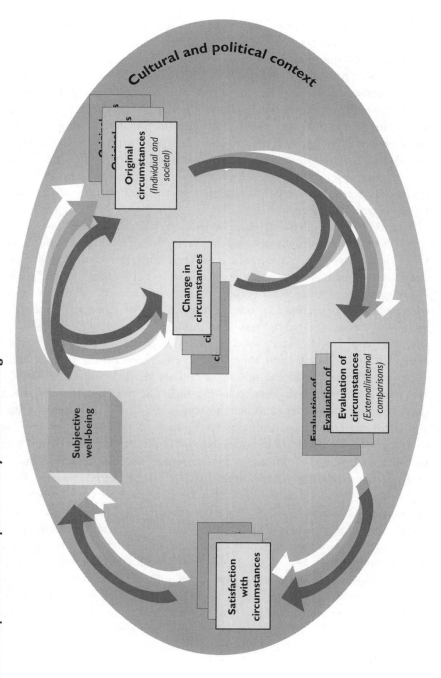

However, these need to be expanded to fully capture the elements that contribute to a positive emotional response – which may be lacking in a single question.

Satisfaction with life overall is a popular well-being measure – indeed, it is quick and easy to administer; however, as has been shown through a review of the literature as well as the new empirical findings, well-being operates at different levels that may not be conducive to measurement on a global scale. An overall global measure of satisfaction with life may be insufficient to capture the components that account for differences in well-being experienced by men and women. Further, it may not adequately capture changes over time and may not be a reliable measurement tool for longitudinal analysis. Although satisfaction with life overall proved to be the most influential factor in determining subjective well-being in the short term (Chapter 3), it is not *the* most important variable for maintaining or promoting subjective well-being (Chapter 4). This fact questions a general consensus that argues that satisfaction with life overall is the best indicator of subjective well-being.

Attaining well-being is a complex affair. It encompasses an evaluation of existing and changing circumstances; comparisons of individual experiences with those of others; and perceived satisfaction resulting from such evaluations. It also combines emotional aspects that transcend different lengths of time, as well as an expression of emotions with varying degrees of intensity. Advances in the field of well-being research are embracing these different emotional components of well-being through new, more diverse methods.

Diener et al (2003) – starting from an hedonic perspective – argue that global measures of life satisfaction may only assess subjective well-being at a more abstract (or higher) level and are unable to capture the complex nature of factors that may influence levels of subjective well-being at a lower level that focus on goals of a more immediate nature. The suggestion here is that there are aspects of well-being that operate within a hierarchy, under four key components: pleasant emotions (below this level includes joy and contentment); unpleasant emotions (including anger, stress); global life judgements (such as life satisfaction and success); and domain satisfaction (covering marriage, work, health and leisure). These four components at the top of the hierarchy compose the concept of subjective well-being itself. Ryff and Keyes (1995) – from a eudaemonic perspective – embrace the notion of 'psychological well-being'. This, they suggest, has six distinct aspects of self-actualisation: autonomy, personal growth, self-acceptance, life purpose, mastery and positive relatedness. Nettle (2005) – who combines these perspectives – identifies three levels of happiness. Level one is momentary feelings such as joy and pleasure; level two is the more considered judgements about the balance of feelings such as contentment and life satisfaction; level three, he suggests, is quality of life – what Aristotle terms 'the good life', where a person flourishes or reaches their full potential.

The trend, then, is to capture well-being as it manifests through different emotional feelings and functionings. This can be done through various measurement tools. The scale chosen here (GHQ12) is a well-validated measure, but it does have its limitations. Returning to Diener et al (2003), they break down well-being into four parts; the GHQ captures two elements, namely positive and negative emotions. The two remaining elements from Diener's work are global life judgements (including satisfaction with life overall) and domain satisfaction. This may account for why domain satisfactions were consistently the most important aspects in explaining variations in subjective well-being (Chapters 3 and 4), and could suggest that they should have been included in the subjective well-being measure (or indeed be used instead of it) as opposed to being treated as factors that may influence subjective well-being. The key point here, however, is that different domains are important to men and women and these vary over time – satisfaction with work and income has given way to satisfaction with the social aspects of life (Figures 3.4 and 3.5; 3.7 and 3.8). The evidence suggests that, while domain satisfactions are important to subjective well-being, they are not the best predictors. A measure of subjective well-being may therefore benefit from the inclusion of questions on life satisfaction, rather than using domain satisfaction in isolation from other elements of subjective well-being; namely, detecting the presence of positive emotion and the absence of negative feelings, as can be done through such psychological measures as the GHQ.

The greater challenge lies in capturing the more subtle elements of well-being. Aspects that are less well explored in the GHQ12 are the components of self-fulfilment and contentment contained in Nettle's (2005) and Ryff and Keyes's (1995) theories. These would best be measured through direct questions on feelings of contentment or ability to accept and cope with negative experiences. However, using the data available it may be possible to capture elements of these through the emergence of – in some instances unexpected – positive aspects of different life experience. For example, higher levels of well-being are associated with those who are in education (Figure 3.4) and, as will be explored in the next chapter, this could be associated with a move towards self-fulfilment. It is interesting to note that educational achievement is commonly included in measures of national and international well-being and development.[1]

More intriguing here, though, is the association with higher levels of well-being among men who are unemployed (Figure 3.8). The findings from the BHPS survey are in line with those of Creed et al (2001), who found that unemployed people were not a homogeneous group and that those who were satisfied with their situation reported similar levels of psychological distress to employed people. Other research, focusing on females, has also found that there were some improvements in psychological health following redundancy, particularly where unemployment had been preceded by a period of uncertainty (Arnetz et al, 1988). It could be speculated that the men in the BHPS study show a strong enough sense of self-worth that they are able to deal with what is generally considered a negative experience. Indeed this positive slant may account for why so few remained unemployed over the long term, as their positive outlook ensured a return to the labour market. These findings are consistent with studies that have shown that unemployment can give rise to positive feelings, particularly where this is associated with the opportunity to escape boring or stressful jobs (Little, 1976; Fineman, 1983), leading some to conclude that no job is better than any job (Rodriguez et al, 2001). Such evidence suggests that, where jobs are not deemed fulfilling, this undermines a sense of self-worth and — under such conditions — not working may be no less damaging to well-being than working in a less than desirable occupation. While it may be possible to speculate on the effects of being content or engaging in activities that may lead to self-fulfilment, there is no doubt that future research would benefit from addressing these different components of well-being by compiling a series of questions that draw out these feelings more directly.

Exploring these different components suggests that future research needs to be more explicit in what it seeks to measure — moving away from the interchangeability of well-being with happiness, life satisfaction and quality of life. Each term taps into a different aspect of well-being, some representing momentary moods, others more considered cognitive aspects that cover a particular period, or the whole of life. Greater consideration needs to be given to the different spatial and temporal components that each term addresses.

The questions asked, then, present restrictions on what conclusions can be drawn from the data. Despite such limitations we can, and should, make the best use of the data that is currently available. While there has been a flurry of analysis over the past few decades, a key consideration is the level at which such analysis is conducted, and in particular the spatial component of measurement: whether this is a more valid representation at the global (national) or local (individual) level. It was suggested in Chapter 3 that average national well-being generally reflects a consistent pattern over time, and this is so for different demographic and socio-economic divisions in society. The consistency of average well-being scores lends support to the existence of a 'set point' of happiness or even the 'happy personality', so that when an event unbalances our sense of well-being, this does not have long-term consequences, because our well-being will return to its equilibrium.

This is the theory proposed by Cummins et al (2003), who suggest that subjective well-being is maintained by a set of psychological devices that function under the control of personality, whereby individuals have a 'set-point' around which their subjective well-being varies (Chapter 2). So despite the experience of positive or negative adverse events, through a process similar to the homeostatic maintenance of blood pressure or temperature, fluctuations in subjective well-being will only be temporary states, and individual psychological functioning will always restore subjective well-being to its original level (Cummins and Nistico, 2002; Cummins et al, 2003).

If subjective well-being is a fixed trait, however, this does raise the difficult question of whether individual levels of subjective well-being could be changed. The evidence reported in Chapter 4 shows us that this may indeed be possible. Changes such as exiting the labour market or deterioration in health had negative consequences; however, many changes such as improvement in satisfaction with life domains, health, social support or becoming employed or an owner–occupier had positive outcomes for subjective well-being.

Such findings suggest that aggregate measures are a poor indicator of subjective well-being. Although national indicators suggest that high or low subjective well-being may be stable over any given period, this is not to say that the same individuals are representative of such states year after year, since changes in individuals' circumstances may mean that they move in and out of different subjective well-being states. And even proponents of the homeostatis theory (Cummins et al, 2003) acknowledge that sufficiently diverse environmental conditions could disrupt the well-being system and that happiness traits are not necessarily genetically determined.

A longitudinal focus on the extreme ends of the scale poses new insights – and new questions – into variations that may in part be explained by changes in individuals' perceptions as they become accustomed to their circumstances, or may be a reflection of the less-than-static nature of human experience. In order to address these issues, research into well-being may consider a change of emphasis away from measures at the aggregate level towards a more individual level – specifically, individual trajectories of well-being experience – with a view to identifying causal pathways. Adopting such an approach here has identified the positive effect that changes in circumstances can have on people's emotional outcomes. Understanding how change becomes a function of well-being is important because this provides a means of intervention and, possibly, enhancement.

Crucially, measures of individual trajectories could work towards unpacking the complex issues of cause and effect – whether people derive well-being from their experiences or whether a certain level of well-being determines courses of action or choices made. The focus of much research – including that reported in this book – is on well-being as an outcome measure. However, research into personality types suggests that well-being may in itself be an explanatory variable, that experiencing positive (or indeed negative) well-being in turn might affect people's opportunities and rewards. For example, research on the relationship between personality traits and the onset of specific forms of illness has led to the view that 'physical illness or disability can be overcome more effectively by patients who are in the right frame of mind' (Huppert et al, 1987, p 51). Further studies would support this view, suggesting that people who display extroversion and internal locus of control are also associated with increased reported subjective well-being (Argyle, 1987; Triemstra et al, 1998). Furthermore, people who are more positive in life tend to adopt different coping strategies and interpretations of situations, and are more likely to avoid stressful situations and seek out positive ones (Veenhoven, 1984; Argyle, 1987). Taylor and Brown (1988) have suggested that having a positive outlook can lead to higher motivation, intellectual creativity and greater success.

However, a positive frame of mind in itself may not always be the route to well-being, particularly where such an approach is adopted as a means of denial.

Boyd-Wilson et al (2002), for example, found that people who are able to live in the present, with accurate perceptions of life, are more likely to experience higher levels of subjective well-being than those who adopt what Taylor and Brown (1988) refer to as a 'positive illusion' or rose-tinted view of the self. They conclude that people experiencing high levels of subjective well-being are more likely to hold a realist's view of life, being more aware of both their negative and positive behaviours, and being more likely to take responsibility for them (Boyd-Wilson et al, 2002). The most effective responses to life experience may therefore arise from holding a realistic view: not to pursue an illusive, permanent hedonic state, but rather to have the ability to counterbalance life's ups and downs, so that not only do we not fall into the depths of despair, from where it is a long way back up, but also perhaps do not climb to some hedonic high from where the only way is down.

There may be some clues, then, to the variations in experiences of well-being in the coping strategies people do or do not adopt. Much of the research done in this area has focused on the alleviation of short-term negative moods. However, another approach would be to consider those aspects of life that are pursued with a view to increasing levels of well-being. Such an approach has been adopted by Tkach and Lyubormirsky (2006). In their research into intentional behaviour and positive mood change, they found that the most frequently used and most influential 'happiness–increasing strategy' was social affiliation, helping or being with others, a fact that has been supported by the research findings reported in Chapters 3 and 4 and is consistent with many studies of happiness or life satisfaction. While social affiliation may be deemed a worthwhile pursuit – something of value in society – not all activities engaged in, in the pursuit of happiness, may be considered in the same light. Although people engage in a variety of activities – adopt strategies – with the belief that they will enhance their mood, not all activities may be considered to be of value at a societal (or individual) level (Offer, 2006). Indeed, over the longer term there may be detriment to other aspects of well-being. This takes the study of well-being into some very difficult terrain, the question of who determines what is 'good' and what is 'bad' in the pursuit of well-being.

Moralising

Things in life may be regarded as being good in themselves and having intrinsic value, or they may be seen as a means of obtaining other things that have worth and, as such, have instrumental value. For example, a good life may be seen as having intrinsic value, while health may be regarded as having instrumental value in achieving a good life (Sirgy et al, 2006). Health presents an interesting example here, not least because it has a long history of measurement in both a social and an economic context, but health means different things to different people, and as such opens up the debate on the moral underpinnings of well-being.

The positive relationship between health status and subjective well-being, reported in Chapters 3 and 4, suggests that subjective assessment of health continues to be important in understanding individual subjective well-being. It would support the continued use of health measures (in particular self-reported health status) as a valid indicator of the psycho-social experience of living in an unequal society. Since the emergence of capitalism, health has been used as a 'sensitive indicator for measuring the social consequence of economic development' (Brennan, 1998, p 23), particularly where the gap in health status has grown in line with increased inequality in Britain (Mitchell et al, 2000). Despite improvements in living standards in western societies, inequalities in health have failed to be eradicated (Elstad, 1998) and this has given rise to a more socially oriented theory of health inequalities. The experience of relative deprivation – the feelings of injustice that arise from living in an unequal society – can have a negative psychological effect, and individuals' health status becomes more a reflection of their perceived rather than their actual material state (Wilkinson, 1996).

A key finding, however, relates to the relationship between health-related behaviour and subjective well-being, which taps into the more complex moral aspects of well-being. The findings on health status and, in particular, (un)healthy related behaviour (such as smoking – discussed in Chapter 4) raise an important question relevant to the moralisation of well-being: is having the right to choose how you live your life indicative of subjective well-being even when this contradicts health-promotion activities? This moral aspect potentially poses the greatest challenge for the study of well-being and for political intervention and enhancement of national levels of well-being. It has already been established that measures of national progress need to address individuals' subjective (as well as actual) circumstances, but well-being may also involve an element of risk-taking behaviour. Policy needs to acknowledge this and, rather than seek to control or determine every aspect of individuals' lives, there should be greater understanding of why people engage in certain behaviour, with a view to tackling the indirect causes.

It is recognised that the pursuit of health promotion may be more beneficial to enhancing subjective well-being than merely focusing on the prevention or cure of ill health. However, where changes in behaviour are sought, this may need to address the underlying emotional issues where activities are engaged in for their perceived psychological benefits; health promotion needs to account for the social and emotional context of some health-related behaviour.

This fundamental philosophical issue underpins how we conceptualise and understand subjective well-being at the individual and societal level. It is beyond this book to attempt to answer this question (and indeed no conclusive answer may ever be forthcoming), but it opens up the space for debate on the moralising of the good life and how we position professional knowledge in relation to lived experiences.

Subjective well-being: individual good or social justice?

The deliberations so far have concentrated on the individual – their personality and response mechanisms. From a policy perspective, where governments seek to devise means of measuring well-being and understanding the factors that influence it, they should consider the extent to which well-being influences (or motivates) people's choices, opportunities and outcomes. While to some extent this may be determined by the individual themselves – and warrant a focus on individual pathways – it should be recognised that many choices and opportunities are determined from the political and social institutions to which they are exposed and the norms that operate within a society. The question, then, is: to what extent is well-being an individual state or a social responsibility?

Throughout this book I have sought to dispel the 'myth of economic progress' (NEF, 2004) by suggesting that economic growth does not make a good proxy measure for a nation's well-being and that many other factors need to be taken into account – including the social as well as environmental costs of economic growth. For societal well-being to be improved it needs to take account of the multiple factors that influence and are influenced by it, and here I suggest that well-being will only progress where it is supported by social justice and not propped up by economic growth.

Subjective well-being is more a reflection of social outcomes than of economic conditions and supports the need for more diverse measures of subjective well-being to be adopted rather than relying on economic factors alone. As discussed previously, although a single global measure of subjective well-being may be sufficient to capture the elements of subjective well-being in the short term, a more diverse measure is needed in order validly to assess the complexities associated with maintaining or promoting subjective well-being. It needs to be understood in terms of the individual set within the context of social systems, and improving well-being will only be achieved where individual and societal level factors are simultaneously embraced.

As alluded to in Chapter 2, social exclusion and poverty are not just about a reduction in income, but represent the deprivation of subjective well-being that comes from lacking the resources that are deemed necessary to enable full participation in society. The nature of such resources, however, is changing. On the one hand, as nations become richer people's expectations also increase, so that what was once deemed a luxury has now become a necessity. But on the other hand, there is also evidence of a move away from fulfilling materialistic needs and desires and towards addressing the more social aspects of life (Chapters 2 and 3). Within this framework poverty has come to be understood in terms of the psychological consequences of interactions with – or exclusion from – the social environment. But, as has been alluded to in Chapter 4, a new pattern is emerging, with feelings of exclusion and subjective deprivation operating at all levels of affluence.

Where the inequalities in society provide the contextual explanations for poor levels of well-being in spite of improved quality of life, there is some evidence emerging of the changing nature of social ideology – a move towards a 'welfare' approach to well-being. This change in attitudes provides the starting point for a reassessment of what we consider to be important in our lives in respect of enhancing our well-being.

The theme to be developed – in line with Smith and Easterlow (2005) – is the extent to which well-being affects the trajectory people take or whether people's life paths affect well-being. People are bound up in their histories, cultural practices and the institutions and political norms of the society in which they live. Although measured as an individual outcome – whether life satisfaction, happiness, or GHQ – well-being is a reflection of a social existence, individuals' response to a collective experience. Well-being research may therefore benefit from a compositional element that psychological or economic-based approaches do not have the capacity to address. A social thesis of well-being may be the way forward.

Whether this is through addressing Offer's (2006) 'economy of regard' or Jordan's (2007) 'relational economy', the emphasis is on the value born of personal relations. This is a value that cannot be traded in a recognised 'market place' but is nonetheless significant for how the economy functions and how we interpret our experiences – whether this adds to or detracts from our well-being. The theory here is for a move towards a welfarist idea of well-being – that the 'subjective' element of well-being is determined as much by social and political systems and how they interact as by individual effort and striving. How such an approach might be developed in practice is the subject of the next chapter.

Notes

1. For example, the World Values Survey (www.worldvaluessurvey.org); the Human Development Index (http://hdr.undp.org).

SIX

Well-being: A welfare ideal?

> I too had acculturated myself to the notion that in a country
> with more money, greater freedom, bigger houses, better
> schools, finer health care, and more unfettered opportunity
> than anywhere else on earth, of course an abundance of its
> population would be out of their minds with sorrow.
>
> (Lionel Shriver, 2005, p 410)

This book started out by suggesting that money and material goods are not the route to happiness. The subsequent chapters have shown that well-being is not a function of economic progress or affluence, but that what matters is the social context of material existence. This is why well-being is more closely associated with income inequality than income levels themselves; it 'is not the direct effects of absolute material living standards so much as the effect of social relativities' (Wilkinson, 1996, p 3) that matters.

Well-being, then, does not emerge from the satisfaction of higher income or consumption opportunities, but is dependent upon one's relative position. The evidence reported in this book together with other research suggests that, where the continual pursuit of happiness is at the expense of others' social immobility, this will never increase the well-being of a nation. This raises the issue of what we deem 'success' to be and whether, in fact, it is ever achievable where it is dependent upon upward advancement in society (Pahl, 1995). This chapter provides explanations for this phenomenon – raising questions about what we *do* and what we *should* consider to be successful and positive progress.

The economics of social justice

The 1990s were arguably a period of reflection, a reconsideration of the politics of the 1980s – living with the consequences of individualisation and privatisation – with a highly visible though (relatively) peaceful reaction against it. The first decade of the millennium has so far been a period of a much different 'experience' – of a real and violent reaction (for example, 11 September 2001 in the US and 7 July 2005 in the UK) to the excess and ideology of western capitalist civilisation.

There is no doubt that there are elements of well-being that operate on a global scale. This is notable in the tendency for studies of well-being to be influenced more by western culture, with an emphasis on 'achieving' – 'work, struggle, striving and purposefulness' – at the expense of 'useless' (expressive, being and growing) behaviour that is more in line with eastern cultures (Maslow, 1970, pp 62–3). Where well-being has previously been understood within this 'climate of economic domination' (Beck et al, 1997, pp 266–7), there is now a growing recognition of a need to engage with the non-economic, social aspects.

A move to embracing well-being is emerging across the political spectrum (Jordan, 2007). But public policy that places well-being at the centre of its agenda will fail to achieve its objectives unless there is a turn to embracing the social and relational aspects of society (Offer, 2006). As discussed in Chapter 5, whether this is through embracing the 'economy of regard' (Offer, 2006) or the 'relational economy' (Jordan, 2007), there is no doubt that a move towards an 'ethics of care' (Smith, 2005a) lies at the centre of improving the well-being of a nation.

The alleviation of deprivation and the enhancement of subjective well-being need to go beyond 'one size fits all' economic growth. As noted earlier, economic growth may be an indication of more production and more consumption, but it does not necessarily follow that everyone benefits to the same extent. Where this has been seen to impact on well-being levels during the 1990s, the implications for future well-being levels are far from optimistic, given that in 2004 the majority of the British population (73%) considered the gap between those with high and low incomes to be too large (Orton and Rowlingson, 2007b). Continual striving to raise a nation's wealth will not – based on such negative public response – raise subjective well-being where the increases continue to be unfairly distributed.

Figure 6.1 illustrates how the rungs of economic progress are not equally spaced and, where economic growth is used to prop up subjective well-being, this is fundamentally flawed. Where economic inputs are not matched by resource

Figure 6.1: Economic growth and subjective well-being

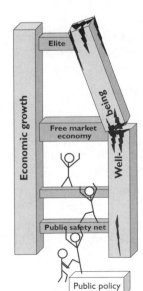

outputs, individuals become stranded and frustrated. Public policy may provide individuals with a 'hand up' onto the first rung, which provides the opportunity to reach the second rung of the ladder. But once outside the public safety net, the gap becomes too large for full participation in the free market economy, with the elite few well out of reach.

As discussed throughout this book, individuals' lives are complex and difficult to simplify into meaningful categories without losing some of the complexity. Similarly, it is difficult to simplify the process by which subjective well-being could be achieved. High subjective well-being is not conditional on a continually ascending trajectory, and should be contained within an area secured by the social justice 'safety net'. Where well-being can only be found at the top of the economic hierarchy, then the costs of losing are high – the existence of a welfare state provides the safety net that stops people falling all the way to the bottom (Offer, 2006). Individuals' circumstances may change, but their subjective well-being will be conditional not only on the impact that this has on their own lives but becomes set within the context of the rest of society. So, where the welfare state is in retreat, this not only reduces the numbers who can be saved and supported, but undermines a sense of well-being for all. Where people are increasingly (forced into) buying out of state provision of housing, education, health and so on, the insecurity of maintaining a given lifestyle increases across the economic spectrum.

Figure 5.1 may be a simplification of a very complicated process. However, it does draw attention to the importance of social (collective and political) understandings in the process of individual levels of well-being. A politics of inequity shows that negative feelings arise in spite of material affluence, and where society deems success and well-being as a move up the ladder – as noted in Chapter 5 – then it is the circumstances of those at the higher end of society we should be concerned with, as well as looking for answers to society's ailments among the most deprived. The political market and institutional processes that undermine achievements in all aspects of life, through a narrow focus on a successful or good life, open up the space for addressing the ethics of well-being and a consideration of how well-being may be compromised by a competition-led market society.

These ideas will be explored further in the rest of this chapter by addressing three key aspects that dominate the political agenda – housing, education and employment – and two that may well come to dominate it in the future – leisure and retirement. These aspects are considered to be important because, although increases in income may bring about short-term improvement in mood, money will not compensate for the lack of opportunity or security in the long term – the loss of self-esteem, identity or secure integration in society associated with poor education, disengagement from the labour market or housing repossession. Education, work and home bring rewards far greater than their monetary or status value and give individuals a sense of identity, purpose and belonging that translates into subjective well-being. As such, these aspects of life are not only important to well-being but also provide insights into the gap between how we do and how we could measure 'success' in society. Finally, this chapter will address the variations in well-being that have been exposed along a gendered division considering the implications for women's well-being in a market system that lacks a 'care-full' component.

Home ownership

Throughout the last century one asset that has become a sign of 'success' is that of owner-occupation. Since the 1950s the proportion of households owning their own home has seen a steady increase, initially at the expense of private renting but more recently also as an alternative to social housing – fuelled by the politicisation of owner-occupation during the 1980s. Today the owner-occupier sector accounts for around 70% of all UK households (DCLG, 2006b). This dominance of home ownership has led it to be seen as the tenure de rigueur (Smith, 2005b) – the 'natural' housing tenure, something to be aspired to – providing the contextual setting for the association of home ownership and a sense of achievement; sustaining a strong psychological connection between housing situation and a sense of self-esteem (Hiscock et al, 2001, p 55).

Housing tenure, then, is an important factor in understanding subjective well-being – supported by findings here that show a positive association with being or becoming an owner-occupier (Chapter 4). This finding is consistent with the positive relationship between housing and health outcomes that has been recognised since *The Black Report* (Townsend and Davidson, 1988). The benefits of owner-occupation, however, may not just be associated with its physical attributes. The home itself may be valued for factors that are themselves pertinent to subjective well-being. These factors embrace the non-financial – emotional – aspects that people value about their home (Searle et al, 2007). These values are reinforced through associated meanings of self, identity, security, protection, a sense of achievement and permanency (Saunders, 1990; Giddens, 1991) particularly when owner-occupation is compared to the rented sector (Hiscock et al, 2001).

Given the current climate of the housing market – which has seen a continued annual increase in prices for over a decade (1996–2006) (based on the Halifax House Price Index) – such a finding has important implications for well-being. In particular, the point of entry into the housing market, the availability of affordable housing and the sustainability of home ownership. Research by Nettleton and Burrows (1998) on the impact of the changes in housing policy and economic circumstances in the UK during the 1980s and 1990s showed that while the availability of Right to Buy enabled more people to get a foot on the housing ladder, this meant more 'at risk' groups were able to enter into home ownership, the owner-occupied sector subsequently accounting for over half of the poor (Burrows, 2003). The implications of this became particularly apparent during the slump of the 1990s where over a tenth of home owners fell into arrears or were having problems paying their mortgage (Nettleton and Burrows, 1998). The same research showed that the new-found wealth and euphoria associated with becoming home owners were soon stripped away, with the onset of mortgage problems being significantly associated with a deterioration in psychological well-being. The results presented here not only reflect the burden of sustaining home ownership during the 1990s but highlight that during this period owner-occupation was no more conducive to well-being than renting (Appendix, Table D1.2). More recent research suggests that, even following a recovery in the housing market, owner-occupation is no guarantee of high well-being (Searle et al, 2007).

So not only is the owner-occupied sector uneven in quality, but the demands of maintaining home ownership may provide the environment in which well-being becomes undermined. Home ownership does not come with the same safety-net provision as the rented sector in the event of loss of income (Ford et al, 2004; Blandy and Hunter, 2005) or deterioration in health (Smith et al, 2003).

The current buoyant housing market may, on the face of it, be beneficial to existing owner-occupiers – indeed the expansion of home ownership and the extent of house price appreciation have evened up the distribution of national wealth. However, the sustainability of home ownership is a risk. The benefits of rising house prices – as with the benefits of economic progress generally – are not evenly spread across society and the difficulties associated with getting on the property ladder give rise to concerns for the increasing polarisation of future generations based on the wealth of the housing haves and have-nots (Thomas and Dorling, 2004).

The turbulent 1990s have been followed by a stable and benign economic period; however, as the end of the first decade of 2000 draws near the housing boom is once again a cause for concern. The signs are that with five interest rate rises (between August 2006 and July 2007) and more speculated (BBC News, 2007) house prices – although not expected to reflect the slump of the 1990s – will certainly slow down. The changing fortunes of owner-occupation reported during the 1990s look set to repeat themselves in the 2000s, as marginal home owners are once again at the mercy of the vagaries of economic conditions and the housing market, leading some to speculate that 'maybe owning a home is not for everyone' (Ferguson, 2007).

The normalisation of home ownership should not, then, be pursued at the expense of the rented sector. Managed property can reduce housing costs and there may be less stress, due to the lack of responsibility for meeting mortgage payments or maintaining housing standards. Research by Oakes and McKee (1997), for example, shows that among certain sectors of society renting is growing in popularity; changes in the job market and the need for geographic mobility, the lack of a substantial deposit, and the lack of responsibility for maintenance or repairs increased the appeal of renting among single people or couples without children. A growing buy-to-let market may fulfil the demands from this sector of society; however, the same research reported that the general standard of rented accommodation was poor (Oakes and McKee, 1997). Evidence from the English House Condition Survey would support this finding. Although the proportion of houses in a decent condition (defined as a house that is warm, weatherproof and has reasonably modern facilities (ODPM, 2003)) has increased, there is still a larger percentage of non-decent houses in the private rented sector compared to other tenures.

National statistics show that while the proportion of homes in the private rented sector in a non-decent standard dropped from 62% to 43% between 1996 and 2004, this still leaves more homes in this sector in an unacceptable standard as compared to the owner-occupied sector, which saw a fall from 40% to 27% over the same period (ODPM, 2004a). So although progress has been made, this is slow and still lags behind those of resident owners. The lack of quality property-to-let suggests that a growing private rented sector – fuelled by the buy-to-let market – may lead to poorer quality of housing stock in the longer term. And where government recognises that a decent home is important to health and well-being (ODPM, 2003), the condition of private as well as public sector housing should be included in measures of national subjective well-being.

The role of 'owner-occupier' potentially, then, is a double-edged sword. Compared to renting, owner-occupiers are more satisfied, but the gain of independence may have detrimental consequences where there is no state fall-back in the event of financial uncertainty. The normalisation of home ownership and its implications for promoting subjective well-being mean the availability of affordable homes should remain a key issue for policy into and beyond 2000. But where home ownership represents a sign of 'success', this needs to be reconsidered in respect of the sustainability of ownership, particularly where at-risk groups have entered the housing market without adequate financial cover.

One possible means of engaging with these issues is through consideration of the 'care-full' thesis that is emerging in the housing and health literature, advanced by Smith et al (2003). This proposes a breaking down of the barriers between the polarisation of a 'care-full' social and 'care-less' private housing sector; the rented sector could benefit from a better quality of housing stock associated with the ownership of homes, while the owner-occupied sector would benefit by incorporation of some of the caring qualities of the social rented sector. Indeed, some would argue that owner-occupation has already claimed the territory of social caring functions previously delivered by the state where this tenure is increasingly being used to house vulnerable groups in society (Smith, 2005b) and where housing wealth is relied upon to meet current and future welfare needs (Searle et al, 2007). This raises the interesting proposal – which may benefit from further debate – of the notion of moving from private ownership to a more social concept of stewardship: a concept and a practice that attends to the care-taking that is needed to preserve the value of the housing stock – as a public welfare resource – for the future (Smith et al, 2006).

Such an approach not only has implications for the quality and condition of the homes of future generations, but may have implications for the well-being of some sectors of the owner-occupied sector. Research shows that where home owners choose to deploy their housing wealth in a 'care-full' way – securing the welfare of the owners or their family members – this is associated with positive well-being outcomes. However, where home-owners' future welfare is dependent upon the performance of one volatile asset – their home – the burden of maintaining the quality and condition of that home in a competitive housing market has been shown to undermine their sense of well-being (Searle et al, 2007). Sharing this responsibility – a move away from individual to collective ownership – may be one means of alleviating the negative emotions arising from such dependency.

The Right to Buy legacy of the 1980s and affordable housing made available during the 1990s need, in future, to be backed up by affordable options in the event of changes in life circumstances and the onset of financial loss. The changing nature of financial services – and mortgage lending in particular – means that homes are no longer an investment for the future but represent a resource to be called upon throughout the life course (Searle et al, 2007). The future of home ownership may, then, lead to greater diversity within this tenure group between those who have alternative resources to call upon in the event of financial difficulties and those whose wealth is restricted and whose home – in the context of increasing withdrawal of public safety nets in many aspects of life – provides their only source of funding in the face of economic shocks.

Education

Another measure of success in modern society is associated with educational achievement. However, this success needs to be considered in a wider context than the formal examinations that feed into league tables. In line with the welfarist approach, access into and out of education should be more flexible and reflect the needs of individuals at any stage of their life rather than being based on financially restricting age zones.

This research has shown that promoting subjective well-being is linked with the fulfilling of basic needs (for example, shelter, in particular becoming an owner-occupier). It also shows that cognitive elements at the higher end of the hierarchy – the desire for knowledge and understanding (Maslow, 1954) – should also be accounted for. The acquisition of knowledge has been linked to the higher elements of well-being for some time. However, education provides a source of social as well as academic learning and experiences of the educational system have the potential to impinge upon as well as enhance subjective well-being.

The benefits of education during the early and compulsory years of life are well rehearsed, but not everyone's experience of the school system is positive or rewarding. Through lifelong learning, on the other hand, there is the capacity to address this problem (potentially reversing the detrimental effects of education experienced during compulsory years) given the right conditions in adult life. The research reported in Chapter 4 shows that returning to education – for women at least – enhances their well-being state. This is consistent with research that reports that even among those whose early experiences of the education system were negative – having lasting and profound effects on confidence and attitudes towards learning – a return to education in later years was associated with indicators of enhanced well-being such as self-esteem, identity and purpose, motivation, confidence and hope. Within this same research by Schuller et al (2004) people also spoke of the social benefits, feelings of belonging to a community, building social networks and broadening experiences through engaging in new activities. This is not to say that all experiences with later learning are positive. Benefits may be dependent upon age, social class, ethnicity and previous life events (Hammond, 2004) among other things. What is key for the study of well-being, however, as Antikainen (1998) reports, is that education has its greatest potential to impact on people's lives during times of change. It has protective benefits during times of adversity and even in stable conditions is enriching, having value for the individual and the community (Hammond, 2004).

Where education becomes a function of well-being, particularly beyond compulsory educational years, this has implications for the changing educational needs of individuals throughout the life course. The positive association of returning to education discussed in Chapter 4 suggests that this may be linked with the opportunity that learning provides to reach one's full potential – a fact that did not escape the attention of the government (DfEE, 1998). However, despite recognition of the benefits of education beyond its immediate knowledge-based and economic benefits, little progress has been made towards the creation of a coherent, engaging, accessible culture of lifelong learning (Hargreaves, 2004, foreword). For Hargreaves the foundations for such a culture need to be set in the formative school years and the policy developments this entails, and while this is a key aspect, the education of individuals needs to be considered as it relates to their opportunities across the life course – a point perhaps recognised by the recent separation of graduate and adult skills from school education, in a policy context. The pursuit of education beyond the formal school years may be associated with a need to fulfil one's potential, and the pursuit of lifelong learning could provide a means of promoting subjective well-being.

While training and education are important aspects of developing well-being, their link to the wider economy for many is inevitable (organisations need to acknowledge the benefits of investing in their workforce, their human capital), while the chances presented in a learning environment need to be matched with secure employment opportunities. The expectations for a constantly mobile, flexible, commuting workforce may result in short-term economic gain; however, such an attitude is not conducive to long-term well-being.

Employment

Within a capitalist system employment status is one of the key markers of 'success', and while it is without doubt pertinent to understanding well-being, this may not be for the most obvious reasons. So, while the positive benefits of employment stem from a comparison with the negative consequences of unemployment, being a source of income, social respect and perceived as rewarding (Veenhoven, 1984), employment per se does not always guarantee satisfaction, nor is it a good predictor of overall life satisfaction (Argyle, 1987). The analysis has shown that unemployed people are no less likely to be among those with high well-being than those who are employed (Chapter 3). There may be several reasons for this and studies have suggested that the increase in stress associated with full-time work or with promotion is not always compensated for by the rewards of economic 'success' (Pahl, 1995; Ferrie, 2001; Rodriguez et al, 2001). Furthermore, the incidence of ill health has been associated with 'job dissatisfaction, boredom, low participation, poor social support from co-workers and supervisors' (WHO, 1979, p 89) and job insecurity (Ferrie et al, 2005).

The issue is further complicated by the imposed boundaries between paid and voluntary work. Studies involving people with disabilities, for example, concluded that the ability to be socially participative (even in voluntary work) was more important than acquiring the professional status associated with paid employment (Ville et al, 2001). There are also emotional rewards underpinning employment, but these again add to the complexity of well-being. Lu and Lin's (1998) study of adults in Taiwan showed that the 'worker role' was both a source of stress, where it was necessary to provide for the family, and a source of satisfaction, where such provision benefited young children. The 'success' that emerges from employment, then, is not necessarily only that linked to status and income, but is bound up in the activity performed, the motivation for being active, and the potential rewards through enhancing the welfare of dependants.

As reported in Chapter 4, there are complex gender-related issues associated with employment status and well-being, with a negative outcome for employed women as compared to a positive association among unemployed men. Such differences may be accounted for in respect of the stress associated with the work environment (Pahl, 1995) or the imposition of multiple roles often encountered by female workers (Ward, 2004), whereas unemployment may be associated with a relief from such stress and responsibilities and be beneficial to (male) subjective well-being at least in the short term.

Flexibility is seen as a key to securing economic progress in a global context (Sennett, 1998; Ferrie et al, 2005); however, the terms are somewhat at opposite ends of the well-being spectrum where, for example, a flexible labour market is anything but secure, with potentially detrimental consequences for well-being. While employment is important in enhancing subjective well-being it has to meet specific requirements, such as those of satisfaction (Veenhoven, 1984) and security (Ferrie et al, 2005). Labour market policies that emphasise the importance of a flexible, mobile workforce within a global economy may therefore be at odds with enhancing well-being.

From the welfarist perspective, providing training and education opportunities in themselves will not increase subjective well-being where the effort is not matched by equally rewarding jobs in a secure employment environment. The employment associations of 'success' and subjective well-being should not only be measured in terms of the levels of participation (or not) in the labour market, but reflect security of employment, for example by offsetting permanent contracts with temporary, casual and seasonal work. Consistent with the findings throughout this research, satisfaction with different aspects of work should also be included, but these should be considered in respect of how time at work impinges on other aspects of individuals' lives – re-emphasising the importance of the work–life balance.

The UK is prone to a culture of long hours (figures for 2000 show that among European nations the average number of hours worked is 40; in the UK the average is 44 (Eurostat, 2002)) and this may be one of the new 'challenges of affluence' (Offer, 2006). Offer (2006) suggests that the choice of working becomes a necessity as the economy responds to rising incomes. For some, keeping pace may be linked to promotion; for others, increasing income in order to maintain a standard of living may only be possible through working longer hours. The 'welfarist' response would be to remove the incentive for excessive work hours. A starting point is Jordan's (2007) suggestion of a 'basic income' payable to those who engage in some form of activity (be it childcare, voluntary work or other activities) deemed 'socially useful'.

A basic income may seem counter-intuitive in a book proclaiming that money doesn't matter; however, it does address the 'care-full' element that needs to be reintroduced into policy. Having the reassurance of a liveable income because all activities are equally recognised for their contribution towards society takes pressure off the need to work (and to work long hours) away from the home. This would enable more time to pursue other activities that underpin well-being – be they fostering social relationships or pursing leisure activities.

Leisure

The importance of 'non-work' social aspects compared to 'work' economic conditions that this and previous research have found has important implications for the goals that individuals pursue and that society endorses. Where the progress of a nation is contained within an economic paradigm, success will continue to be measured in terms of individual financial gain. Technological developments and materialistic values have come to denote success, whereby societies with the highest per capita resources are held to be the most successful (Pahl, 1995). However, as the analysis reported in Chapter 4 shows, income is not pertinent to sustaining high subjective well-being, and the positive benefits associated with upward social mobility have not been borne out. In contrast, access to good social support, social relationships, participation in community groups and the availability of leisure time are all beneficial (Chapters 3 and 4). These findings support Pahl's (1995) and Jordan's (2007) argument that we need to redefine success in more universalistic terms, where the advantages of upward mobility are set in the context of long hours, stress, the loss of leisure time and the fear of losing ties to family, friends and familiar surroundings.

The emphasis placed on success associated with income, and the means of earning income, has infiltrated many aspects of life. As Hirsch (1977) argues, where time commands a price in the labour market, this is subsumed into leisure time. Good social behaviour becomes costly and time consuming and is liable to be economised; a good gesture is less likely to be returned and social interaction is seen as a cost with no benefit. As the subjective costs of our time rise due to its scarcity, this makes it 'more pressing to pass by on the other side' rather than to engage in 'friendliness and mutual concern that would be to everyone's worthwhile' (Hirsch, 1977, p 79). Scitovsky (1976), Hirsch (1977), and more recently Offer (2006) and Jordan (2007), among others, argue that the social costs of economic culture occur where time given to maintaining social relationships becomes reduced as the benefit is offset by the cost of lost earning potential through giving up work hours and losing pay. This principle underpins the 'individualisation' of society whereby the emphasis on flexibility and mobility in the interests of economic wealth has led to a breaking down of trust, community ties and social relationships (Giddens, 1991; Beck and Beck-Gernsheim, 1995; Sennett, 1998), creating the downside to economic growth that is detrimental to well-being.

In such a climate the importance of leisure time takes a back seat. However, the pursuit of leisure activities has been associated with social motivation and the benefits from social support and social interaction, as well as with providing a source of identity for people who are otherwise disengaged from society (Argyle, 1987). The positive outcomes associated with leisure activities (Chapter 3) are in line with previous research (Marsh et al, 1986; Fenner, 1987; Milligan et al, 2004), and have implications for policy that seeks to promote well-being. This may not only be in respect of formal, building-based facilities, but informal, leisure-friendly environments encompassing open public space, walking and cycling routes, and ensuring such environments are safe to access. While the outcomes may be measured in terms of the health benefits of physical activity or the social benefits of integration and community participation, the psychological benefits of green space and therapeutic landscapes are a growing area of research literature (Gesler, 2005) and may enhance any national well-being measures.

The ability to take 'time out' and participate in non-work-related activities also poses a different challenge – the solution to which may be found in non-monetary-based market systems. The adoption of a 'welfarist' approach already exists in the form of time-banking systems – where labour and services are all assigned the same value. Jordan's (2007) suggestion of a 'basic income' for all work undertaken would be a bold step, but reflects a welfarist approach to enable equity of choice across the activities that matter to us most. What matters is how we spend our time, not how much an hour of our time is worth.

Retirement

The ultimate time of leisure – or time out – within a capitalist system may be considered as being that point in life when we can withdraw from the pressures of work and pursue a more relaxed lifestyle during retirement. The analysis showed that entering the stage of their life associated with retirement had a significant bearing on those participants' well-being, eliciting and maintaining scores which put them at the high end of the well-being scale. This is consistent with the view that retirement is increasingly seen in a positive way where individuals become released from the demands of work and financial commitment (Scales and Scase, 2001) – which in itself has implications for the extent to which employment brings about well-being. However, a caveat may exist within the current political system where individual economic success provides the means for later welfare. Current retirees are potentially financially better off than future ones may be, and an emerging polarisation is developing between affluent early retirees and disadvantaged older workers (Scales and Scase, 2001). This will have significant implications for well-being levels in future years, as research is already showing that retirement among higher earners leads to the kinds of improvement in mental health and well-being that are not experienced by lower occupational groups (Chandola et al, 2007).

Security in retirement increasingly depends upon employment patterns, age of exit from the labour market and the extent to which individuals have the opportunities to make provision during their working lives. The (in)ability to acquire financial security for later life has implications for the quality of life that retired people experience. Future generations may not experience the high levels of subjective well-being of those in retirement at the end of the twentieth century within a 'care-less' market system.

Where a pensions crisis is potentially looming, the 'oasis' of retirement may be more of a mirage. The demographic shift towards an aging population – rising on average by 1% per decade (ONS, 2006b) – has implications for the extent to which public monies can fund retirement, giving rise to three main options: raise taxes, raise the retirement age or raise your own finances (Turner, 2004). These options lie within the realms of the political arena and will determine the opportunities that are available within society and provide the springboard to (in)equality across the life course. The opportunities to raise personal finances are dependent, within a capitalist society, on sustained access to the labour market, and the accumulation of capital assets. As discussed earlier the 'flexibilisation' of employment (Pahl, 1995) means that there is less stability and security in the labour market; where incomes cannot be guaranteed to meet day-to-day expenditure, there is little incentive or opportunity to save or invest money over the life course.

The accumulation of capital assets is increasingly seen as an alternative means of pension planning to the more traditional pension funds or investment in stocks and shares. Research by Thomas and Dorling (2004), for example, shows that housing has become the greatest repository of wealth in the United Kingdom and exceeds all other forms of savings or pension funds. Furthermore, the buoyant housing market means that many people are investing in property as a form of pension planning (Rhodes and Bevan, 2003). However, while rising house prices may benefit existing owner-occupiers and those investing in second homes through the buy-to-let initiative, the rise in house price to earnings ratio – which reached an all-time high of 4.59 in 2003, rising from 3.42 in 1991 (ODPM, 2004b) – means that current generations are finding it increasingly difficult to become established on the property ladder.

So we are entering a stage where, increasingly, alternative personal resources need to be found to fund retirement, conditional on the opportunities that are available within society. The polarisation of the housing market, the insecurities of the labour market and gendered divisions within the domestic arena mean that not everyone is able to accumulate the resources during their working lives that will sustain them in later life. The gendered inequalities that exist within society have implications for females who suffer from fragmented careers or complete absence from the labour market, limiting their ability to build the resources necessary for retirement within a capitalist-based system.

The gender divide

Longitudinal analysis highlights the importance of these findings, particularly as they impinge on the well-being of women. As identified in Chapter 4, the age variable may be representative of a combination of several other important life circumstances that would appear to have a greater impact on women's subjective well-being in the longer term. Parenthood, financial commitments and employment status have all individually – and in combination – been associated with the negative impact of middle age. The research into stress and coping has been concerned with the different social roles individuals acquire or have imposed upon them, and the extent to which people are integrated into a society. Multiple social roles provide the opportunity to adopt different identities and may provide a buffer to stress and enhance well-being; where roles are conflicting, however, this may add to stress and reduce well-being. This would still appear to operate along a gendered division.

Women, through their propensity to experience fragmented careers based around their roles as care givers, are less likely to build up financial resources through their working-age years, putting them at greater risk of poverty in later life (Fawcett, 2003). Where the means of providing security in retirement are – in the present market-based system – conditional on the ability to acquire assets across the life course, research suggests that women are feeling more pressured to remain a part of the labour market. Research by the National Family and Parenting Institute, for example, has found that between 1994 and 2004 more mothers were returning to work – and returning sooner, resulting in 'role strain'. Although the report found that fathers' roles had shifted, they did not do so as dramatically as mothers', and for many women balancing work and family was still a sizeable challenge (Ward, 2004).

Women then are still more likely to have dual-worker status, or are still relied upon as main care givers. As reported in Chapter 4, women suffer through having family care responsibilities and, while parenthood was detrimental to both genders, analysis on childcare shows that, whereas women have full childcare responsibilities, this is not the case among men (although men did suffer psychologically through being lone parents) (Searle, 2005). These findings have implications for the impact that caring responsibilities have on subjective well-being, particularly where the conditions of a market society mean that participation in employment is needed in order to provide the means of caring for dependants and the assets that will sustain existence during retirement. Adopting a welfarist approach, an enhancement of the social, collective responsibility for caring would alleviate the need to accumulate the resources – the private assets, including housing – that are increasingly being considered as the basis of welfare provision, providing an important step forward in securing the current and future well-being of the nation.

The implications for well-being here are immense, with many potential areas for further research into the roles of individuals and how such roles interact. There is scope to develop measures that not only assess the quality of individuals' social relationships but combine individuals' social roles and assess the extent to which they feel fulfilled or inhibited by them. This would focus our understanding of the impact of social relations on psychological health. In combination, the different areas of literature show that our lives are complex and ever changing, and in order to understand well-being it follows that the measure here needs to be flexible enough to capture fluctuations in mood and emotion. Life, as we have seen, is not always a smooth, upward progression and measures of well-being should not assume that this is so. Well-being is not just a function of what is earned and consumed but about who people are – how they perceive themselves, and how they fit into the different social contexts of everyday living. While the research reported here has taken account of some of the roles that individuals may acquire throughout the life course, it has not sought to combine them – or investigate the motivations for taking on certain roles – and this may provide a vital step forward in accounting for variations in well-being.

Well-being: the pursuit of contentment?

Since the beginning of the twentieth century the route to happiness has been implicit in the economic approach to well-being. The accumulation of wealth fulfils a 'need' to consume, wherein lies the source of satisfaction. But this theory has not been borne out in practice. The economic aspects that underpin experiences of subjective well-being may reflect a desire for social participation or the accumulation of customary resources, rather than the desire for the resources per se. This suggests that there is a disjuncture between economic progress and securing subjective well-being.

Through measuring relative poverty, research has shown how the luxuries of one generation have become the necessities of the next. It is increasingly recognised that, in order to understand what people are being deprived of, social science should not be focusing on the poor in isolation. Rather, it needs to secure a better understanding of the circumstances of those with whom the poor are being compared – those whose circumstances exceed a 'national average'. The constant drive to achieve and improve the standard of living is motivated by those in power who, through constant exposure to new temptations, create false needs that can never be filled and lead to certain disappointment.

The last century saw tremendous growth within a capitalist paradigm, whereby success and happiness have become associated with economic growth and the trappings of modern living. But economic growth simply raises the norm of a 'decent' standard of living and, therefore, the point at which satisfaction is achieved. Higher income/consumption has not resulted in higher levels of well-being and will fail to do so where the route to satisfaction is always on the next rung of the economic ladder. The key argument here is that sharp increases in material standards – and consequent unequal distribution of resources – can lead to reductions in well-being because they seem to be unjust.

Although economic measures may not provide a sufficient explanation for subjective well-being, this is not to say that they are not important or even unnecessary – simply that they should not be considered in isolation. The sense of injustice fuelled by living in an unequal society should form the basis for progress in understanding well-being. However, the true gap in inequality in society will only be known where we can compare the circumstances of the rich against the circumstances of the poor (Townsend, 1979; Orton and Rowlingson, 2007a). Although income may not be important to everyone, there is a false sense of poverty felt at all levels of affluence – where people look to those who are excessive consumers as their comparator group, with inevitable negative consequences. The study of well-being should – and indeed could – redress this imbalance, through showing that a sense of exclusion – and indeed inclusion – does not operate purely along a poor/affluent divide but occurs at all levels of the social hierarchy.

The hierarchical structure embedded in an economic idea of well-being is unable to embrace the rediscovery of the social welfare approach that is being adopted in some sectors of society. That is not to say that we should all downsize and live in a remote community – but that there would be benefits from embracing some of the collective ideals underpinning such a way of life. Subjective well-being is not an individual but a collective experience – as such, while everyone should have the right to experience high levels of well-being there should also be a shared, collective responsibility for the well-being of others. There is the capacity here to embrace the move towards the 'caring' components of a social existence – to embrace respect and regard (Offer, 2006) – and an acceptance that our actions have implications for the well-being of others and that continually striving to keep up with (or indeed surpass) the Joneses will not necessarily realise the hedonic feelings we aspire to. The quest, then, may not be to raise happiness levels but to seek a more sustainable emotion – that of contentment.

Appendix

Regression tables

Table A1: Operationalising subjective well-being: dependent variables

Subjective well-being

Reason for inclusion: Subjective well-being is operationalised as the psychological outcome of everyday experience. The extent to which individuals are able to cope, make decisions, feel worthwhile and generally feel happy about themselves are considered to be different elements of psychological state, which combine to produce a measure of overall subjective well-being. All these factors are measured in the GHQ12.

BHPS variables	Data description and transformation
HLGHQ1	**Subjective well-being.** This measure has converted the answers to the 12 GHQ questions into one overall score and the polarity of the scores has been reversed, whereby an increased score relates to higher levels of subjective well-being on a scale from 0 (Low subjective well-being) to 36 (High subjective well-being).

Cross-sectional measures combine individuals' annual subjective well-being scores into a single score for each of the 3-year periods 1991–93, 1994–96 and 1997–99, and are categorised as:

Low	scores of 0–65
Medium	scores of 66–84
High	scores of 85–360

Longitudinal measure looks at individuals' subjective well-being across each of the 3 periods

Stable high	High subjective well-being in each of the 3 periods
Mostly high	High subjective well-being in 2 out of the 3 periods
Stable moderate	Moderate subjective well-being in each of the 3 periods
Mostly moderate	Moderate subjective well-being in 2 out of the 3 periods
Stable low	Low subjective well-being in each of the 3 periods
Mostly low	Low subjective well-being in 2 out of the 3 periods
Mixed	A different level of subjective well-being in each of the 3 periods

Change measure is based on a change in subjective well-being status across 2 time periods: from low/moderate in 1993 to high in 1996 and from low/moderate in 1996 to high in 1999.

Regression analysis is based on these measures being recoded into dichotomous variables to reflect those with high subjective well-being, stable high subjective well-being or subjective well-being that had become high.

Cross-sectional analysis		Longitudinal analysis		Change analysis	
swb31t3h	High subjective well-being 1991-93	swb7ah	Stable high subjective well-being 1991-99	swbeh1	Subjective well-being became high 1993-96
swb32t3h	High subjective well-being 1994-96			swbeh2	Subjective well-being became high 1996-99
swb33t3h	High subjective well-being 1997-99		0 Not stable high well-being		
			1 Stable high well-being		0 Not high well-being
	0 Not high well-being				1 Well-being became high
	1 High well-being				

Table A2: Operationalising the independent variables

BHPS variables	Data description and transformation
Demographic	
	Reason for inclusion: Demographic information will be useful in the process of describing the circumstances associated with different levels of subjective well-being. It may also highlight variations in subjective well-being in respect of gender differences or life-course effects as shown by variations in subjective well-being status by different age groups. Age and ethnicity will be used as control variables throughout the regression analysis.
SEX	**Gender:** Analysis is based on an individual's gender: 1 Male 2 Female

AGE	**Age:** The age variable was recoded into 6 different groups. Cross-sectional analysis is based on the age group an individual was in at 1993, 1996 and 1999. Longitudinal analysis is based on the age group an individual was in at 1999. Change analysis is based on the age group an individual was in at 1996 and 1999.
	
	cage7 Age in 1993
	fage7 Age in 1996
	iage7 Age in 1999
	      1 25-34
	      2 35-44
	      3 45-54
	      4 55-64
	      5 65-74
	      6 75+

RACE	**Ethnicity:** Individuals' ethnicity is only recorded in the year in which they join the BHPS. A new variable was created to combine this information and ensure it was carried over into each subsequent year of the BHPS. Due to the low numbers of different ethnic status this variable was recoded to 'white' and the remaining groups all collapsed into one category of 'ethnic minority'.
	
	Cross-sectional analysis is based on an individual's ethnic status in 1993, 1996 and 1999. **Longitudinal analysis** is based on ethnicity status in 1999. **Change analysis** is based on ethnicity status in 1996 and 1999
	
	c2race Ethnicity 1993
	f2race Ethnicity 1996
	i2race Ethnicity 1999
	      1 White
	      2 Ethnic minority

(continued)

BHPS variables	Data description and transformation
HHTYPE	**Household type:** The original 9 categories were recoded into 4 groups: Single (combining elderly and non-elderly); Couple with children (including those with non-dependent and dependent children); Lone parent (including those with non-dependent and dependent children); Couple no children; Couple with children (including those with non-dependent and dependent children). Households with 2 or more unrelated adults, and other households, were assigned as missing due to the low number of cases.
	Cross-sectional analysis is based on an individual's household type in 1993, 1996 and 1999
	Longitudinal analysis is based on an individual's movement in and out of different household formations, looking at data for each year from 1991 to 1999. The categorisation reflects stability in household type and the household type that an individual person changed to rather than the household type they had changed from.
	Change analysis is based on the change in an individual's household status between 1993 and 1996, and between 1996 and 1999. The categorisation reflects stability in household type and the household type that an individual person changed to rather than the household type they had changed from.

chhtype1 Household type 1993
fhhtype1 Household type 1996
ihhtype1 Household type 1999

1 Single
2 Couple no children
3 Couple with children
4 Lone parent

hhtype99a Household type 1991 to 1999

1 Single
2 Couple no children
3 Couple with children
4 Lone parent (or become l p)
5 Moved into relationship
6 Become single
7 Become couple with/without children
8 Multiple changes

hhtype1a Change in household type from 1993 to 1996
hhtype2a Change in household type from 1996 to 1999

1 Single
2 Couple no children
3 Couple with children
4 Lone parent
5 Become single
6 Become couple without children
7 Become couple with children
8 Become lone parent

Socio-economic

Reason for inclusion: Economic prosperity has been associated with improvements in subjective well-being. Actual levels of income will reflect the importance of economic measures in experiencing subjective well-being. In addition to income, economic wealth can also be inferred by social standing or material possession as represented by social class or housing tenure. Education can influence employment status, which in turn will influence income levels. Income levels can be correlated with subjective measures of financial circumstances to find the importance of income levels in respect of subjective well-being. Relative wealth has been identified as being more important to subjective well-being than objective wealth and can be inferred by subjective measures of financial circumstances such as perceived financial situation.

(continued)

BHPS variables	Data description and transformation
FIHHYR	**Household annual income after housing costs:** Income is equivalised, deflated to 1991 prices and combined into quintile groups.

Cross-sectional analysis is based on a household's income quintile group in 1993, 1996 and 1999.

Longitudinal analysis is based on changes in income quintile between 1993, 1996 and 1999. Change in quintiles was categorised by those who moved up one or more quintiles, down one or more quintiles or experienced movement up and down one or more quintiles.

Change analysis is based on changes in income quintile between 1993 and 1996, and between 1996 and 1999. Change in quintiles was categorised by those who moved up one or more quintiles, or moved down one or more quintiles.

cquina	Hh income after housing costs 1993
fquina	Hh income after housing costs 1996
iquina	Hh income after housing costs 1999

1 Bottom quintile
2 2nd
3 3rd
4 4th
5 Top quintile

incaft3a	Hh income after housing costs 1991 to 1999

1 Bottom quintile
2 2nd
3 3rd
4 4th
5 Top quintile
6 Increase quintile(s)
7 Decrease quintile(s)
8 Fluctuation

incaft1a	Hh income after housing costs 1993 to 1996
incaft2a	Hh income after housing costs 1996 to 1999

1 Bottom quintile
2 2nd
3 3rd
4 4th
5 Top quintile
6 Increase quintile(s)
7 Decrease quintile(s)

FISIT	**Self-reported financial situation:** The 5 original categories of this variable were collapsed into 3: Comfortable ('Living comfortably' and 'Doing alright'); Just about getting by; Having difficulty ('Finding it quite difficult' and 'Finding it very difficult').

Cross-sectional analysis is based on an individual's perceived financial situation in 1993, 1996 and 1999.

Longitudinal analysis is based on similar categories to the cross-sectional analysis, although allocation to the groups is based on the following criteria:

	First criteria: at least 6 years	**Second criteria: if less than 6 years**
Comfortable	'Comfortable'	No years of 'having difficulty'
Having difficulty	'Having difficulty'	No years of 'comfortable'
Getting by	All other combinations	

Change analysis is based on changes in an individual's perceived financial situation between 1993 and 1996, and between 1996 and 1999.

(continued)

BHPS variables	Data description and transformation		
	Cross-sectional analysis	**Longitudinal analysis**	**Change analysis**
FISIT (continued)	cfinsit Financial situation 1993 ffinsit Financial situation 1996 ifinsit Financial situation 1999 1 Comfortable 2 Just about getting by 3 Having difficulty	finsit9a Financial situation 1991 to 1999 1 Comfortable 2 Just about getting by 3 Having difficulty	finsit1a Financial situation 1993 to 1996 finsit2a Financial situation 1996 to 1999 1 Having difficulty 2 Started having difficulty 3 Were having difficulty now getting by 4 Getting by 5 Were comfortable now getting by 6 Become comfortable 7 Comfortable
JBSTAT	**Current economic status:** The original 9 categories were collapsed into 6: Employed (Self-employed, In paid employment, On maternity leave); Unemployed; Retired; Family care; Student (full time student, government training scheme); Long-term sick/disabled.		
	Cross-sectional analysis is based on employment status in 1993, 1996 and 1999.	**Longitudinal analysis** is based on employment status in 6 out of the 9 years between 1991 and 1999. Changes in employment status were very complex and difficult to categorise, resulting in a single category of mixed employment status.	**Change analysis** is based on changes in employment status between 1993 and 1996, and between 1996 and 1999. The categorisation reflects stability in employment status and the employment status that an individual person changed to rather than the employment status they had changed from. Although this gave rise to a small number of cases within some categories, the potential impact that different employment status might have on subjective well-being was considered important enough to retain all categories.

(continued)

BHPS variables	Data description and transformation
JBSTAT (continued)	cjbstat1 Employment status 1993 fjbstat1 Employment status 1996 ijbstat1 Employment status 1999 1 Employed 2 Unemployed 3 Retired 4 Family care 5 Student 6 Long-term sick/disabled empsum99 Employment status 1991 to 1999 1 Employed 2 Unemployed 3 Retired 4 Family care 5 Student 6 Long-term sick/disabled 7 Mixed empst1a Employment status 1993 to 1996 empst2a Employment status 1996 to 1999 1 Employed 2 Unemployed 3 Retired 4 Family care 5 Student 6 Long-term sick/disabled 7 Become employed 8 Become unemployed 9 Become retired 10 Become family care 11 Become student 12 Become long-term sick/disabled
JBFT	**Employment commitment:** This variable is based on whether people work full or part time. Data are available for 1992–97 only. **Cross-sectional analysis** is based on employment commitment 1993, 1996 and 1999. **Longitudinal analysis** is based on whether people spent all or most of their time not employed; more or the same number of years in full-time; more or the same number of year in part-time employment, using data for each year between 1992 and 1997. **Change analysis** is based on employment commitment in 1993, 1996 and 1997. It was recoded into an ordinal variable reflecting the range of status from not being employed (not applicable) through to being employed full time. cjbft Employment commitment 1992–93 fjbft Employment commitment 1994–96 ijbft 0 Not applicable 1 Full time (30 hrs+) 2 Part time (<30 hrs) jbnoft1 Employment commitment 1992 to 1997 0 Not applicable 1 More years full than part time 2 More years part than full time 3 Same number of years full and part time ft1a Employment commitment 1993 to 1996 ft2a Employment commitment 1996 to 1997 0 Not applicable 1 Become not applicable 2 Become part time 3 Part time 4 Become full time 5 Full time

(continued)

BHPS variables	Data description and transformation		
JBTERM	**Employment security**: This was based on whether people were in permanent or temporary (including fixed-term and seasonal contracts) employment.		
	Cross-sectional analysis is based on employment security status in 1993, 1996 and 1999.	**Longitudinal analysis** is based on the majority number of years not in employment or in either permanent or temporary employment, using data for each year between 1991 and 1999.	**Change analysis** is based on employment security in 1993, 1996, and 1999. Data was recoded into an ordinal variable reflecting the range of status from not being employed (not applicable) through to being employed on a permanent basis.
	cjbterm2 Employment security 1993 fjbterm2 Employment security 1996 ijbterm2 Employment security 1999 0 Not applicable 1 Permanent 2 Temporary	tempsum Employment security 1991 to 1999 0 Not applicable 1 More years permanent than temporary 2 More years temporary than permanent	perm1a Employment security 1993 to 1996 perm2a Employment security 1996 to 1999 0 Not applicable 1 Become not applicable 2 N/A to temporary/stayed temporary 3 Permanent to temporary 4 Become permanent 5 Permanent
JBRGSC	**Registrar General's social class:** Values were re-labelled to represent the numeric values of social classes I to V.		
	Cross-sectional analysis is based on social class in 1993, 1996 and 1999	**Longitudinal analysis** is based on changes in social class using data from 1993, 1996 and 1999 only. Due to the low number of cases reflecting change in social class these categories were collapsed into Manual classes and Non-manual classes.	**Change analysis** uses the same categorisation as the longitudinal analysis, based on change in social class from 1993 to 1996, and from 1996 to 1999.
	cjbrgsc Social class 1993 fjbrgsc Social class 1996 ijbrgsc Social class 1999 0 Not applicable 1 I 2 II 3 III non-manual 4 III manual 5 IV 6 V	scmove Social class 1991 to 1999 0 Not applicable 1 Become not applicable 2 Become manual 3 Manual 4 Become non-manual 5 Non-manual	sclass1a Social class 1993 to 1996 sclass2a Social class 1996 to 1999 0 Not applicable 1 Become not applicable 2 Become manual 3 Manual 4 Become non-manual 5 Non-manual

(continued)

BHPS variables	Data description and transformation			
TENURE	**Housing tenure:** The original 8 categories were collapsed into 4: Owned outright; Owned with mortgage; LA/HA rented; Private rented (employer rented, private rented unfurnished, private rented furnished, other rented)			
	Cross-sectional analysis is based on housing tenure in 1993, 1996 and 1999	**Longitudinal analysis** is based on housing tenure in 1993, 1996 and 1999 only. The original categories were collapsed to show the difference between those who were owner-occupiers (combining owned outright with owned with a mortgage) and those who rented their accommodation (including social and private rented sectors).	**Change analysis** is based on change in housing tenure between 1993 and 1996, and 1996 and 1999 using the same collapsed categories as the longitudinal analysis.	
	ctenure Housing tenure 1993 ftenure Housing tenure 1996 itenure Housing tenure 1999 1 Owned outright 2 Owned with mortgage 3 LA/HA rented 4 Private rented	tenstat2 Housing tenure 1991 to 1999 1 Owner-occupied 2 Rented 3 Owner-occupied to rented 4 Rented to owner-occupied 5 Mixed	tenure1a Housing tenure 1993 to 1996 tenure2a Housing tenure 1996 to 1999 1 Rented 2 Owner-occupier to rented 3 Rented to owner-occupier 4 Owner-occupier	
QFEDHI	**Highest educational qualification:** The original 13 categories were collapsed into 5: Higher qualifications (Higher degree, 1st degree, Teaching qualification, Other higher qualification, Nursing qualification); A-level; O-level (inc CSE grade 1); Lower qualifications (Commercial, CSE grade 2–5, Apprenticeship, Other qualification); No qualifications.			
	Cross-sectional analysis is based on educational status in 1993, 1996 and 1999.	**Longitudinal analysis** is based on a comparison of individuals' educational status in 1991 with that in 1999. Due to the small number of cases it was not possible to record every move in educational status, therefore any improvement in education is combined within the single category of 'increased qualifications'.	**Change analysis** uses the same categories as the longitudinal analysis, based on change in education from 1993 to 1996 and from 1996 to 1999.	
	ced Educational status 1993 fed Educational status 1996 ied Educational status 1999 1 Higher qualifications 2 A-levels 3 O-levels 4 Lower qualifications 5 No qualifications	edstart1 Educational status 1991 to 1999 1 Higher qualifications 2 A-levels 3 O-levels 4 Lower qualifications 5 No qualifications 6 Increased qualification(s)	educat1a Educational qualifications 1993 to 1996 educat2a Educational qualifications 1996 to 1999 1 Higher qualifications 2 A-levels 3 O-levels 4 Lower qualifications 5 No qualifications 6 Increased qualifications	

(continued)

BHPS variables	Data description and transformation
Social	
	Reason for inclusion: Social relationships and social support have been recognised as important to an individual's life satisfaction or happiness levels. Social relationships and integration have been shown to act as an important source of personal identification and may provide a buffer to the experiences of stress. However, different social roles may also be a source of stress, thereby impacting on experiences of subjective well-being.
MASTAT	**Marital status:** The 7 original categories were recoded into 4: Couple (married and living as couple); Widowed; Marital breakdown (divorced and separated); Single never married. The remaining category (2+ unrelated adults) was assigned as missing due to the low percentage of the population within that group.

Cross-sectional analysis is based on marital status in 1993, 1996 and 1999.	**Longitudinal analysis** is based on marital status using data for each year between 1991 and 1999. Some combinations of marital experience were common enough to enable separate categories; however, many combinations were too complex or individual and were combined into a single category of mixed experience.	**Change analysis** is based on data for 1993, 1996 and 1999. The categorisation reflects stability in marital status and the marital status that an individual person changed to rather than what they had changed from. Although this gave rise to a small number of cases within some categories, the potential impact that different marital status might have on subjective well-being was considered important enough to retain all categories.
cmastat1 Marital status 1993 fmastat1 Marital status 1996 imastat1 Marital status 1999 1 Couple 2 Widow 3 Marital breakdown 4 Single never married	mar99a Marital status 1991 to 1999 1 Couple 2 Widow 3 Marital breakdown 4 Single never married 5 Couple to widow 6 Couple to single 7 Single to couple 8 Mixed	marst1a Marital status 1993 to 1996 marst2a Marital status 1996 to 1999 1 Couple 2 Widow 3 Marital breakdown 4 Single never married 5 Become couple 6 Become widow 7 Become marital breakdown 8 Become single never married

(continued)

BHPS variables	Data description and transformation		
YPPAR	**Parental responsibilities** (whether parent of young person): This is a binary variable based on data for 1995 and 1998.		
	Cross-sectional	**Longitudinal analysis** was not done.	**Change analysis**

	eyppar Parental responsibility 1994
	hyppar Parental responsibility 1998
	
	  1 Parent
	  2 Not a parent
			Parent1a Parental responsibilities 1995 to 1998
			
			  1 Parent
			  2 Become parent
			  3 Stop being parent
			  4 Not a parent

HUSITS HUNURS	**Childcare responsibility:** Individuals are considered to have 'full responsibility' if they are the person responsible for 'looking after children', and 'when a child is ill'. If they are responsible in only one of these circumstances they have 'partial responsibility', otherwise they have 'no responsibility'. Data are not available for 1993.		

	Cross-sectional analysis is based on childcare responsibility in 1992, 1996 and 1999.
	
	chcare92 Childcare responsibility 1992
	chcare96 Childcare responsibility 1996
	chcare99 Childcare responsibility 1999
	
	  0 Not applicable
	  1 No responsibility
	  2 Partial responsibility
	  3 Full responsibility
		Longitudinal analysis is based on individuals' level of childcare responsibility for each year between 1991 and 1999. Individuals had either limited responsibility (combining no or partial responsibility) or full responsibility.
		
		chres99b Childcare responsibility 1991 to 1999
		
		  0 Not applicable
		  1 Limited responsibility
		  2 Full responsibility
			Change analysis is based on data for 1992, 1996 and 1999. Change in responsibility is recorded in respect of those who gained or increased their responsibility, and those who lost or reduced their level of responsibility.
			
			chcare1a Childcare responsibility 1992 to 1996
			chcare2a Childcare responsibility 1996 to 1999
			
			  0 Not applicable
			  1 Not responsible
			  2 Lose/reduce responsibility
			  3 Gain/increase responsibility
			  4 Partial responsibility
			  5 Full responsibility

(continued)

BHPS variables	Data description and transformation
SSUPA SSUPB SSUPC SSUPD SSUPE	**Social support:** This is based on the number of situations where an individual had someone: who was available to listen; to help in a crisis; to relax with; who appreciated them; whom they could count on. People having someone in 2 or fewer areas were categorised as having 'Poor support'; people having someone in 3 to 4 areas were categorised as having 'Moderate support'; and those having someone for all 5 areas were categorised as having 'Good support'. Information on social support is only collected every other year in the BHPS.
	Longitudinal analysis is based on social support for each year 1991, 1993, 1995, 1997 and 1999	**Cross-sectional analysis** is based on level of support in 1993, 1995 and 1999.	**Change analysis** is based on data for 1993, 1995 and 1999. Due to the low level of cases those with no, poor or reduced levels of support, were combined.
	ssup99a Social support 1991 to 1999 1 Poor/mixed support 2 Moderate support 3 Good support 4 Improved support 5 Worsened support	csocsup Social support 1991 esocsup Social support 1995 isocsup Social support 1999 0 Poor support 1 Moderate support 2 Good support	socsup1a Social support 1993 to 1995 socsup2a Social support 1995 to 1999 0 None/poor/reduced 1 Improved 2 Moderate 3 Good
JBTIME	**Times of day worked:** The original 10 categories were collapsed into 4: Day time (combining mornings only, afternoons only, during the day); Evenings/nights (combining evenings only, at night, lunch/evening); Regular shifts; Varied work patterns (combining other times, varies/no pattern and other). People who were not in paid employment were coded as 'not applicable'. Data is only available for 1992 to 1997.
	Longitudinal analysis is based on times of day worked each year between 1992 and 1997.	**Cross-sectional analysis** is based on times of day worked in 1992, 1994 and 1997.	**Change analysis** is based on data for 1992, 1995 and 1997. Changes were recorded to reflect the time of day people changed to as opposed to what they changed from. Although this gave rise to a small number of cases within some categories, the potential impact that working at different times of the day might have on subjective well-being was considered important enough to retain all categories.

(continued)

BHPS variables	Data description and transformation
JBTIME (continued)	time92 Time of day worked 1992 time94 Time of day worked 1994 time97 Time of day worked 1997 0 Not applicable 1 Day time 2 Evenings/nights 3 Regular shifts 4 Varied times time99a Time of day worked 1992 to 1997 0 Not applicable 1 Day 2 Varied but mostly in work 3 Mixed wktime1a Time of day worked 1992 to 1995 wktime2a Time of day worked 1995 to 1997 0 Not applicable 1 Become n/a 2 Day 3 Evening/nights 4 Shifts 5 Start/change to day 6 Start/change to evening/nights 7 Start/change to shifts 8 Remained varied or start/change to varied
JBHRS JBOT	**Total number of hours in paid work:** The number of hours worked in a normal week was combined with the number of hours overtime worked in a normal week to produce the total number of hours worked. Data are available for 1992 to 1997 only. People who were not in paid employment were coded as 'not applicable'. **Cross-sectional analysis** is based on data for 1992, 1995 and 1997. tohrs92 Total hours in paid work 1992 tohrs95 Total hours in paid work 1995 tohrs97 Total hours in paid work 1997 0 Not applicable 1 u30 2 30–39 3 40–49 4 50+ **Longitudinal analysis** is based on data for each year between 1992 and 1997. thrs99a Total hours in paid work 1992 to 1997 0 Not applicable 1 u30 2 30–39 3 40+ 4 Mixed **Change analysis** is based on data for 1992, 1995 and 1997 hrswk1a Total hours worked per week 1992 to 1995 hrswk2a Total hours worked per week 1995 to 1997 0 Not applicable 1 u30 2 30–39 3 40+ 4 Become n/a 5 Change to u30 6 Change to 30+ 7 Was working 30–39 and increased to 40+ 8 Was working 40+ and decreased to 30–39

(continued)

BHPS variables	Data description and transformation		
HOWLING	**Number of hours on housework:** Data are available for 1992 to 1999 only. Analysis is based on the average number of hours on housework for each of the 3-year periods 1992–93, 1994–96 and 1997–99.		
	Cross-sectional analysis	Longitudinal analysis	Change analysis
	hwork31a Hours of housework 1992–93 hwork32a Hours of housework 1994–96 hwork33a Hours of housework 1997–99 0 None 1 u5 2 5–9 3 10–19 4 20+	hwork99a Hours of housework 1992 to 1999 1 u5 2 5–9 3 10–19 4 20–29 5 30+ 6 Increased hours 7 Decreased hours 8 Varied hours	hwork1a Hours of housework 1993 to 1996 hwork2a Hours of housework 1996 to 1999 1 u5 2 5–9 3 10–19 4 20+ 5 Increase hours 6 Decrease hours
LACTK	**Participation in local groups:** Data are available for 1996 and 1998 only.		
	Cross-sectional analysis	Longitudinal analysis: The original 5 categories were reduced to 3: Frequent (several times a year or more); Irregular (varied between several times a year or more, and once a year or fewer); Infrequent (once a year or fewer, or almost never).	**Change analysis:** The original 5 categories were reduced to 2: Frequent (several times per year or more) and Not frequent (once a year or fewer and never/almost never).
	flactk Participation in local groups 1996 hlactk Participation in local groups 1998 1 Once per week 2 Once per month 3 Several times a year 4 Once a year or less 5 Never/almost never	org99a Participation in local groups 1996 and 1998 1 Frequent 2 Irregular 3 Infrequent	org1a Participation in local groups 1996 and 1998 1 Frequent 2 Not frequent 3 Frequent to not frequent 4 Not frequent to frequent

(continued)

BHPS variables	Data description and transformation
VOTE	**Political interest:** This is derived from an individual's support for a political party. The original categories of Scottish National, Plaid Cymru, Green Party and Other were all combined into a single category of 'other' due to the low number of cases within each.

Cross-sectional analysis is based on data for each year of the 3-year periods 1991–93, 1994–96 and 1997–99, and records change in support.

vote31a Political interest 1991–93
vote32a Political interest 1994–96
vote33a Political interest 1997–99

1	Conservative	6	change to Con
2	Labour	7	change to Lab
3	Liberal	8	change to Lib
4	Other	9	change to other
5	None	10	change to none

Longitudinal analysis is based on an individual's party-political preference for 6 out of the 9 years 1991 to 1999.

vote99a Political interest 1991 to 1999

1 Conservative
2 Labour
3 Liberal
4 None
5 Mixed

Change analysis is based on changes in political support between 1993 and 1996, between 1996, and between 1996 and 1999.

vote1a   Political interest 1991 to 1999
vote2a

1	Conservative	6	change to Con
2	Labour	7	change to Lab
3	Liberal	8	change to Lib
4	Other	9	change to other
5	None	10	change to none

| OPRLG2 ORGAF | **Religious activity.** Individuals are deemed to be religiously active if they attend a religious service at least once a month or more frequently, or they are active in a religious group. Data are only available on attendance at a religious service for 1993, 1994, 1995, 1997 and 1999. Analysis is based on data for 1993, 1995 and 1997. |

Cross-sectional analysis

rlgn93 Religious activity 1993
rlgn95 Religious activity 1995
rlgn9   Religious activity 1999

0 Not active
1 Active

Longitudinal analysis

rlgn99a Religious activity 1991 to 1999

1 Always active
2 Sometimes active
3 Never active

Change analysis analysis

rlgn1a Religious activity 1993 to 1995
rlgn2a Religious activity 1995 to 1999

0 Not active
1 Become not active
2 Become active
3 Active

(continued)

145

BHPS variables	Data description and transformation
Spatial	
	Reason for inclusion: Physical environment will not only determine opportunities for education or employment that will influence objective circumstances, but may also be related to subjective well-being where neighbourhood resources or problems may influence an individual's satisfaction with their neighbourhood.
REGION	**Regional residency:** The original 19 regions were regrouped into 11 categories, reflecting the Government Offices for the Regions of Great Britain. Inner and outer London were combined; the West Midlands included the conurbation, and Greater Manchester; the North West included Merseyside; South and West Yorkshire were combined with Yorkshire and the Humber; and Tyne and Wear and the Rest of North were combined to give the North East group. Other groups remained as originally coded. Data for Northern Ireland did not commence until 1997 and have therefore been omitted from this analysis.

Cross-sectional analysis is based on an individual's region of residency for 2 out of 3 years 1991–93, 1994–96 and 1997–99.

regn31a	Regional residency 1991–93
regn32a	Regional residency 1994–96
regn33a	Regional residency 1997–99

  1 London
  2 Rest of the South East
  3 South West
  4 East Anglia
  5 East Midlands
  6 West Midlands
  7 North West
  8 Yorkshire and Humberside
  9 North East
10 Wales
11 Scotland

Longitudinal analysis is based on an individual's regional residency for 6 out of the 9 years between 1991 and 1999.

regn99a Regional residency 1991 to 1999

  1 London
  2 Rest of the South East
  3 South West
  4 East Anglia
  5 East Midlands
  6 West Midlands
  7 North West
  8 Yorkshire and Humberside
  9 North East
10 Wales
11 Scotland
12 Mixed

Change analysis is based on region of residency in 1993, 1996 and 1999. The 11 Government Regions from the cross-sectional analysis were regrouped into 7 categories: South East (combining London and the Rest of the South East); South West; East (East Anglia); Midlands (combining East and West Midlands); North (combining North West, North East, and Yorkshire and Humberside); Wales; and Scotland.

regn32a	Regional residency 1993 to 1996
regn33a	Regional residency 1996 to 1999

  1 South East
  2 South West
  3 East
  4 Midlands
  5 North
  6 Wales
  7 Scotland
  8 Changed regions

(continued)

BHPS variables	Data description and transformation
LADISTC	**Area classification:** Each Local Authority was recoded according to the Office of National Statistics 2001 Area Classification of Local Authorities based on the 'supergroup' level (ONS, 2001).
	Cross-sectional analysis is based on an individual's area of residency in 1993, 1996 and 1999.	**Longitudinal analysis** is based on an individual's area of residency in 2 out of the 3 years 1993, 1996 and 1999.	**Change analysis** is based on residency in 1993 and 1996, and 1996 and 1999. The separate categories for London were combined.

	claclas3 Area of residency 1993
	fiaclas3 Area of residency 1996
	ilaclas3 Area of residency 1999
	
	  1 Centres and services
	  2 London suburbs
	  3 London centre
	  4 London cosmopolitan
	  5 Prospering UK
	  6 Coastal and countryside
	  7 Mining and manufacturing
		lacl99a Area of residency 1993 to 1999
		
		  1 Centres and services
		  2 London suburbs
		  3 London centre
		  4 London cosmopolitan
		  5 Prospering UK
		  6 Coastal and countryside
		  7 Mining and manufacturing
		  8 Mixed
			area1 Area of residency 1996
			area2 Area of residency 1999
			
			  1 Centres and services
			  2 London
			  3 Prospering UK
			  4 Coastal and countryside
			  5 Mining and manufacturing
			  6 Changed area

HSBRPH HSPRBI HSBRBP HSBRPQ	**Neighbourhood problems:** A binary variable was created according to whether individuals had neighbourhood problems in at least one area, ie they suffered from noise from neighbours, or street noise, or pollution/environmental problems, or vandalism or crime. Data are only available for 1996 to 1999.
	Cross-sectional analysis	**Longitudinal analysis** Not done	**Change analysis**

	env96a Environmental problems 1996
	env99a Environmental problems 1999
	
	  0 No problems
	  1 Have problems
			nprob1a Neighbourhood problems 1996 to 1999
			
			  1 Have problems
			  2 Gain problems
			  3 Lost problems
			  4 No problems

(continued)

BHPS variables	Data description and transformation		
LOCCHD LOCSERA LOCSERB LOCSERC LOCSERD LOCSERE	**Neighbourhood resources:** Individuals were considered to have good neighbourhood resources if they thought the standard of local services in respect of schools, medical, transport, shopping or leisure or the suitability of the area for raising children was excellent or good. Individuals who classified these areas as fair or poor were considered to have poor neighbourhood resources. Data are only available for 1998, therefore it was not possible to conduct longitudinal or change analysis.		
	Cross-sectional analysis	**Longitudinal analysis** not done	**Change analysis** not done
	Locchd Suitability of area for raising children locsera Standard of local services: schools locserb Standard of local services: medical locserc Standard of local services: transport locserd Standard of local services: shopping locsere Standard of local services: leisure 1 Good 2 Poor		

Health

Reason for inclusion: Good health and ability to function have important implications for an individual's subjective well-being where reductions in health status may prevent participation in the kind of daily activities enjoyed by others in society. Development of health problems may therefore become a psychological burden where individuals are not able to engage in social or work activities. Health may be defined in terms of medically determined categories, by subjective measures of self-reported status or functioning ability or certain lifestyle behaviours.

HLDSBL	**Registered disabled:**		
	Cross-sectional analysis is based on whether an individual was registered disabled in 1993, 1996 and 1999.	**Longitudinal analysis** is based on registered disability status for each year between 1991 and 1999. Analysis is based on whether people have been registered for: 5 years or more (mostly/always); 4 years or fewer (mostly not); or never registered.	**Change analysis** is based on the same categories created for the longitudinal analysis
	chldsbl Registered disabled 1993 fhldsbl Registered disabled 1996 ihldsbl Registered disabled 1999 1 Yes 2 No	dis99a Registered disabled 1991 to 1999 1 Mostly/always 2 Mostly not 3 Never	dis99a Registered disabled 1991 to 1999 1 Mostly/always 2 Mostly not 3 Never

(continued)

BHPS variables	Data description and transformation
HLPRBA to HLBRBM	**Number of health problems:** For each year between 1991 and 1999 a count was made of the number of problems that each individual had from a list of problems with: arms, legs, hands, etc; sight; hearing; skin conditions/allergy; chest/breathing; heart/blood pressure; stomach or digestion; diabetes; anxiety, depression, etc; alcohol or drugs; migraine; other. This gave a range of between 0 and 8 problems. Due to the low number of people who had 4 or more health problems, these were combined into one group.

Cross-sectional analysis is based on the number of health problems an individual had in 1993, 1996 and 1999.

Longitudinal analysis is based on the number of problems between 1991 and 1999 and is categorised based on 2 criteria:

	First criteria: 6 yrs with	**Second criteria: if <6 yrs**
None/infrequent	No problems	No >1 problem
Mild	1 problem	No >2 problems
Moderate	2 problems	No >3 problems and no <1 problem
Severe	3 or 4 problems	No <2 problems
Mixed	All other combinations	

Change analysis is based on data for 1993, 1996 and 1999 and is categorised to show those who had 0, 1, 2, 3 or more problems, had stopped having problem(s), or had started to have problem(s); among those who continued to have health problems categories were also created to show whether the number of problems they reported had gone up or down.

Cross-sectional analysis		Longitudinal analysis		Change analysis	
chprob	Number of health problems 1993	hprob99a	Number of health problems 1991 to 1999	hprob1a	Number of health problems 1993 to 1996
fhprob	Number of health problems 1996			hprob2a	Number of health problems 1996 to 1999
ihprob	Number of health problems 1999		0 None/infrequent		
	0		1 Mild		0 No problems
	1		2 Moderate		1 1 problem
	2		3 Severe		2 2 problems
	3		4 Mixed		3 3 or more problems
	4 or more				4 Gain problems
					5 Lose problems
					6 Increase number of problems
					7 Decrease number of problems

(continued)

149

BHPS variables	Data description and transformation
HLSTAT	**Self-reported health status.** Individuals were asked to rate their health status over the last 12 months. Data are used for 1991 to 1998 only (the question in 1999 was worded differently and the options for answering were also coded differently, therefore these data were not included in the analysis). **Cross-sectional analysis** is based on self-reported health status in 1993, 1996 and 1998. **Longitudinal analysis** is based on self-reported health status between 1991 and 1998 and is categorised based on 2 criteria: **First criteria: 6 yrs with** **Second criteria: if <6 yrs** Excellent Combinations of excellent/good only Good Combinations of excellent/good/fair Fair Combinations of good/fair or good/fair/poor Poor/very poor Combinations of fair/poor only All other combinations **Change analysis:** The original 5-point Likert scale from 1 (very poor) to 5 (excellent) was collapsed into 3 categories: Poor (combining poor and very poor); Fair; Good (combining good/excellent). Changes in health status were then coded as an ordinal variable ranging from poor/very poor to good.

Cross-sectional analysis		Longitudinal analysis		Change analysis	
chlstat	Self-reported health status 1993	hstat99a	Self-reported health status 1991 to 1999	hstat1a	Self-reported health status 1993 to 1996
fhlstat	Self-reported health status 1996			hstat2a	Self-reported health status 1996 to 1999
ihlstat	Self-reported health status 1999				
	1 Very poor		1 Mixed		1 Poor/very poor
	2 Poor		2 Poor		2 Become poor
	3 Fair		3 Fair		3 Poor to fair
	4 Good		4 Good		4 Fair
	5 Excellent		5 Excellent		5 Good to fair
					6 Become good
					7 Good

(continued)

BHPS variables	Data description and transformation		
HLLT	**Health limits daily functioning:** This is a binary variable with a Yes/No dichotomy. Data are available for 1991 to 1998 only.		
	Cross-sectional analysis is based on data for 1993, 1996 and 1998. chllt Health limits daily functioning 1993 fhllt Health limits daily functioning 1996 hhllt Health limits daily functioning 1998 1 Yes 2 No	**Longitudinal analysis** is based on whether health has limited daily functioning for 8 years (Always limiting), 7–5 years (Mostly limiting), 4 years (Equal), fewer than 4 years (Mostly not limiting), or never between 1991 and 1998. limit99a Health limits daily functioning 1991–98 1 Always limiting 2 Mostly limiting 3 Equal 4 Mostly not limiting 5 Never limiting	**Change analysis** is based on health functioning in 1993, 1996 and 1998. limits1a Health limits daily functioning 1993 to 1996 limits2a Health limits daily functioning 1996 to 1998 1 Yes 2 Started to limit 3 Stopped limiting 4 No
LACTA	**Health behaviour: Leisure activity.** Leisure activity is based on one question, which asks individuals how often they walk/swim or do sport. Data is available for 1996 and 1998 only.		
	Cross-sectional analysis is based on frequency of leisure activity in 1996 and 1998. flacta Leisure activity 1996 hlacta Leisure activity 1998 1 At least once per week 2 At least once per month 3 Several times per annum 4 Once per annum or fewer 5 Never/almost never	**Longitudinal analysis:** Individuals are categorised as: Regular leisure (several times a year or more); Increase leisure (change from once a year or less to several times a year or more); Decrease leisure (change from several times a year or more to once a year or fewer); Irregular/no leisure (once a year or fewer). leis99a Leisure activity 1996 to 1998 1 Regular leisure 2 Increase leisure 3 Decrease leisure 4 Irregular/no leisure	**Change analysis:** The original 5 categories were reduced to 2: Frequent (combining at least once per week, at least once per month, and several times per year) and non-frequent (combining once a year or fewer and never/almost never). leisure1a Leisure activity 1996 to 1998 1 Frequent 2 Non-frequent 3 Frequent to non-frequent 4 Non-frequent to frequent

(continued)

BHPS variables	Data description and transformation
SMOKER	**Health behaviour: Smoking.** Individuals were asked whether they smoked cigarettes each year between 1991 and 1998. (In 1999 the question was changed to ask if they 'smoked cigarettes at all nowadays'; this question gave a marked difference in frequencies from previous years and data for this year was therefore not used.)
	Cross-sectional analysis is based on data for 1993, 1996 and 1998. csmoker Smoking behaviour 1993 fsmoker Smoking behaviour 1996 hsmoker Smoking behaviour 1998 1 Yes 2 No	**Longitudinal analysis** is based on the number of years an individual smoked between 1991 and 1998. smoke9a Smoking behaviour 1991-98 1 Smoker 2 Smoker 4 years or more 3 Smoker <4 years 4 Non-smoker	**Change analysis:** This variable was coded according to whether individuals reported being a smoker/non-smoker in 1993, 1996 and 1998 and whether they had started or stopped smoking between each period. smoke1a Smoker 1993 to 1996 smoke2a Smoker 1996 to 1998 1 Smoker 2 Started smoking 3 Stopped smoking 4 Non-smoker

Domain satisfaction

Reason for inclusion: Subjective measures of well-being have been shown to be better predictors of experiences of well-being than objective measures. Subjective measures can be used to explain differences in well-being over and above actual circumstances. The subjective element is represented by individuals' perceived satisfaction with different domains of their lives.

LFSAT1 to LSFST8 and LFSATO	**Life satisfaction:** Satisfaction with life was measured on a 7-point Likert scale from 1 (not at all satisfied) to 7 (completely satisfied) in respect of income, work, accommodation, spouse/partner, social life, amount and use of leisure time and health, as well as a global measure of satisfaction with life overall. Satisfaction with spouse/partner and work may not apply to all participants in the study; where this is the case these individuals have been coded as 'not applicable'. Questions on life satisfaction were only included in the BHPS from 1996.
	Cross-sectional analysis is based on satisfaction in 1996 and 1999.	**Longitudinal analysis** is based on changes in individuals' satisfaction levels using data for each year between 1996 and 1999. The original Likert scales were recoded as: not satisfied (rating 1–4); or satisfied (rating 5–7).	**Change analysis** is based on change in satisfaction ratings between 1996 and 1999. It uses the methodology adopted for the longitudinal analysis to create categories of satisfied and not satisfied.

(continued)

BHPS variables	Data description and transformation		
LFSAT1 to LSFST8 and LFSATO (continued)	flfsat1 — Satisfaction with health 1996 ilfsat1 — Satisfaction with health 1999	sfhlth99 — Satisfaction with health 1996–99	htsat1a — Satisfaction with health 1996 to 1999
	flfsat2 — Satisfaction with income 1996 ilfsat2 — Satisfaction with income 1999	sfinc99 — Satisfaction with income 1996–99	lncsat1a — Satisfaction with income 1996 to 1999
	flfsat3 — Satisfaction with accommodation 1996 ilfsat3 — Satisfaction with accommodation 1999	sfhse99 — Satisfaction with accommodation 1996–99	accsat1a — Satisfaction with accommodation 1996 to 1999
	flfsat6 — Satisfaction with social life 1996 ilfsat6 — Satisfaction with social life 1999	sfsoc99 — Satisfaction with social life 1996–99	socsat1a — Satisfaction with social life 1996 to 1999
	flfsat7 — Satis with amount of leisure time 1996 ilfsat7 — Satis with amount of leisure time 1999	sftime99 — Satisfaction with amount of leisure time 1996–99	timsat1a — Satisfaction with amount of leisure time 1996 to 1999
	flfsat8 — Satis with use of leisure time 1996 ilfsat8 — Satis with use of leisure time 1999	sfuse99 — Satisfaction with use of leisure time 1996–99	usesat1a — Satisfaction with use of leisure time 1996 to 1999
	1 Not at all satisfied 2 3 4 5 6 7 Completely satisfied	1 Not satisfied 2 Reduced satisfaction 3 Mixed satisfaction 4 Increased satisfaction 5 Satisfied	lfesat1a — Satisfaction with life overall 1996 to 1999
			1 Not satisfied 2 Satisfied to not satisfied 3 Not satisfied to satisfied 4 Satisfied
	flfsat4a — Satisfied with spouse/partner 1996 ilfsat4a — Satisfied with spouse/partner 1999	sfspse99 — Satisfaction with spouse/partner 1996–99	spssat1a — Satisfaction with spouse/partner 1996 to 1999
	flfsat5a — Satisfaction with work 1996 ilfsat5a — Satisfaction with work 1999	sfjob99 — Satisfaction with work 1996–99	
	0 Not applicable 1 Not at all satisfied 2-6 7 Completely satisfied	1 Not applicable 2 Not satisfied 3 Satisfied 4 Mixed	0 Not applicable 1 Becomes not applicable 2 N/A to not satis/remained not satisfied 3 Satisfied to not satisfied 4 Not applicable to not satisfied 5 Not satisfied to satisfied 6 Satisfied
			jobsat1a — Satisfaction with work 1996 to 1999
			0 Does not apply 1 Becomes not applicable 2 Not applicable to not satisfied 3 Not satisfied 4 Satisfied to not satisfied 5 Not applicable to satisfied 6 Not satisfied to satisfied 7 Satisfied

Table B1.1: High subjective well-being: females 1991–93

Total n (High well-being n)			3106 (534)	3102 (534)
		Adjusted odds: regression analysis		
Variable	**Odds bivariate analysis**	**Model 1 (n/a)**	**Model 2ᵃ**	**Model 3ᵇ**
Self-reported health status			***ΔLLR 75.7	N/A
Very poor	0.3		0.5	
Poor	0.5**		0.5*	
Fair	0.9		0.9	
Good	2.0***		1.5*	
Excellent	3.7***		2.9***	
Financial situation			***ΔLLR 52.8	N/A
Having difficulty	1.0		1.0	
Just about getting by	1.9**		1.5	
Comfortable	3.7***		2.9***	
Age			***ΔLLR 30.1	***ΔLLR 44.8
25–34	1.1		1.0	0.8
35–44	0.7**		0.6***	0.6***
45–54	1.1		1.0	0.8
55–64	1.4**		1.3*	1.4**
65–74	1.2		1.5**	1.7***
75+	0.7*		0.9	1.1
Social support			***ΔLLR 19.3	***ΔLLR 25.8
Poor	1.0		1.0	1.0
Moderate	1.0		1.3	1.2
Good	3.5**		3.1*	3.2*
Health limits daily activity			**ΔLLR 8.3	***ΔLLR 29.9
No	1.0		1.0	1.0
Yes	0.3***		0.5**	0.4***
Household income after housing costs				***ΔLLR 27.0
Bottom quintile	0.8**			0.8
2nd	0.8**			0.8*
3rd	0.9			0.8
4th	1.4***			1.4**
Top quintile	1.4**			1.4***
Number of health problems				**ΔLLR 15.6
None	1.0			1.0
1	0.7***			0.8
2	0.6***			0.6**
3	0.4***			0.6*
4 or more	0.2***			0.4*
Ethnicity				
White	1.0			
Ethnic minority	0.9			
Household type				
Single	1.0			
Couple with no children	1.4***			
Couple with children	1.0			
Lone parent	0.7**			
Employment status				
Employed	1.3*			
Unemployed	0.6			
Retired	1.4**			
Family care	1.0			
Student	2.2**			
Long-term sick/disabled	0.4**			
Political party supported				
Conservative	1.4**			
Labour	0.9			
Liberal	1.1			
Other	0.9			
None	0.8			

ᵃ Excluding domain satisfaction variables.
ᵇ Excluding domain satisfaction, financial situation and self-reported health status variables.
Odds are significant at *p < 0.05, **p < 0.01, ***p < 0.001.

Table B1.2: High subjective well-being: males 1991–93

Variable	Odds bivariate analysis	Total n (High well-being n) 2551 (694)	2550 (694)	
		Adjusted odds: regression analysis		
		Model 1 (n/a)	Model 2[a]	Model 3[b]
Self-reported health status			***ΔLLR 96.9	N/A
Very poor	0.4*		0.6	
Poor	0.4**		0.4**	
Fair	0.9		0.9	
Good	1.9***		1.6**	
Excellent	3.6***		3.1***	
Financial situation			***ΔLLR 69.8	N/A
Having difficulty	1.0		1.0	
Just about getting by	1.7**		2.3**	
Comfortable	3.6***		4.3***	
Social class			**ΔLLR 23.3	*ΔLLR 16.2
N/A	0.9		1.2	1.0
I	0.8		0.7	0.9
II	0.9		0.9	1.0
III non-manual	1.1		0.9	0.9
III manual	1.3**		1.5***	1.5***
IV	1.2		1.3	1.1
V	1.0		0.8	0.8
Number of health problems			***ΔLLR 22.2	***ΔLLR 43.5
None	1.0		1.0	1.0
I	0.7**		0.9	0.8*
2	0.6***		0.8	0.6***
3	0.3***		0.4**	0.3***
4 or more	0.1***		0.2**	0.1***
Age			***ΔLLR 22.1	***ΔLLR 32.8
25–34	1.1		0.9	0.8
35–44	0.8**		0.7**	0.6***
45–54	0.9		0.8	0.7**
55–64	1.1		1.2	1.2
65–74	1.3**		1.6**	1.7***
75+	0.9		1.0	1.3
Health limits daily activity			N/A	***ΔLLR 23.2
No	1.0			1.0
Yes	0.3***			0.4*
Social support				**ΔLLR 10.8
Poor	1.0			1.0
Moderate	1.2			1.1
Good	1.9*			1.7
Political party supported				*ΔLLR 10.5
Conservative	1.2*			1.2
Labour	0.8*			0.8*
Liberal	1.1			1.1
Other	0.8			0.9
None	1.2			1.1
Ethnicity				*ΔLLR 4.8
White	1.0			1.0
Ethnic minority	0.4*			0.4
Household type				
Single	1.0			
Couple with no children	1.4***			
Couple with children	1.1			
Lone parent	0.7*			
Employment status				
Employed	1.2			
Unemployed	0.9			
Retired	1.4*			
Family care	1.7			
Student	1.5			
Long-term sick/disabled	0.3***			

(continued)

Table B1.2: High subjective well-being: males 1991–93 (continued)

Total n (High well-being n)		2551 (694)	2550 (694)	
		Adjusted odds: regression analysis		
Variable	**Odds bivariate analysis**	**Model 1 (n/a)**	**Model 2ᵃ**	**Model 3ᵇ**
Total no of hrs in paid work				
N/A	0.8**			
U30	1.4			
30–39	1.0			
40–49	0.9			
50+	0.9			
Household income after housing			N/A	
Bottom	0.7***			
2nd	1.0			
3rd	1.0			
4th	1.1			
Top	1.3**			
Religion			N/A	
Not active	1.0			
Active	1.4*			

ᵃ Excluding domain satisfaction variables.
ᵇ Excluding domain satisfaction, financial situation and self-reported health status variables.
Odds are significant at *p < 0.05, **p < 0.01, ***p < 0.001.

Table B2.1: High subjective well-being: females 1994–96

Total n (High well-being n)		3058 (494)	3090 (498)	3087 (498)
		Adjusted odds: regression analysis		
Variable	**Odds bivariate analysis**	**Model 1**	**Model 2[a]**	**Model 3[b]**
Satisfaction with life overall		***ΔLLR 113.6	N/A	N/A
Not at all satisfied	0.5	2.3		
2	0.4	0.7		
3	0.3**	0.4*		
4	0.5**	0.3***		
5	1.4	0.8		
6	4.0***	2.0***		
Completely satisfied	7.4***	3.4***		
Self-reported health status		***ΔLLR 24.0	***ΔLLR 78.9	N/A
Very poor	0.4*	0.6	0.3*	
Poor	0.4**	0.6	0.5*	
Fair	0.9	0.9	1.0	
Good	1.9***	1.4	1.9**	
Excellent	3.7***	2.1***	3.5***	
Satisfaction with amount of leisure time		**ΔLLR 19.2	N/A	N/A
Not at all satisfied	0.1***	0.2*		
2	0.8	1.4		
3	1.1	1.4		
4	0.9	0.9		
5	1.6**	1.3		
6	2.3***	1.5*		
Completely satisfied	3.3***	1.8**		
Satisfied with income		**ΔLLR 18.2	N/A	N/A
Not at all satisfied	0.4***	0.5**		
2	0.5**	1.0		
3	0.7**	1.0		
4	0.9	1.1		
5	1.3**	1.2		
6	2.1***	1.6***		
Completely satisfied	2.3***	1.0		
Satisfaction with health		*ΔLLR 15.6	N/A	N/A
Not at all satisfied	0.2***	0.3*		
2	0.6	1.1		
3	0.6*	0.9		
4	0.9	1.3		
5	1.3*	1.2		
6	2.3***	1.4*		
Completely satisfied	4.1***	1.4**		
Employment status		**ΔLLR 15.3	***ΔLLR 34.6	***ΔLLR 32.8
Employed	1.1	0.7*	0.6**	0.7**
Unemployment	0.6	0.5	0.5	0.4*
Retired	1.3	0.8	1.2	1.2
Family care	0.9	0.6**	0.6*	0.6*
Student	2.2*	4.5**	2.7*	2.7*
Long-term sick/disabled	0.8	1.5	1.7	1.8
Financial situation			**ΔLLR 23.5	
Having difficulty	1.0		1.0	
Just about getting by	2.4***		1.7	
Comfortable	4.5***		2.7**	
Number of health problems			*ΔLLR 10.2	***ΔLLR 28.4
None	1.0		1.0	1.0
1	0.6**		0.8*	0.6***
2	0.6**		0.8	0.6**
3	0.5***		0.7	0.5*
4 or more	0.2***		0.4*	0.3***
Limits daily activity		N/A	N/A	***ΔLLR 22.5
No	1.0			1.0
Yes	0.4***			0.4***

(continued)

Table B2.1: High subjective well-being: females 1994–96 (continued)

Total n (High well-being n)		3058 (494)	3090 (498)	3087 (498)
		Adjusted odds: regression analysis		
Variable	**Odds bivariate analysis**	**Model 1**	**Model 2**[a]	**Model 3**[b]
Political party supported			*ΔLLR 10.5	*ΔLLR 13.2
Conservative	1.2		1.0	1.1
Labour	0.8**		0.8**	0.7**
Liberal	1.0		0.9	0.9
Other	1.1		1.3	1.3
None	1.0		1.1	1.1
Social support			*ΔLLR 8.1	**ΔLLR 11.7
Poor	1.0		1.0	1.0
Moderate	1.7		2.5	2.8
Good	3.9**		4.0	4.8*
Household type				*ΔLLR 8.8
Single	1.0			1.0
Couple without children	1.4**			1.3**
Couple with children	1.0			1.1
Lone parent	0.7**			0.7*
Parental role			**ΔLLR 6.8	**ΔLLR 5.0
Not a parent	1.0		1.0	1.0
Parent	0.6***		0.7*	0.7*
Neighbourhood problems			*ΔLLR 4.2	*ΔLLR 4.7
No	1.0		1.0	1.0
Yes	0.7***		0.8*	0.8*
Ethnicity			*ΔLLR 3.4	
White	1.0		1.0	
Ethnic minority	0.9		2.6*	
Age				
25–34	1.0			
35–44	0.8**			
45–54	0.8			
55–64	1.2*			
65–74	1.3*			
75+	1.0			
Participation in local groups				
Once per week	1.4*			
Once per month	1.2			
Several times a year	1.2			
Once a year or less	0.7			
Never/almost never	1.0			

[a] Excluding domain satisfaction variables.
[b] Excluding domain satisfaction, financial situation and self-reported health status variables.
Odds are significant at *$p < 0.05$, **$p < 0.01$, ***$p < 0.001$.

Table B2.2: High subjective well-being: males 1994–96

Total n (High well-being n)		2548 (685)	2604 (701)	2598 (701)
		Adjusted odds: regression analysis		
Variable	Odds bivariate analysis	Model 1	Model 2[a]	Model 3[b]
Satisfaction with life overall		***ΔLLR 59.6	N/A	N/A
Not at all satisfied	0.5	1.4		
2	0.3*	0.8		
3	0.3***	0.3**		
4	0.6**	0.6		
5	1.2	0.9		
6	3.4***	1.6*		
Completely satisfied	6.6***	3.0***		
Self-reported health status		***ΔLLR 38.3	***ΔLLR 90.7	N/A
Very poor	0.3*	0.5	0.3	
Poor	0.4***	0.5	0.4*	
Fair	1.0	1.0	1.0	
Good	2.2***	1.7*	1.9**	
Excellent	4.5***	2.6***	3.8***	
Age		**ΔLLR 18.9	***ΔLLR 42.5	***ΔLLR 57.2
25–34	1.3**	1.5**	1.1	0.9
35–44	0.7***	0.8	0.6***	0.6***
45–54	0.7***	0.8	0.6***	0.6***
55–64	1.0	0.9	1.2	1.2
65–74	1.3*	1.0	1.4**	1.5**
75+	1.2	1.1	1.5*	1.8*
Satisfaction with use of leisure time		**ΔLLR 18.6	N/A	N/A
Not at all satisfied	0.3*	0.9		
2	0.4**	0.6		
3	0.6**	0.7		
4	0.9	1.1		
5	1.5**	1.1		
6	2.7***	1.6**		
Completely satisfied	3.8***	1.6**		
Satisfaction with work		*ΔLLR 18.1	N/A	N/A
N/A	1.2*	1.2		
Not at all satisfied	0.6	0.6		
2	0.7*	1.0		
3	0.5***	0.7		
4	0.7*	1.0		
5	1.0	1.0		
6	2.0***	1.2		
Completely satisfied	3.8***	1.9***		
Financial situation		***ΔLLR 17.7	***ΔLLR 45.1	
Having difficulty	1.0	1.0	1.0	
Just about getting by	1.7*	1.3	1.8*	
Comfortable	3.5***	2.1**	3.2***	
Household income after housing				**ΔLLR 17.5
Bottom	0.7***			0.6***
2nd	1.0			1.0
3rd	1.0			1.1
4th	1.1			1.1
Top	1.3***			1.3**
Times of day worked		*ΔLLR 12.3	*ΔLLR 12.2	**ΔLLR 13.6
N/A	1.0	1.0	1.0	1.0
Day time	1.0	0.8	0.8	0.8
Evenings/nights	1.8*	2.4*	2.2*	2.1*
Shifts	1.3	1.2	1.1	1.1
Varied	1.0	0.8	0.8	0.8
No of health problems		*ΔLLR 11.7	*ΔLLR 10.8	***ΔLLR 37.9
None	1.0	1.0	1.0	1.0
1	0.6***	0.7**	0.7**	0.6***
2	0.6***	1.0	0.9	0.6**
3	0.4***	0.7	0.6	0.4***
4 or more	0.2***	0.6	0.6	0.2**

(continued)

Table B2.2: High subjective well-being: males 1994–96 (continued)

Total n (High well-being n)		2548 (685)	2604 (701)	2598 (701)
		Adjusted odds: regression analysis		
Variable	**Odds bivariate analysis**	**Model 1**	**Model 2ᵃ**	**Model 3ᵇ**
Household type		*ΔLLR 8.2		
Single	1.0	1.0		
Couple no children	1.4**	1.3*		
Couple with children	1.0	0.9		
Lone parent	0.7**	0.8		
Social support		*ΔLLR 7.2	***ΔLLR 25.4	***ΔLLR 31.1
Poor	1.0	1.0	1.0	1.0
Moderate	1.8	1.2	1.1	1.2
Good	4.2***	1.9	2.6*	3.0**
Neighbourhood problems		*ΔLLR 5.2	**ΔLLR 7.1	**ΔLLR 10.6
No	1.0	1.0	1.0	1.0
Yes	0.7***	0.8*	0.8**	0.7**
Health limits daily activity		*ΔLLR 4.2	*ΔLLR 4.6	***ΔLLR 37.1
No	1.0	1.0	1.0	1.0
Yes	0.3***	0.6*	0.6*	0.3***
Satisfaction with income			N/A	N/A
Not satisfied	0.5**			
2	0.5***			
3	0.6***			
4	0.9			
5	1.4***			
6	2.4***			
Completely satisfied	2.6***			
Ethnicity				
White	1.0			
Ethnic minority	0.7			
Political party supported				
Conservative	1.3**			
Labour	0.9			
Liberal	0.9			
Other	1.0			
None	1.0			
Employment status				
Employed	1.5**			
Unemployed	1.1			
Retired	1.8***			
Family care	0.7			
Student	1.7			
Long-term sick/disabled	0.3***			

ᵃ Excluding domain satisfaction variables.
ᵇ Excluding domain satisfaction, financial situation and self-reported health status variables.
Odds are significant at *p < 0.05, **p < 0.01, ***p < 0.001.

Table B3.1: High subjective well-being: females 1997–99

Total n (High well-being n)		3955 (651)	3986 (660)	3989 (660)
		Adjusted odds: regression analysis		
Variable	**Odds bivariate analysis**	**Model 1**	**Model 2[a]**	**Model 3[b]**
Satisfaction with life overall		***ΔLLR 116.3	N/A	N/A
Not at all satisfied	0.8	1.9*		
2	0.3*	0.6		
3	0.2***	0.3**		
4	0.5**	0.5**		
5	1.2	0.8		
6	4.6***	2.2***		
Completely satisfied	8.3***	3.5***		
Self-reported health status		***ΔLLR 35.2	***ΔLLR 93.2	N/A
Very poor	0.2**	0.4	0.3*	
Poor	0.5**	0.7	0.6*	
Fair	1.2	1.1	1.1	
Good	2.2***	1.4*	1.7**	
Excellent	4.5***	2.2***	3.3***	
Satisfaction with health		***ΔLLR 34.2	N/A	N/A
Not at all satisfied	0.2***	0.4*		
2	0.4**	0.8		
3	0.6**	0.8		
4	0.9	1.0		
5	1.5***	1.2		
6	3.1***	1.8***		
Completely satisfied	5.1***	1.8***		
Satisfaction with social life		**ΔLLR 17.6	N/A	N/A
Not at all satisfied	0.3**	0.8		
2	0.3**	0.8		
3	0.4***	0.7		
4	1.0	1.1		
5	1.5**	1.0		
6	3.5***	1.4**		
Completely satisfied	4.7***	1.5*		
Marital status		**ΔLLR 17.0	*ΔLLR 8.1	
Couple	1.1	0.8*	0.9	
Widowed	0.8	0.7**	0.7*	
Marital breakdown	0.9	1.4*	1.2	
Single never married	1.2	1.2	1.2	
Financial situation		**ΔLLR 14.1	*ΔLLR 47.3	
Having difficulty	1.0	1.0	1.0	
Just about getting by	2.2**	1.2	1.8	
Comfortable	4.7***	1.9*	3.3***	
Social support		*ΔLLR 8.1	***ΔLLR 24.0	***ΔLLR 27.9
Poor	1.0	1.0	1.0	1.0
Moderate	2.2	1.8	1.9	1.8
Good	4.4**	2.5*	3.5**	3.5**
Parental role		**ΔLLR 6.4	*ΔLLR 6.2	**ΔLLR 6.9
Not a parent	1.0	1.0	1.0	1.0
Parent	0.6***	0.7*	0.7*	0.7*
Health limits daily functioning				***ΔLLR 25.3
No	1.0			1.0
Yes	0.3***			0.5***
Age			**ΔLLR 21.4	***ΔLLR 24.5
25–34	1.1		0.8	0.8
35–44	0.8*		0.8**	0.7**
45–54	0.9		0.8*	0.8*
55–64	1.1		1.1	1.1
65–74	1.3**		1.6***	1.6***
75+	0.9		1.1	1.1

(continued)

Table B3.1: High subjective well-being: females 1997–99 (continued)

Variable	Odds bivariate analysis	Model 1	Model 2[a]	Model 3[b]
Total n (High well-being n)		3955 (651)	3986 (660)	3989 (660)
		Adjusted odds: regression analysis		
Number of health problems			**ΔLLR 14.7	***ΔLLR 36.3
None	1.0		1.0	1.0
1	0.8**		0.8	0.7**
2	0.6***		0.7*	0.6***
3	0.4***		0.6*	0.4***
4 or more	0.2***		0.4**	0.3***
Participation in local groups			*ΔLLR 10.4	*ΔLLR 12.2
At least once a week	1.7***		1.6**	1.7**
At least once a month	1.1		1.0	1.0
Several times a year	1.4		1.3	1.3
Once a year or less	1.2		1.1	1.1
Never/almost never	1.0		1.0	1.0
Household income after housing				*ΔLLR 9.9
Bottom	0.8*			0.9
2nd	0.8*			0.8*
3rd	0.9			1.0
4th	1.1			1.1
Top	1.4***			1.3**
Standard of medical			*ΔLLR 6.4	**ΔLLR 8.8
Good	1.6***		1.3*	1.3**
Poor	1.0		1.0	1.0
Neighbourhood problems			*ΔLLR 6.1	**ΔLLR 9.4
No problems	1.0		1.0	1.0
Have problems	0.6***		0.8*	0.7**
Ethnicity				
White	1.0			
Ethnic minority	0.8			
Employment status				
Employed	1.3*			
Unemployed	0.7			
Retired	1.5**			
Family care	1.3			
Student	1.4			
Long-term sick/disabled	0.4**			

[a] Excluding domain satisfaction variables.
[b] Excluding domain satisfaction, financial situation and self-reported health status variables.
Odds are significant at *p < 0.05, **p < 0.01, ***p < 0.001.

Table B3.2: High subjective well-being: males 1997–99

Total n (High well-being n)		3014 (839)	3038 (848)	3045 (851)
		Adjusted odds: regression analysis		
Variable	Odds bivariate analysis	Model 1	Model 2[a]	Model 3[b]
Satisfaction with life overall		***ΔLLR 84.1	N/A	N/A
Not at all satisfied	0.4	1.7		
2	0.3**	0.6		
3	0.3***	0.4*		
4	0.6**	0.5**		
5	1.5**	1.0		
6	4.5***	1.9**		
Completely satisfied	7.8***	2.7***		
Satisfaction with health		***ΔLLR 38.3	N/A	N/A
Not at all satisfied	0.2***	0.2**		
2	0.4**	1.0		
3	0.5***	0.8		
4	0.9	1.0		
5	1.7***	1.5**		
6	2.7***	1.6**		
Completely satisfied	5.8***	2.3***		
Self-reported health status		***ΔLLR 35.1	***ΔLLR 114.5	N/A
Very poor	0.4*	1.1	0.8	
Poor	0.4***	0.7	0.5***	
Fair	0.9	0.7*	0.7*	
Good	1.8***	1.2	1.4**	
Excellent	3.6***	1.7***	2.7***	
Satisfaction with social life		**ΔLLR 22.3	N/A	N/A
Not at all satisfied	0.4*	1.5		
2	0.1***	0.3*		
3	0.7	1.2		
4	0.9	0.8		
5	1.9***	1.2		
6	3.4***	1.4*		
Completely satisfied	5.0***	1.6**		
Age		*ΔLLR 13.4	***ΔLLR 50.3	**ΔLLR 21.2
25–34	1.2*	1.1	0.9	0.9
35–44	0.7***	0.8*	0.6***	0.6***
45–54	0.8*	1.0	0.8*	0.9
55–64	1.0	0.8	0.9	1.0
65–74	1.3**	1.3*	1.7***	1.6**
75+	1.2	1.1	1.5**	1.4
Financial situation		*ΔLLR 9.1	***ΔLLR 24.9	N/A
Having difficulty	1.0	1.0	1.0	
Just about getting by	2.9***	1.6	1.2	
Comfortable	5.6***	2.0*	2.1**	
Number of health problems			**ΔLLR 15.4	***ΔLLR 31.8
None	1.0		1.0	1.0
1	0.8		1.0	0.9
2	0.7**		0.8	0.6**
3	0.5***		0.6*	0.5***
4 or more	0.2***		0.3**	0.2***
Health limits daily activity				***ΔLLR 18.1
No	1.0			1.0
Yes	0.3***			0.5***
Employment status				**ΔLLR 15.4
Employed	2.0***			1.2
Unemployed	1.1			1.8*
Retired	2.3***			0.6
Family care	0.7			0.7
Student	0.7			0.6
Long-term sick/disabled	0.4***			0.6**
Parental role		**ΔLLR 7.4	**ΔLLR 10.0	**ΔLLR 10.0
Not a parent	1.0	0.7**	0.6**	0.6**
Parent	0.5***	1.0	1.0	1.0

(continued)

Table B3.2: High subjective well-being: males 1997–99 (continued)

Variable	Odds bivariate analysis	Model 1	Model 2[a]	Model 3[b]
Total n (High well-being n)		3014 (839)	3038 (848)	3045 (851)
		Adjusted odds: regression analysis		
Social support		*ΔLLR 6.4	***ΔLLR 35.2	***ΔLLR 36.0
Poor	1.0	1.0	1.0	1.0
Moderate	1.3	1.2	2.2**	1.2
Good	2.6***	1.6	3.3***	2.2**
Neighbourhood problems			*ΔLLR 5.9	**ΔLLR 9.6
No	1.0		1.0	1.0
Yes	0.7**		0.8*	0.8**
Neighbourhood resources				
Standard of leisure			*ΔLLR 5.5	**ΔLLR 7.1
Good	1.4***		1.2*	1.3**
Poor	1.0		1.0	1.0
Ethnicity				
White	1.0			
Ethnic minority	1.1			
Number of hours on housework				
under 5	1.2*			
5–9	1.1			
10–19	1.1			
20+	0.7*			
Suitability of area for raising children				
Good	1.4***			
Poor	1.0			
Satisfaction with income			N/A	N/A
Not satisfied	0.5**			
2	0.4***			
3	0.5***			
4	1.0			
5	1.5***			
6	2.4***			
Completely satisfied	3.3***			

[a] Excluding domain satisfaction variables.
[b] Excluding domain satisfaction, financial situation and self-reported health status variables.
Odds are significant at *p < 0.05, **p < 0.01, ***p < 0.001.

Table C1.1: Maintaining high subjective well-being 1991–99: females

Total n (Stable high well-being n)		2521 (145)	2624 (154)	2624 (155)
		Adjusted odds: regression analysis		
Variable	**Odds bivariate analysis**	**Model 1**	**Model 2ᵃ**	**Model 3ᵇ**
Satisfaction with life overall		***ΔLLR 36.1	N/A	N/A
Not satisfied	0.03	0.1		
Reduced satisfaction	0.03	0.01		
Mixed	8.5	10.4		
Increased satisfaction	2.6	3.2		
Satisfied	73.6	33.8		
Satisfaction with use of leisure time		***ΔLLR 32.0	N/A	N/A
Not satisfied	0.2*	0.01		
Reduced satisfaction	0.7	2.5		
Mixed	0.8	2.4		
Increased satisfaction	1.2	3.0		
Satisfied	6.0***	7.9		
Self-reported health status		***ΔLLR 31.2	***ΔLLR 74.6	N/A
Mixed	1.8	5.4	2.5	
Poor	0.02	0.001	0.01	
Fair	0.9	1.7	0.9	
Good	4.1	6.1	4.7	
Excellent	8.6	11.6	9.7	
Age		***ΔLLR 24.4	***ΔLLR 54.1	***ΔLLR 67.3
25–34	0.7	0.7	0.6*	0.5**
35–44	0.6**	0.7	0.5**	0.4***
45–54	0.7	0.7	0.7*	0.6*
55–64	1.0	0.9	0.9	0.9
65–74	2.5***	2.3***	2.9***	3.2***
75+	1.4	1.3	1.9**	2.2***
Number of health problems		N/A	N/A	***ΔLLR 21.0
None/infrequent	1.0			1.0
Mild	0.8			0.8
Moderate	0.7			0.5*
Severe	0.4			0.4
Mixed	0.2**			0.2***
Health limits daily activity		ΔLLR 9.0		**ΔLLR 18.4
Always limiting	0.5	5.6*		0.5
Mostly limiting	0.2**	0.9		0.2*
Equal	0.4	0.8		0.5
Mostly not limiting	0.3***	0.5		0.4**
Never limiting	1.0	1.0		1.0
Financial situation			***ΔLLR 15.8	N/A
Having difficulty	1.0		1.0	
Just about getting by	3.9		2.8	
Comfortable	10.9*		6.1	
Social support			**ΔLLR 15.7	***ΔLLR 22.8
Poor/moderate/mixed	1.0		1.0	1.0
Moderate/good support	1.8		1.9	1.9
Good support	3.1		2.2	2.7
Improved support	0.6		0.7	0.5
Decline in support	0.7		0.5	0.6
Ethnicity				
White	1.0			
Ethnic minority	0.3			
Satisfaction with health			N/A	N/A
Not satisfied	0.3*			
Reduced satisfaction	0.8			
Mixed	0.9			
Increased satisfaction	1.2			
Satisfied	3.8***			

ᵃ Excluding domain satisfaction variables
ᵇ Excluding domain satisfaction, financial situation and self-reported health status variables.
Odds are significant at *p < 0.05, **p < 0.01, ***p < 0.001.

Table C1.2: Maintaining high subjective well-being 1991–99: males

Variable	Odds bivariate analysis	Model 1	Model 2[a]	Model 3[b]
Total n (Stable high well-being n)		1619 (206)	1687 (217)	1685 (215)
		Adjusted odds: regression analysis		
Self-reported health status		***ΔLLR 53.2	***ΔLLR 73.3	
Mixed	1.3	1.4	1.4	
Poor	0.2*	0.4	0.3	
Fair	0.6	0.5*	0.5*	
Good	1.6*	1.2	1.3	
Excellent	4.7***	3.2***	3.9***	
Employment status		***ΔLLR 28.7	**ΔLLR 22.7	
Employed	3.6	2.8	1.6	
Unemployed	3.9	10.9	5.8	
Retired	6.8	6.7	4.8	
Family care	0.1	0.02	0.05	
Student	0.1	0.01	0.04	
Long-term sick/disabled	0.8	3.0	2.8	
Mixed	4.1	7.1	4.8	
Satisfaction with life overall		**ΔLLR 17.6	N/A	N/A
Not satisfied	0.01	0.02		
Reduced satisfaction	2.3	2.1		
Mixed	1.9	2.2		
Increased satisfaction	1.8	1.7		
Satisfied	10.4*	5.7		
Social support		**ΔLLR 17.2	***ΔLLR 28.3	***ΔLLR 43.8
None/poor/mixed	1.0	1.0	1.0	1.0
Moderate support	1.1	0.9	0.9	0.9
Good support	3.5***	2.4	2.9*	3.8**
Improved support	2.3	2.4	2.3	2.4
Decrease in support	1.4	1.1	1.2	1.3
Satisfaction with social life		*ΔLLR 10.3	N/A	N/A
Not satisfied	0.3**	0.8		
Reduced satisfaction	0.7	0.8		
Mixed	1.2	1.2		
Increased satisfaction	1.2	0.7		
Satisfied	3.5***	1.7**		
Financial situation		*ΔLLR 9.3	***ΔLLR 33.7	N/A
Comfortable	1.0	411.0	387.0	
Just about getting by	217.7	222.1	124.4	
Having difficulty	712.5	1.0	1.0	
Satisfaction with income		ΔLLR 8.2	N/A	N/A
Not satisfied	0.4***	0.7		
Reduced satisfaction	1.0	1.1		
Mixed	1.0	1.1		
Increased satisfaction	0.9	0.8		
Satisfied	3.0***	1.5**		
Health limits daily activity		N/A	N/A	**ΔLLR 40.3
Always limiting	0.002			0.001
Mostly limiting	0.2*			0.1**
Equal	0.6			0.4
Mostly not limiting	0.6**			0.5*
Never limiting	1.0			1.0
Household type			*ΔLLR 17.7	**ΔLLR 21.9
Single	2.0**		2.5**	2.4**
Couple no children	2.1***		2.0**	3.8**
Couple with children	1.1		1.4	2.3*
Lone parent	0.2*		0.2	0.1*
Moved into relationship	1.2		0.5	0.7
Become single	0.8		0.8	0.5
Couple with/without children	1.3		1.3	2.1*
Mixed	1.1		1.2	1.0

(continued)

Table C1.2: Maintaining high subjective well-being 1991–99: males (continued)

Total n (Stable high well-being n)		1619 (206)	1687 (217)	1685 (215)
		Adjusted odds: regression analysis		
Variable	**Odds bivariate analysis**	**Model 1**	**Model 2ᵃ**	**Model 3ᵇ**
Social class			*ΔLLR 14.3	**ΔLLR 18.0
N/A or become n/a	1.0		1.0	1.0
Non-manual	0.5**		0.7	0.4**
Manual	1.2		1.8	1.0
Increase class(es)	0.6*		0.8	0.5*
Decrease class(es)	0.9		1.5	0.8
Mixed	0.7		1.3	0.6
Marital status				*ΔLLR 15.2
Couple	1.3			3.8
Widow	2.6*			3.4
Marital breakdown	1.3			2.8
Single	1.8*			2.1
Couple to widow	0.9			0.01
Couple to single	0.2*			1.1
Single to couple	1.1			1.6
Mixed	1.0			
Political party supported				*ΔLLR 12.3
Conservative	1.3**			1.2
Labour	0.8*			0.7*
Liberal	1.0			0.8
None	1.3			1.6
Mixed	0.8			0.9
Registered disability			*ΔLLR 7.1	
Always/mostly registered	0.2*		0.4	
Mostly not registered	0.3***		0.4*	
Never registered	1.0		1.0	
Age				
25–34	1.0			
35–44	0.7*			
45–54	0.7*			
55–64	0.9			
65–74	1.3			
75+	1.6**			
Ethnicity				
White	1.0			
Ethnic minority	0.01			
Household income				
Bottom quintile	0.7			
2nd	1.1			
3rd	0.9			
4th	1.4			
Top quintile	1.2			
Increase quintile(s)	1.2			
Decrease quintile(s)	0.9			
Income fluctuated	0.8			
Number of health problems		N/A	N/A	
None/infrequent	1.0			
Mild	1.0			
Moderate	0.7			
Severe	0.2			
Mixed	0.4**			

ᵃ Excluding domain satisfaction variables.
ᵇ Excluding domain satisfaction, financial situation and self-reported health status variables.
Odds are significant at *p < 0.05, **p < 0.01, ***p < 0.001.

Table D1.1: Improved subjective well-being: females 1993–96

Variable	Odds bivariate analysis	Model 1 (n/a)	Model 2ᵃ	Model 3ᵇ
Total n (Improved well-being n)			3008 (213)	3008 (213)
		Adjusted odds: regression models		
Employment status			*ΔLLR 23.9	**ΔLLR 25.4
Employed	1.0		1.0	1.0
Unemployed	3.9		2.0	1.8
Retired	0.7		0.8	0.7
Family	0.5*		0.6	0.5*
Student	0.02		0.02	0.02
Long-term sick/disabled	0.7		1.3	0.7
Become employed	1.5		1.7*	1.7*
Become unemployed	0.2		0.4	0.3
Become retired	1.2		1.4	1.3
Become family care	0.7		0.7	0.7
Become student	3.6*		4.8**	4.9**
Become long-term sick/dis	1.2		2.3	1.2
Self-reported health status			**ΔLLR 18.6	N/A
Poor	1.0		1.0	
Become poor	2.4		2.6	
Poor to fair	3.4		3.9	
Fair	5.2		6.5	
Good to fair	3.9		4.7	
Become good	7.3		8.9*	
Good	6.2		7.1	
Smoking			**ΔLLR 12.2	*ΔLLR 11.2
Smoker	1.4*		1.5*	1.4*
Started smoking	1.2		1.3	1.4
Stopped smoking	0.3		0.8	0.2
Non-smoker	1.0		1.0	1.0
Age				
25–34	1.2			
35–44	1.0			
45–54	0.9			
55–64	1.2			
65–74	0.9			
75+	0.8			
Ethnicity				
White	1.0			
Ethnic minority	1.3			
Health limits daily activity		N/A		
Yes	0.6			
Start to limit	0.6			
Stopped limiting	1.4			
No	1.0			

ᵃ Excluding domain satisfaction variables.
ᵇ Excluding domain satisfaction, financial situation and self-reported health status variables.
Odds are significant at *p < 0.05, **p < 0.01, ***p < 0.001.

Table D1.2: Improved subjective well-being: males 1993–96

Total n (Improved well-being n)			2358 (222)	2358 (221)
		Adjusted odds: regression analysis		
Variable	**Odds bivariate analysis**	**Model 1 (n/a)**	**Model 2ª**	**Model 3ᵇ**
Self-reported health status			***ΔLLR 39.2	N/A
Poor	1.0		1.0	
Become poor	92.0		94.2	
Poor to fair	158.7		81.4	
Fair	183.5		169.1	
Good to fair	173.8		151.5	
Become good	511.6		450.9	
Good	450.9		392.7	
Social support			***ΔLLR 18.6	***ΔLLR 20.4
None/poor/reduced support	1.0		1.0	1.0
Improved support	4.1**		6.0**	6.4**
Moderate support	1.7		2.4	2.5
Good support	3.3**		4.9**	5.2**
Social class			**ΔLLR 17.6	*ΔLLR 14.5
N/A	1.0		1.0	1.0
Become n/a	1.4		1.2	1.1
Become manual	3.1***		2.3**	2.7**
Manual	1.3		1.0	1.1
Become non-manual	2.7***		2.1*	2.1*
Non-manual	1.3		0.9	1.0
Region				ΔLLR 13.5
S East	0.9			0.9
S West	1.5*			1.7**
East	1.1			1.0
Midlands	1.0			1.1
North	0.8			0.8
Wales	0.5			0.6
Scotland	0.7			0.7
Changed region	2.2*			1.7
Housing tenure			*ΔLLR 11.4	*ΔLLR 10.4
Rented	0.6**		0.7*	0.6*
Owner-occupier to rented	1.2		1.2	1.2
Rented to owner-occupier	1.9**		1.9**	1.9*
Owner-occupier	0.8		0.7*	0.7*
Health limits daily activity			N/A	*ΔLLR 9.5
Yes	0.4**			0.4*
Started to limit	0.5*			0.6
Stopped limiting	1.1			1.3
No	1.0			1.0
Age				
25–34	1.4**			
35–44	1.0			
45–54	0.9			
55–64	1.1			
65–74	0.9			
75+	0.9			
Ethnicity				
White	1.0			
Ethnic minority	1.8			
Times of day worked				
N/A	1.0			
Become n/a	1.4			
Day	1.6*			
Evening/nights	0.02			
Shift	0.02			
Start/change to day	1.1			
Start/change to evenings/night	2.8**			
Start/change to shift	1.0			
Start/change to varied	1.1			

ª Excluding domain satisfaction variables.
ᵇ Excluding domain satisfaction, financial situation and self-reported health status variables.
Odds are significant at *p < 0.05, **p < 0.01, ***p < 0.001.

Table D2.1: Improved subjective well-being: females 1996–99

Total n (Become high well-being n)		2790 (248)	2835 (251)	2835 (251)
		Adjusted odds: regression analysis		
Variable	**Odds bivariate analysis**	**Model 1**	**Model 2ᵃ**	**Model 3ᵇ**
Satisfaction with health		***ΔLLR 32.1	N/A	N/A
Not satisfied	1.0	1.0		
Satisfied to not satisfied	1.5	1.8		
Not satisfied to satisfied	4.9***	4.0***		
Satisfied	4.9***	3.6***		
Satisfaction with life overall		***ΔLLR 18.9	N/A	N/A
Not satisfied	1.0	1.0		
Satisfied to not satisfied	1.3	1.4		
Not satisfied to satisfied	7.6***	4.4**		
Satisfied	6.7***	3.7**		
Self-reported health status			***ΔLLR 39.7	N/A
Poor	1.0		1.0	
Become poor	0.8		1.4	
Poor to fair	2.0		3.3	
Fair	1.7		2.3	
Good to fair	3.4		5.3	
Become good	5.5*		7.6*	
Good	5.1*		7.2	
Household income after housing costs		**ΔLLR 17.0	***ΔLLR 20.5	***ΔLLR 21.5
Bottom quintile	1.0	1.0	1.0	1.0
2nd	0.8	0.6	0.7	0.7
3rd	0.9	0.7	0.8	0.8
4th	0.5	0.4*	0.5*	0.5*
Top quintile	1.8*	1.2	1.5	1.5
Increase quintile(s)	1.4	1.1	1.3	1.3
Decrease quintile(s)	1.0	0.9	1.0	1.0
Satisfaction with amount of leisure time		**ΔLLR 15.6	N/A	N/A
Not satisfied	1.0	1.0		
Satisfied to not satisfied	1.4	1.2		
Not satisfied to satisfied	3.4***	2.2***		
Satisfied	2.0***	1.2		
Satisfaction with income		*ΔLLR 10.0	N/A	N/A
Not satisfied	1.0	1.0		
Satisfied to not satisfied	0.8	0.7		
Not satisfied to satisfied	2.8***	1.6*		
Satisfied	2.4***	1.3		
Health limits daily activity			N/A	***ΔLLR 20.8
Yes	0.3***			0.4*
Started to limit	0.3**			0.3*
Stopped limiting	1.2			1.3
No	1.0			1.0
Social support				*ΔLLR 9.8
None/poor/reduced support	1.0			1.0
Improved support	0.7			0.9
Moderate support	0.4			0.5
Good support	1.8*			1.7*
Education				
Higher qualifications	1.3			
A-levels	1.3			
O-levels	1.7**			
Lower qualifications	1.0			
Increased qualifications	1.8*			
None	1.0			
Suitability of leisure facilities			N/A	N/A
Good	1.3*			
Poor	1.0			

(continued)

Table D2.1: Improved subjective well-being: females 1996–99 (continued)

Total n (Become high well-being n)		2790 (248)	2835 (251)	2835 (251)
		Adjusted odds: regression analysis		
Variable	Odds bivariate analysis	Model 1	Model 2ᵃ	Model 3ᵇ
Number of health problems	**			
None	1.0			
1	0.9			
2	1.1			
3 or more	0.3*			
Gain problems	0.6*			
Lose problems	0.7			
Increase no of problems	0.4***			
Decrease no of problems	0.8			
Age				
25–34	1.6***			
35–44	1.1			
45–54	1.0			
55–64	1.0			
65–74	0.8			
75+	0.6*			
Ethnicity				
White	1.0			
Ethnic minority	1.0			

ᵃ Excluding domain satisfaction variables.
ᵇ Excluding domain satisfaction variables and self-reported health status.
Odds are significant at *p < 0.05, **p < 0.01, ***p < 0.001.

Table D2.2: Improved subjective well-being: males 1996–99

Total n (Become high well-being n)		2423 (263)	2509 (269)	2512 (269)
		Adjusted odds: regression analysis		
Variable	**Odds bivariate analysis**	**Model 1**	**Model 2**[a]	**Model 3**[b]
Satisfaction with work		***ΔLLR 29.8	N/A	N/A
N/A	1.0	1.0		
Become N/A	1.0	0.9		
N/A to not satisfied	1.7	2.1		
Not satisfied	0.5*	0.6		
Satisfied to not satisfied	0.4*	0.5		
N/A to satisfied	3.7***	3.2***		
Not satisfied to satisfied	1.9**	1.6		
Satisfied	1.6**	1.2		
Satisfaction with health		**ΔLLR 14.5	N/A	N/A
Not satisfied	1.0	1.0		
Satisfied to not satisfied	0.8	0.7		
Not satisfied to satisfied	3.3***	2.1*		
Satisfied	3.2***	1.7		
Employment status			**ΔLLR 31.8	**ΔLLR 39.3
Employed	1.0		1.0	1.0
Unemployed	0.002		0.002	0.002
Retired	0.8		1.0	0.9
Family care	0.002		0.002	0.002
Student	1.3		1.4	1.3
Long-term sick/disabled	0.3*		0.8	0.4
Become employed	2.5***		2.9***	2.6***
Become unemployed	0.7		0.8	0.7
Become retired	1.3		1.4	1.2
Become family care	2.7		2.8	2.9
Become student	0.002		0.003	0.002
Become long-term sick/disabled	0.002		0.004	0.002
Self-reported health status			***ΔLLR 25.8	N/A
Poor	1.0		1.0	
Become poor	1.8		2.2	
Poor to fair	0.03		0.01	
Fair	3.5		3.3	
Good to fair	4.3		4.3	
Become good	6.3*		5.8*	
Good	5.2*		5.0*	
Social support		*ΔLLR 11.4	**ΔLLR 15.9	**ΔLLR 15.9
No/poor/reduced support	1.0	1.0	1.0	1.0
Improved support	2.4**	2.2*	2.4**	2.4**
Moderate support	2.9*	3.8**	3.1*	2.8*
Good support	2.2**	1.7*	2.1**	2.1**
Satisfaction with life overall		**ΔLLR 11.4	N/A	N/A
Not satisfied	1.0	1.0		
Satisfied to not satisfied	0.9	0.9		
Not satisfied to satisfied	5.7***	2.6*		
Satisfied	6.0***	2.6*		
Satisfaction with use of leisure time		*ΔLLR 9.2	N/A	N/A
Not satisfied	1.0	1.0		
Satisfied to not satisfied	1.3	1.1		
Not satisfied to satisfied	3.0***	1.7		
Satisfied	3.3***	1.8*		
Health limits daily activity				
Yes	0.6*			
Start to limit	0.4*			
Stopped limiting	1.3			
No	1.0			
Age				
25–34	1.1			
35–44	0.9			
45–54	1.2			
55–64	0.9			
65–74	1.3			
75+	0.8			
Ethnicity				
White	1.0			
Ethnic minority	0.9			

[a] Excluding domain satisfaction variables.
[b] Excluding domain satisfaction variables and self-reported health status.
Odds are significant at *p < 0.05, **p < 0.01, ***p < 0.001.

References

Acheson, D. (1998) *Independent inquiry into inequalities in health*, London: The Stationery Office.

Ahmed, P.I. and Coelho, G.V. (eds) (1979) *Towards a new definition of health: Psychosocial dimensions*, New York: Plenum Press.

Alderson, A.S. and Nielson, F. (2002) 'Globalization of the great u-turn: income inequality trends in 16 OECD countries', *American Journal of Sociology*, vol 107, no 5, pp 1244–99.

Andrews, F.M. and Withey, S.B. (1976) *Social indicators of well-being*, New York: Plenum Press.

Angelou, M. (2001) *I know why the caged bird sings*, Folio Society, first published 1969, New York: Random House.

Antikainen, A. (1998) 'Between structure and subjectivity: life-histories and lifelong learning', *International Review of Education*, vol 44, no 2–3, pp 215–34.

Antonovsky, A. (1974) 'Conceptual and methodological problems in the study of resistance resources and stressful life events', in B.S. Dohrenwend and B.P. Dohrenwend (eds) *Stressful life events: Their nature and effect*, New York: John Wiley and Sons, pp 245–58.

Arber, S. (1991) 'Class, paid employment and family roles: Making sense of structural disadvantage, gender and health status', *Social Science and Medicine*, vol 32, no 4, pp 425–36.

Argyle, M. (1987) *The psychology of happiness*, London: Metheun and Co.

Argyle, M. and Lu, L. (1990) 'The happiness of extroverts', *Personality and Individual Differences*, vol 11, no 10, pp 1011–17.

Armstrong, D. (1983) *The political anatomy of the body*, Cambridge: Cambridge University Press.

Armstrong, D. (1995) 'The rise of surveillance medicine', *Sociology of Health and Illness*, vol 17, no 3, pp 393–404.

Arnetz, B.B., Brenner, S., Hjelm, R., Levi, L. and Petterson, I. (1988) 'Stress reactions in relations to threat of job loss and actual unemployment: physiological, psychological and economic effects of job loss and unemployment', Stress Research Reports, Karolinska Institute, Stockholm, No 206. Cited in J.E. Ferrie (2001) 'Commentary: do social programmes contribute to mental well-being? The long-term impact of unemployment on depression in the US', *International Journal of Epidemiology*, vol 30, no 1, pp 170–2.

Back, K. (1971) 'Transition to aging and self-image', *Aging and Human Development*, vol 2, no 4, pp 296–304. Cited in M.A. Shields and S.W. Price (2003) *The labour market outcomes and psychological well-being of ethnic minority migrants in Britain*, Economics and Resources Analysis Unit, Home Office online report 07/03, www.homeoffice.gov.uk (accessed 28 October 2004).

Baggott, R. (1991) 'Looking forward to the past? The politics of public health', *Journal of Social Policy*, vol 20, no 2, pp 191–213.

Barron, L. and Mellor, M. (2003) 'Can sociology embrace sufficiency as well as desire?', Paper presented to the British Sociological Society Annual Conference, York, 11–14 April.

Baudrillard, J. (1998) *The consumer society: Myths and structures*, London: Sage.

Bauman, Z. (1998) *Work, consumerism and the new poor*, Buckingham: Open University Press.

Baumeister, R.F. (1986) *Identity, cultural change and the struggle for self*, New York: Oxford University Press. Cited in A. Giddens (1991) *Modernity and self-identify: Self and society in the late modern age*, Cambridge: Polity Press.

Baumeister, R.F., Campbell, J.D., Krueger, J.I. and Vohs, K.D. (2003) 'Does high self-esteem cause better performance, interpersonal success, happiness or healthier lifestyles?' *Psychological Science in the Public Interest*, vol 4, no 1, pp 1–44.

BBC News (2007) 'UK interest rates rise to 5.75%', 5 July, www.bbc.co.uk (accessed 5 July 2007).

Beck, U. (2000) *The brave new world of work*, Cambridge: Polity Press.

Beck, U. and Beck-Gernsheim, E.B. (1995) *The normal chaos of love*, Cambridge: Polity Press.

Beck, W., Maesen, L. and Walker, A. (eds) (1997) *The social quality of Europe*, The Netherlands: Kluwer Law International.

Becker, L.C. (1992) 'Good lives: prolegomena', *Social Philosophy and Policy*, vol 9, no 2, pp 15–37.

Begg, D., Fisher, S. and Dombrusch, R. (1997) *Economics*, 5th edn, London: McGraw-Hill.

Beiser, M. (1974) 'Components and correlates of mental well-being', *Journal of Health and Social Behavior*, vol 15, no 4, pp 320–7.

Bennet, K.M., Smith, P.T. and Hugh, G.M. (2002) 'Older widow(er)s: bereavement and gender effects on lifestyle and participation', *Research Findings: 6*, Growing Older Programme, ESRC.

Beveridge, A. (1942) *Social insurance and allied services*, Cmd 6404, London: HMSO.

BHPS (1991–2000) *British Household Panel Survey, Waves 1 – 9*, www.iser.essex.ac.uk/bhps.

BHPS (2002) *British Household Panel Survey user manual: Volume A: Introduction, technical report and appendices*, Appendix 2: Notes on derived variables, www.iser.essex.ac.uk/bhps/doc/index.html.

Blanchflower, D.G. and Oswald, A.J. (2002) 'Well-being over time in Britain and the USA', www.warwick.ac.uk/fac/soc/economics/oswald (accessed 18 November 2002).

Blandy, S. and Hunter, C. (2005) 'Shifting risks and changing patterns of tenure', Paper presented to the Housing Studies Association special anniversary conference, University of York, 6–8 April.

Blaxter, M. (1987) 'Beliefs about the causes of health and ill-health' and 'Attitudes to health', in B.D. Cox, M. Blaxter, A.L.J. Buckle, N.P. Fenner, J.F. Golding, M. Gore, F.A. Huppert, J. Nicklson, M. Roth, J. Stark, M.E.J. Wadson, M. Wichelow, *The health and lifestyle survey*, London: Health Promotion Research Trust, pp 131–40.

Blum, R.W., McNeely, C. and Nonnemaker, J. (2002) 'Vulnerability, risk and protection', *Journal of Adolescent Health*, vol 31 (1 suppl), pp 28–39.

Bok, D.C. (1993) *The cost of talent: How executives and professionals are paid and how it affects America*, New York: The Free Press. Cited in R.H. Frank, and P.J. Cook (1995) *The winner-take-all society*, New York: The Free Press.

Bond, M. (2003) 'The pursuit of happiness', *New Scientist*, no 2415, 4 October, pp 40–7.

Booth, C. (1902–03) *Life and labour of the people in London*, 17 vols, London: Macmillan and Co.

Boyd-Wilson, B.M., Walkey, F.H. and McClure, J. (2002) 'Present and correct: we kid ourselves less when we live in the moment', *Personality and Individual Differences*, vol 33, no 5, pp 691–702.

Bradburn, N.M. and Caplowitz, D. (1965) *Reports on happiness*, Chicago: Aldine.

Bradshaw, J. (2001) 'Methodologies to measure poverty: more than one is best?', Paper for the international symposium Poverty: Concepts and Methodologies, Mexico City, 28–29 March.

Brennan, M. (1998) 'Choosing ill health? Gender, class and health behaviour', *Sociology Review*, vol 7, no 3, pp 23–6.

Brickman, P. and Campbell, D.T. (1971) 'Hedonic relativism and planning the good society', in M.H. Apley (ed), *Adaptation-level theory: A symposium*, New York: Academic Press, pp 287–302.

British Medical Association (BMA) (1987) *Living with risk*, Chichester: John Wiley and Sons.

Bryman, A. and Cramer, D. (1994) *Quantitative data analysis for social scientists*, rev edn, London: Routledge.

Burchardt, T., Le Grand, J. and Piachaud, D. (1999) 'Social exclusion in Britain 1991–1995', *Social Policy and Administration*, vol 33, no 3, pp 227–44.

Burrows, R. (2003) 'How the other half lives: an exploratory analysis of the relationship between home ownership and poverty in Britain', *Urban Studies*, vol 40, no 7, pp 1223–42.

Butzel, J.S. and Ryan, R.M. (1997) 'The dynamics of volitional reliance: a motivational perspective on dependence, independence and social support', in G.R. Pierce, B. Lakey, I.G. Sarason and B.R. Sarason (eds), *Sourcebook of social support and personality*, New York: Plenum, pp 49–67.

Cameron. E., Mathers, J. and Parry, J. (2006) 'Being well and well-being: the value of community and professional concepts in understanding positive health', in L. Bauld, K. Clark, and T. Maltby, *Social Policy Review 18: Analysis and debate in social policy, 2006*, Bristol: The Policy Press, pp 121–43.

Campbell, A. (1981) *The sense of well-being in America: Recent patterns and trends*, New York: McGraw-Hill.

Campbell, A., Converse, P.E. and Rodgers, W.L. (1976) *The quality of American life*, New York: Russell Sage Foundation.

Campbell, C. (1997) 'The romantic ethic and the spirit of modern consumerism; reflection on the reception of a thesis covering the origin of the continuing desire for goods', in S.M. Pearce (ed), *Experiencing material culture in the western world*, London: Leicester University Press, pp 36–48.

Cannon, W.B. (1929) *Bodily changes in pain, hunger, fear and rage*, New York: D. Appleton and Company.

Carley, M. (1981) *Social measurement and social indicators: Issues of policy and theory*, London: George Allen and Unwin.

Carver, D.J., Chapman, C.A., Thomas, V.S., Sladnyk, K.J. and Rockwood, K. (1999) 'Validity and reliability of the medical outcomes study short form-20 questionnaire as a measure of quality of life of elderly people living at home', *Age and Ageing*, vol 28, no 2, pp 169–74.

Chadwick, E. (1842) *Report to Her Majesty's Principal Secretary of State for the Home Department. From the Poor Law Commissioners, on an Inquiry into the Sanitary Condition of the Labouring Population of Great Britain*, London: W. Clowes and Sons.

Chandola, T., Ferrie, J., Sacker, A. and Marmot, M. (2007) 'Social inequalities in self reported health in early old age: follow-up of prospective cohort study', *BMJ*, vol 334, no 7601, available at www.bmj.com (accessed 17 July 2007).

Cheng, H. and Furnham, A. (2003) 'Personality, self-esteem, and demographic predictions of happiness and depression', *Personality and Individual Difference*, vol 34, no 6, pp 921–42.

Clarke, M. and Islam, S.M.N. (2002) 'Measuring social welfare: application of social choice theory', *Journal of Socio-Economics*, vol 32, no 1, pp 1–15.

Coase, R. (1960) 'The problems of social cost', *Journal of Law and Economics*, vol 3, no 1, pp 1–44.

Coleson, E. (1973) 'Tranquility for the decision maker', in L. Nader and T.W. Maretzki (eds) *Culture, illness and health*, Washington, DC: American Anthropological Association.

Commission on Critical Choices, The (1976) *Qualities of life: Critical choices for Americans Vol VII*, Lexington, MA: Lexington Books.

Cook, S. (2002) 'Horn of plenty', *Guardian, Society*, 6 November, p 5.

Cooper, H., Okamura, X. and Gurka, X. (1992) 'Social activities and subjective well-being', *Personality and Individual Differences*, vol 13, no 5, pp 573–83.

Copeland, A.L., Brandon, T.H. and Quinn, E.P. (1995) 'The Smoking Consequences Questionnaire-Adult: measurement of smoking outcome expectancies of experienced smokers', *Psychological Assessment*, vol 7, no 4, pp 484–94.

Costa, D. (1998) *The evolution of retirement: An American economic history 1880–1990*, Chicago: Chicago University Press.

Costa, P.J. Jr. and McCrae, R. (1980) 'Influence of extroversion and neuroticism on subjective well-being; happy and unhappy people', *Journal of Personality and Social Psychology*, vol 38, no 4, pp 668–78.

Court, M. (2003) 'City shareholders take a swipe at the corporate fat cats', *The Times*, 20 May, www.timesonline.co.uk/article/0,,2–686239,00.html (accessed 20 May 2003).

Creed, P.A., Muller, J. and Machin, M.A. (2001) 'The role of satisfaction with occupational status, neuroticism, financial strain and categories of experience in predicting mental health in the unemployed', *Personality and Individual Difference*, vol 30, no 3, pp 435–47.

Csikszentmihalyi, M. (1975) *Beyond boredom and anxiety*, San Francisco, CA: Jossey-Bass.

Csikszentmihalyi, M. (1999) 'If we are so rich, why aren't we happy?' *American Psychologist*, vol 54, no 10, pp 821–7.

Csikszentmihalyi, M. and Rathunde, K. (1992) 'The measurement of flow in everyday life: toward a theory of emergent motivation', *Nebraska Symposium on Motivation*, no 40, pp 57–97.

Cummins, R.A. and Nistico, H. (2002) 'Maintaining life satisfaction: the role of positive cognitive bias', *Journal of Happiness Studies*, vol 3, no 1, pp 37–69.

Cummins, R.A., Eckersley, R., Pallant, J., van Vugt, J. and Masijon, R. (2003) 'Developing a national index of subjective wellbeing: the Australian Unity Wellbeing Index', *Social Indicators Research*, vol 64, no 2, pp 159–90.

Dahlgren, G. and Whithead, M. (1991) *Policies and strategies to promote social equity in health*, Stockholm: Institute of Futures Studies. Cited in Sir Donald Acheson (1998) *Independent inquiry into inequalities in health*, London: The Stationery Office.

Dale, A., Arber, S. and Procter, M. (1988) *Doing secondary analysis*, London: Unwin Hyman.

Davidson, R. (1992) 'Emotion and affective style: hemispheric substrates', *Psychological Science*, vol 3, no 1, pp 39–43.

Davidson, R., Jackson, D.C., and Kalin, N.H. (2000) 'Emotion, plasticity, context and regulation: perspectives from affective neuroscience', *Psychological Bulletin*, vol 126, no 6, pp 890–909.

DCLG (Department for Communities and Local Government) (2006a) *English House Condition Survey Annual Report 2004*, London: DCLG.

DCLG (2006b) *Trends in tenure and cross tenure topics (General)*, Table S101, http://www.communities.gov.uk (accessed 5 August 2006).

de Vaus, D. (2002) *Analysing social science data: 50 key problems in data analysis*, London: Sage.

Defra (Department of Environment, Food and Rural Affairs) (2005) *Securing the future: delivering the UK Sustainable Development Strategy*, London: The Stationery Office.

Dempster, M. and Donnelly, M. (2001) 'A comparative analysis of the SF12 and the SF36 among ischaemic heart disease patients', *Journal of Health Psychology*, vol 6, no 6, pp 707–11.

DfEE (Department for Education and Employment) (1998) *The learning age: A renaissance for new Britain*, London: The Stationery Office.

DHSS (Department of Health and Social Security) (1976) *Prevention and health: Everybody's business: A reassessment of public and personal health*, London: HMSO.

Diener, E. (1984) 'Subjective well-being', *Pscyhological Bulletin*, vol 95, no 3, pp 542–75.

Diener, E. (1993) 'Most Americans are happy', unpublished manuscript, Department of Psychology, University of Illinois. Cited in C.D. Ryfe and C.L.M. Keyes (1995) 'The structure of psychological well-being revisited', *Journal of Personality and Social Psychology*, vol 69, no 4, pp 719–27.

Diener, E. and Lucas, R.E. (1999) 'Personality and subjective well-being', in D. Kahneman, E. Diener and N. Schwarz (eds) *Well-being: The foundations of hedonic psychology*, New York: Russell Sage Foundation, pp 213–29.

Diener, E., Scollon, C.N. and Lucas, R.E. (2003) 'The evolving concept of subjective well-being: the multifaceted nature of happiness', *Advances in Cell Aging and Gerontology*, vol 15, pp 187–219.

Diez Roux, A.V. (2004) 'Estimating neighbourhood health effects: the challenges of causal inference in a complex world', *Social Science and Medicine*, vol 58, no 10, pp 1953–60.

Dirksen, S.R. (2000) 'Predicting well-being among breast cancer survivors', *Journal of Advanced Nursing*, vol 32, no 4, pp 937–43.

Dobash, R.E. and Dobash, R. (1979) *Violence against wives: A case against the patriarchy*, London: Open Books.

Dobson, S. (2002) 'History of anti-capitalism protests', *Guardian*, 1 May, www.guardian.co.uk/mayday/story (accessed 28 November 2002).

Dohrenwend, B.S. and Dohrenwend, B.P. (eds) (1974) *Stressful life events: Their nature and effect*, John Wiley and Sons, New York.

Donovan, N., Halpern, D. and Sargeant, R. (2002) *Life satisfaction: The state of knowledge and implications for government*, Strategy Unit, London: The Cabinet Office.

Dorling, D., Rigby, J., Wheeler, B., Ballas, D., Thomas, B., Fahmy, E., Gordon D. and Lupton, R. (2007) *Poverty and wealth across Britain 1968 to 2005*, York: Joseph Rowntree Foundation Findings, July.

Durkheim, E. (1952) *Suicide: A study in sociology*, edited with an introduction by George Simpson, London: Routledge and Kegan Paul.

Economic and Social Research Council Research Centre on Micro-Social Change, British Household Panel Survey. Colchester, Essex: UK Data Archive, 10 April 2002. SN: 4505.

Elstad, J.I. (1998) 'The psycho-social perspective on social inequalities in health', in M. Bartley, D. Blane and G. Davey Smith (eds) *The sociology of health inequalities*, Oxford: Blackwell, pp 39–58.

Etzioni, A. (1998) 'Voluntary simplicity: characterization, select psychological implications and societal consequences', *Journal of Economic Psychology*, vol 19, no 4, pp 619–43.

Eurostat (2002) *The social situation in the European Union*, Eurostat.

Fawcett (2003) *Pay, pensions and poverty*, joint briefing by Fawcett and the Women's Budget Group, available at www.fawcettsociety.org.uk (accessed 2 December 2004).

Feather, N.T. (1990) *The psychological impact of unemployment*, Berlin: Springer-Verlag.

Feinstein, A.R. (1988) 'Scientific standards in epidemiological studies of the menace of daily life', *Science*, vol 242, no 4883, pp 1257–63.

Fenner, N. (1987) 'Leisure, exercise and work', in B.D. Cox, M. Blaxter, A.L.J. Buckle, N.P. Fenner, J.F. Golding, M. Gore, F.A. Huppert, J. Nicklson, M. Roth, J. Stark, M.E.J. Wadson and M. Wichelow, *The health and lifestyle survey*, London: Health Promotion Research Trust, pp 85–96.

Ferguson, N. (2007) 'Maybe owning a home is not for everyone', *Telegraph*, available at www.telegraph.co.uk (accessed 16 July 2007).

Ferrie, J.E. (2001) 'Commentary: Do social programmes contribute to mental well-being? The long-term impact of unemployment on depression in the US', *International Journal of Epidemiology*, vol 30, no 1, pp 170–2.

Ferrie, J.E., Shipley, M.J., Newman, K., Stansfeld, S.A., Marmot, M. (2005) 'Self-reported job insecurity and health in the Whitehall II study: potential explanations of the relationship', *Social Science and Medicine*, vol 60, no 7, pp 1593–602.

Findhorn Community, www.findhorn.org (accessed 2 November 2006).

Fineman, S. (1983) *White collar unemployment: Impact and stress*, Chichester: John Wiley and Sons. Cited in E. Rodriguez, E.A. Frongillo and P. Changra (2001) 'Do social programmes contribute to mental well-being? The long-term impact of unemployment on depression in the United States', *International Journal of Epidemiology*, vol 30, no 1, pp 163–70.

Flint, J. (2004) 'The responsible tenant: housing governance and the politics of behaviour', *Housing Studies*, vol 19, no 6, pp 893–909.

Ford, J., Quilgars, D., Burrows, R. and Rhodes, D. (2004) *Homeowners risk and safety-nets: Mortgage payment protection and beyond*, London: ODPM.

Foucault, M. (1991) 'Governmentality', in G. Burchell, C. Gordon and P. Miller (eds) *The Foucault effect: Studies in governmentality*, Hemel Hempstead: Harvester Wheatsheaf, pp 87–104.

Frank, R.H. and Cook, P.J. (1995) *The winner-take-all society*, New York: The Free Press.

Fujita, F., Diener, E. and Sandvik, E. (1991) 'Gender differences in negative affect and well-being: the case for emotional intensity', *Journal of Personality and Social Psychology*, vol 61, no 3, pp 427–34.

Furnham, A. (1991) 'Work and leisure satisfaction', in F. Strack, M. Argyle and N. Schwarz (eds), *Subjective well-being: An interdisciplinary approach*, Oxford: Pergamon Press, pp 235–59.

Gardner, C. and Sheppard, J. (1989) *Consuming passion: The rise of retail culture*, London: Unwin Hyman.

Gerston, J.C., Langner, T.S., Eisenberg, J.G. and Orzeck, L. (1974) 'Child behaviour and life events: undersirable change or change per se?' in B.S. Dohrenwend and B.P. Dohrenwend (eds), *Stressful life events: Their nature and effect*, New York: John Wiley and Sons, pp 159–70.

Gesler, W. (2005) 'Therapeutic landscapes: an evolving theme' (Editorial), *Health and Place*, vol 11, no 4, pp 295–7.

Giddens, A. (1991) *Modernity and self-identify: Self and society in the late modern age*, Cambridge: Polity Press.

Giddens, A. (1998) *The third way: The renewal of social democracy*, Cambridge: Polity Press.

Glennerster, H. and Hills, J. (eds) (1998) *The state of welfare: The economics of social spending*, Oxford: Oxford University Press.

Goldberg, D.P. (1972) 'The detection of psychiatric illness by questionnaire', Institute of Psychiatry, Maudsley Monographs, No 21, London: Oxford University Press.

Goldberg, D.P. and Hillier, V.F. (1979) 'A scaled version of the General Health Questionnaire', *Psychological Medicine*, vol 9, no 1, pp 139–45.

Goldberg, D.P. and Williams, P. (1991) *A user's guide to the General Health Questionnaire, Windsor, NFER-Nelson*. Cited in S. Donath (2001) 'The validity of the 12-item General Health Questionnaire in Australia: a comparison between three scoring methods', *Australian and New Zealand Journal of Psychiatry*, vol 35, no 3, pp 231–5.

Golderg, D.P., Gater, R., Sartorius, N., Ustun, T.B., Piccinelli, M., Gureje, O. and Rutter, C. (1997) 'The validity of two versions of the GHQ in the WHO study of mental illness in general health care', *Psychological Medicine*, vol 27, no 1, pp 191–7.

Goodchild, M.E. and Duncan-Jones, P. (1985) 'Chronicity and the General Health Questionnaire', *The British Journal of Psychiatry*, vol 146, no 1, pp 55–61.

Gordon, D. and Pantazis, C. (1998) *Breadline Britain in the 1990s*, Aldershot: Ashgate.

Gordon, D., Adelman, L., Ashworth, K., Bradshaw, J., Levitas, R., Middleton, S., Pantazis, C., Patsios, D., Payne, S., Townsend, P. and Williams, J. (2000) *Poverty and social exclusion in Britain*, York: Joseph Rowntree Foundation.

Grundy, E. and Sloggett, A. (2003) 'Health inequalities in the older population: the role of personal capital, social resources and socio-economic circumstances', *Social Science and Medicine*, vol 56, no 5, pp 935–47.

Gurin, G., Veroff, J. and Field, S. (1960) *Americans view their mental health*, New York: Basic Books.

Hadaway, C.K. (1978) 'Life satisfaction and religion: a reanalysis', *Social Forces*, vol 57, no 2, pp 636–43.

Hall, S. and du Gay, P. (eds) (1996) *Questions of cultural identity*, London: Sage.

Hamilton, C. (2003) *Overconsumption in Britain: A culture of middle-class complaint?*, Manuka, The Australia Institute.

Hammond, C. (2004) 'Mental health and well-being throughout the life course', in T. Schuller, J. Preston, C. Hammond, A. Brasset-Grundy and J. Bynner (eds), *The benefits of learning: The impact of education on health, family life and social capital*, London: RoutledgeFalmer, pp 57–79.

Hargreaves D. (2004) *Learning for life: The foundations for lifelong learning*, Bristol: Policy Press.

Heise, D.R. (1970) 'The semantic differential and attitude research', in G.F. Summers (ed), *Attitude measurement*, Chicago: Rand McNally, pp 235–53.

Hemingway, H., Stafford, M., Standfeld, S., Shipley, M. and Marmot, M. (1997) 'Is the SF-36 a valid measure of change in population health? Results from the Whitehall II Study', *British Medical Journal*, vol 315, no 7118, pp 1273–9.

Herper, M. (2004) 'Money won't buy you happiness', *Forbes*, 21 September, www.forbes.com (accessed 17 October 2006).

Hills, P. and Argyle, M. (1998) 'Positive moods derived from leisure and their relationship to happiness and personality', *Personality and Individual Differences*, vol 25, no 3, pp 523–35.

Hills, P. and Argyle, M. (2002) 'The Oxford Happiness questionnaire: a compact scale for the measurement of psychological well-being', *Personality and Individual Difference*, vol 33, no 7, pp 1073–82.

Hinkle, L.E. (1974) 'The effect of exposure to cultural change, social change and changes in interpersonal relationships on health', in B.S. Dohrenwend and B.P. Dohrenwend (eds) *Stressful life events: Their nature and effect*, New York: John Wiley and Sons, pp 9–43.

Hirsch, F. (1977) *Social limits to growth*, London: Routledge and Kegan Paul.

Hiscock, R., Kearns, A., MacIntyre, S. and Ellaway, A. (2001) 'Ontological security and psycho-social benefits from the home: qualitative evidence on issues of tenure,' *Housing, Theory and Society*, vol 18, no 1, pp 50–66.

Holmes, T.H. and Masuda, M. (1974) 'Life change and illness susceptibility', in B.S. Dohrenwend and B.P. Dohrenwend (eds), *Stressful life events: Their nature and effect*, New York: John Wiley and Sons, pp 45–72.

Huppert, A., Roth, M. and Gore, M. (1987) 'Psychological factors', in B.D. Cox, M. Blaxter, A.L.J. Buckle, N.P. Fenner, J.F. Golding, M. Gore, F.A. Huppert, J. Nicklson, M. Roth, J. Stark, M.E.J. Wadson and M. Wichelow, *The health and lifestyle survey*, London: Health Promotion Research Trust, pp 51–8.

Inglehart, R. (1990) *Culture shift in advanced industrial society*, Princeton: Princeton University Press.

Jin, R.L., Shah, C.P. and Svoboda, T.J. (1995) 'The impact of unemployment on health: a review of the evidence', *Canadian Medical Association Journal*, vol 153, no 5, pp 529–40.

Johnston, R., Jones, K., Sarker, R., Propper, C., Burgess, S. and Bolster, A. (2004) 'Party support and the neighbourhood effect: spatial polarisation of the British electorate, 1991–2001', *Political Geography*, vol 23, no 4, pp 367–402.

Jones, G. (2002) *The youth divide: Diverging paths to adulthood*, York: Joseph Rowntree Foundation.

Jones, H. (1994) *Health and society in twentieth century Britain*, Essex: Longman.

Jordan, B. (2007) *Rewarding company, enriching life: The economics of relationships and well-being*, available at www.billjordan.co.uk/pages/introduction.htm (accessed 23 May 2007).

Kahn, R.L. and Juster, F.T. (2002) 'Well-being: concepts and measures', *Journal of Social Issues*, vol 58, no 4, pp 627–44.

Kashdan, T.B. (2004) 'The assessment of subjective well-being (issues raised by the Oxford Happiness Questionnaire)', *Personality and Individual Difference*, vol 36, no 5, pp 1225–32.

Kassel, J.D., Stroud, L.R. and Paronis, C.A. (2003) 'Smoking, stress and negative affect: correlation, causation and context across stages of smoking, *Psychological Bulletin*, vol 129, no 2, pp 270–304.

Kellan, S.G. (1974) 'Stressful life events and illness: a research area in need of conceptual development', in B.S. Dohrenwend and B.P. Dohrenwend (eds) *Stressful life events: Their nature and effect*, New York: John Wiley and Sons, pp 207–14.

Kessel, N. and Shepherd, M. (1965) 'The health and attitudes of people who seldom consult a doctor', *Medical Care*, vol 3, no 1, pp 6–10.

Khantzian, E.J. (1997) 'The self-medication hypothesis of substance use disorders: a reconsideration and recent applications,' *Harvard Review of Psychiatry*, vol 4, no 5, pp 231–44. Cited in J.D. Kassel, L.R. Stroud and C.A. Paronis (2003) 'Smoking, stress and negative affect: correlation, causation and context across stages of smoking', *Psychological Bulletin*, vol 129, no 2, pp 270–304.

Klein, N. (2001) *No logo*, London: Flamingo.

La Barbara, P. and Gurhan, Z. (1997) 'The role of materialism, religiosity and demographics in subjective well-being', *Psychology and Marketing*, vol 14, no 1, pp 71–97. Cited in P. Schyns (2002) 'Wealth of nations, individual income and life satisfaction in 42 countries: a multilevel approach', *Social Indicators Research*, vol 60, no 1–3, pp 4–50.

Lawlor, S. (2004) Contribution to 'Freedom and choice', third in a series of three seminars on 'Richer not happier: a 21st century search for the good life', Royal Society of Arts, London, 25 February.

Layard, R. (2003) 'Happiness: has social science a clue?', Paper presented at the Lionel Robbins Memorial Lectures 2003, London School of Economics, 3–5 March.

Layard, R. (2004) Contribution to 'Have we solved the economic problem?', second in a series of three seminars on 'Richer not happier: a 21st century search for the good life', Royal Society of Arts, London, 18 February.

Layard, R. (2005) *Happiness: Lessons from a new science*, London: Allen Lane, Penguin.

Lazarus, R., Kanner, A. and Folkman, S. (1980) 'Emotions. A cognitive phenomenological analysis', in R. Plutchik and H. Kellerman (eds) *Emotion, theory, research and experience*, New York: Academic Press, pp 189–217.

LetsLinkUK (2006) www.letslinkuk.net (accessed 2 November 2006).

Lewis, T. (1933) 'Harveian oration on clinical science', *British Medical Journal*, vol 2, no 717, p 720. Cited in D. Armstrong (1993) *The political anatomy of the body*, Cambridge: Cambridge University Press.

Lief, A. (ed) (1948) *The commonsense psychiatry of Dr Adolf Meyer*, New York: McGraw-Hill Book Company.

Lim, L.L.Y. and Fisher, J.D. (1999) 'Use of the 12 item short form (SF12) health survey in an Australian stroke population', *Quality of Life Research*, vol 8, no 1, pp 1–8.

Little, C.B. (1976) 'Technical-professional unemployment: middle class adaptability to personal crisis', *Sociological Quarterly*, vol 17, no 2, pp 262–74.

Little, I.M.D. (1950) *A critique of welfare economics*, 2nd edn, Oxford: Oxford University Press.

Lu, L. and Lin, Y.Y. (1998) 'Family roles and happiness in adulthood', *Personality and Individual Differences*, vol 25, no 2, pp 195–207.

Lupton, R. (2003) *'Neighbourhood effects': Can we measure them and does it matter?* CASEPaper 73, London School of Economics.

MacIntyre, S., Ellaway, A. and Cummins, S. (2002) 'Place effects on health: how can we conceptualise, operationalise and measure them?' *Social Science and Medicine*, vol 55, no 1, pp 123–39.

MacIntyre, S., Ellaway, A., Der, G., Ford, G. and Hunt, K. (1998) 'Do housing tenure and car access predict health because they are simply markers of income or self esteem? A Scottish study', *Journal of Epidemiology and Community Health*, vol 52, no 10, pp 657–64.

MacIntyre, S., Ellaway, A., Hiscock, R., Kearns, A., Der, G. and McKay, L. (2003) 'What features of the home and the area might help to explain observed relationships between housing tenure and health? Evidence from the west of Scotland', *Health and Place*, vol 9, no 3, pp 207–18.

Mack, J. and Lansley, S. (1985) *Poor Britain*, London: George Allen and Unwin.

Marcuse, H. (1968) *One dimensional man*, London: Sphere Books. Cited in B. Smart (2003) *Economy, culture and society*, Birmingham: Open University Press.

Marmot, M. (2005) *Status syndrome; How your social standing directly affects your health and life expectancy*, London: Bloomsbury.

Marsh, H.W., Richards, G.E. and Barnes, J. (1986) 'Multidimensional self-concepts: the effect of participation in an Outward Bound program', *Journal of Personality and Social Psychology*, vol 50, no 1, pp 195–204.

Maslow, A. (1954) *Motivation and personality*, New York: Harper and Row.

Maslow, A. (1970) *Motivation and personality*, 3rd edn, rev R. Frager, J. Fadimen, C. McKeynolds and R. Cox, New York: Harper Collins.

Mather, A.S. and Chapman, K. (1995) *Environmental resources*, Essex: Longman.

Mayhew, H. (1861) *London labour and the London poor*, 4 vols, London: Griffin Bohn and Co.

McClements, L. (1978) *The economics of social security*, London: Heinemann.

McCulloch, A. (2000) *Ward level deprivation and individual social and economic outcomes in the British Household Panel Survey*, Institute for Economic and Social Research, University of Essex.

Mechanic, D. (1974) 'Discussion of research programs on relations between stressful life events and episodes of physical illness', in B.S. Dohrenwend and B.P. Dohrenwend (eds) *Stressful life events: Their nature and effect*, New York: John Wiley and Sons, pp 87–98.

Meyer, A. (1951) 'The life chart and the obligation of specifying positive data in psychopathalogical diagnosis', in E.E. Winters (ed) (1951) *The collected papers of Adolf Meyer Vol III, Medical Teaching*, Baltimore, MD: Johns Hopkins University Press, pp 52–6. Cited in B.S. Dohrenwend and B.P. Dohrenwend (eds) (1974) *Stressful life events: Their nature and effect*, New York: John Wiley and Sons.

Milligan, C., Gatrell, A. and Bingley, A. (2004) 'Cultivating health: therapeutic landscapes and older people in Northern England', *Social Science and Medicine*, vol 58, no 9, pp 1781–93.

Mills, M. (ed) (1993) *Prevention, health and British politics*, Aldershot, Hants: Averbury.

Mitchell, R., Dorling, D. and Shaw, M. (2000) *Inequalities in life and death: What if Britain were more equal?* Bristol: The Policy Press.

Moen, P., Robinson, J. and Dempter-McClain, D. (1995) 'Caregiving and women's well-being: a life course approach', *Journal of Health and Social Behaviour*, vol 36, no 3, 259–73.

Murray, C. (1994) *Underclass: The crisis deepens*, London: Institute for Economic Affairs Health and Welfare Unit. Cited in W.A. Mitchell, P. Crawshaw, R. Bunton and E.E. Green (2001) 'Situating young people's experiences of risk and identity', *Health, Risk and Society*, vol 3, no 2, pp 217–33.

Nazroo, J. (1997a) *The health of Britain's ethnic minorities*, London: PSI.

Nazroo, J. (1997b) *Ethnicity and mental health: Findings from a national community survey*, London: PSI.

Nettle, D. (2005) *Happiness: The science behind your smile*, Oxford: Oxford University Press.

Nettleton, S. (1997) 'Governing the risky self. How to become healthy, wealthy and wise', in A. Peterson and R. Bunton (eds) *Foucault, health and medicine*, London: Routledge, pp 207–22.

Nettleton, S. and Burrows, R. (1998) 'Mortgage debt, insecure home ownership and health: an explanatory analysis', in M. Bartley, B. Blane and G.D. Smith (eds) *The sociology of health inequalities*, Oxford: Blackwell, pp 171–92.

New Economics Foundation (NEF) (2004) *Chasing progress: Beyond measuring economic growth*, NEF, www.neweconomics.org (accessed 6 May 2004).

Newman, Sir George (1931) *Health and social evolution*, London: George Allen and Unwin.

Oakes, C. and McKee, E. (1997) 'The market for a new private rented sector', *Findings, Housing Research 214*, York: Joseph Rowntree Foundation.

Oakes, J.M. (2004) 'The (mis)estimation of neighbourhood effects: causal inference for a practicable social epidemiology', *Social Science and Medicine*, vol 58, no 10, pp 1929–52.

ODPM (Office of the Deputy Prime Minister) (2003) *English House Condition Survey 2001: Key facts*, London: HMSO [further information on 'decent homes' is available at www.odpm.gov.uk].

ODPM (2004a) *English House Condition Survey 2004: Headline report – Decent homes and decent places*, London: ODPM.

ODPM (2004b) *Housing Statistics: Housing Market Tables 517 and 522*, available at www.odpm.gov.uk (accessed 30 November 2004).

OECD (Organization for Economic Cooperation and Development) (1976) *Measuring social well-being: A progress report on the development of social indicators*, Paris: OECD.

OECD (2001) *Society at a glance: OECD social indicators*, Paris: OECD.

Offer, A. (2006) *The challenge of affluence: Self-control and well-being in the United States and Britain since 1950*, Oxford: Oxford University Press.

ONS (Office for National Statistics) (2001) *National Statistics 2001 area classification for local authority user guide*, www.statistics.gov.uk/about/methodology_by_theme/area_classification/svg/index.htm (accessed 29 February 2004).

ONS (2003) *Households below average incomes: An analysis of the income distribution from 1994/5 to 2001/2*, London: Department of Work and Pensions [Table A1 and Opportunities for All indicators].

ONS (2006a) Retail Price Index – RPO4 Table http://www.statistics.gov.uk/StatBase (accessed 5 August 2006).

ONS (2006b) Population statistics at www.statistics.gov.uk/ (accessed 5 August 2006).

Oppenheim, A.N. (1992) *Questionnaire design, interviewing and attitude measurement*, London: Pinter.

Orton, M. and Rowlingson, K. (2007a) 'A problem of riches: towards a new social policy research agenda on the distribution of economic resources', *Journal of Social Policy*, vol 36, no 1, pp 59–77.

Orton, M. and Rowlingson, K. (2007b) *Public attitudes to economic inequality*, York: Joseph Rowntree Foundation.

Osgood, C.E., Suci, C.J. and Tannenbaum, P.H. (1957) *The Measurement of Meaning*, Ubranall: University of Illinois Press, Cited in A. N. Oppenheim (1992) *Questionnaire design, interviewing and attitude measurement*, London: Pinter.

Oswald, A.J. (1983) 'Altruism, jealousy and the theory of optimal non-linear taxation', *Journal of Public Economics*, vol 20, no 1, pp 77–87.

Pahl, R. (1995) *After success*, Cambridge: Polity Press.

Parker, S. (2002) 'Fair exchange', *Guardian, Society*, 30 October, p 10.

Parkes, A., Kearns, A. and Atkinson, R. (2002) *The determinants of neighbourhood dissatisfaction*, CNR Paper 1, ESRC Centre for Neighbourhood Research.

Parkes, C.M. (1996) *Bereavement: Studies of grief in adult life*, London: Routledge.

Pearlin, L.I. (1989) 'The sociological study of stress', *Journal of Health and Social Behaviour*, vol 30, no 3, pp 241–56.

Pearlin, L.I. and Lieberman, M.A. (1979) 'Social sources of emotional distress', in R. Simmons (ed) *Research in community and mental health*, vol 1, Greenwich, CT: JAI Press, pp 217–48.

Pearlin, L.I. and Schooler, C. (1978) 'The structure of coping', *Journal of Health and Social Behavior*, vol 19, no 1, pp 2–31.

Pearlin, L.I., Lieberman, M.A., Menghan, E.G. and Mullan, J.T. (1981) 'The stress process', *Journal of Health and Social Behavior*, vol 22, no 4, pp 337–56.

Pfautz, H.W. (ed) (1967) *Charles Booth, on the city: Physical pattern and social structure*, Chicago: University of Chicago Press.

Phares, E.J. (1991) *Introduction to personality*, 3rd edn, New York: Harper Collins.

Pigou, A.C. (1920) *The economics of welfare*, London: Macmillan.

Porritt, J. (2005) *Capitalism as if the world matters*, London: Earthscan.

Putnam, R. (2000) *Bowling alone*, New York: Touchstone.

Rees, J. (2001) 'Anti-capitalism, reformism and socialism', *International Socialism Journal*, no 90, www.isj1text.ble.org.uk/pubs/isj90/rees.htm (accessed 28 November 2002).

Reeves, R. (2002a) 'It's not the economy, stupid', *Guardian*, 17 April, p 16.

Reeves, R. (2002b) 'What's a fireman worth?' *Observer*, 3 November, www.observer.guardian.co.uk/futureforpublicservices/comment (accessed 18 November 2002).

Reich, J.W. and Zautra, A.J. (1988) 'Direct and stress-moderating effects of positive life experiences', in L.H. Cohen (ed) *Life events and psychological functioning; theoretical and methodological issues*, London: Sage, pp 149–80.

Rhodes, D. and Bevan, M. (2003) 'Private landlords and buy-to-let', *Findings, Ref 013*, York: Joseph Rowntree Foundation (Full report published by the Centre for Housing Policy, University of York).

Rodriguez, E., Frongillo, E.A. and Chandra, P. (2001) 'Do social programmes contribute to mental well-being? The long-term impact of unemployment on depression in the US', *International Journal of Epidemiology*, vol 30, no 1, pp 163–70.

Rose, D. (ed) (2000) *Researching social and economic change*, London: Routledge.

Rose, M.E. (1972) The relief of poverty 1834–1914, London: Macmillan.

Rose, N. (1990) *Governing the soul: The shaping of the private self*, London: Routledge.

Roseneil, S. (2004) 'Why we should care about friends: an argument for queering the care imaginary in social policy', *Social Policy and Society*, vol 3, no 4, pp 409–19.

Rotter, J.B. (1966) 'Generalized expectations for internal vs external control of reinforcement', *Psychological Monographs*, vol 80, no 1 (Whole No 609).

Rotter, J.B. and Hochreich, D.J. (1975) *Personality*, USA: Scott, Foresman and Company.

Rowntree, B.S. (1902) *Poverty: A study of town life*, London: Macmillan and Co.

Rowntree, B.S. (1941) *Poverty and progress: A second social survey of York*, London: Longmans Green.

Rowntree, B.S. and Lavers, G.R. (1951) *Poverty and the welfare state: A third social survey of York dealing only with economic questions*, London: Longmans Green.

Ryan, R. and Deci, E. (2001) 'On happiness and human potentials: a review of research on hedonic and eudaimonic well-being', *Annual Review of Psychology*, vol 52, no 1, pp 141–66.

Ryff, C.D. and Keyes, C.L.M. (1995) 'The structure of psychological well-being revisited', *Journal of Personality and Social Psychology*, vol 69, no 4, pp 719–27.

Saunders, P. (1990) *A nation of home owners*. London: Unwin Hyman.

Scales, J. and Scase, R. (2001) *Fit and fifty*, Swindon: ESRC. Cited in C. Phillipson (2004), 'Work and retirement transitions: changing sociological and social policy contexts', *Social Policy and Society*, vol 3, no 2, pp 155–62.

Schuller, T., Preston, J., Hammond, C., Brasset-Grundy, A. and Bynner, J. (2004) *The benefits of learning: The impact of education on health, family life and social capital*, London: RoutledgeFalmer.

Schwartz, B. (2004) Contribution to 'Freedom and Choice', third in a series of three seminars on 'Richer not happier: a 21st century search for the good life', Royal Society of Arts, London, 25 February.

Schwarz, N. and Strack, F. (1999) 'Reports of subjective well-being: judgmental processes and their methodological implications', in D. Kahneman, E. Diener and N. Schwarz (eds) *Well-being: The foundations of hedonic psychology*, New York: Russell Sage, pp 61–84.

Schwarzer, R. (1994) 'Optimism, vulnerability and self-beliefs as health related cognitions: a systematic over-view', *Psychology and Health*, vol 9, no 2, pp 161–80.

Schyns, P. (2002) 'Wealth of nations, individual income and life satisfaction in 42 countries: a multilevel approach', *Social Indicators Research*, vol 60, no 1, pp 5–40.

Scitovsky, T. (1976) *The joyless economy*, London: Oxford University Press.

Searle, B.A. (2005) 'Understanding well-being: a study of British adults aged 25 years and over', unpublished thesis, Department of Social Policy and Social Work, University of York, UK.

Searle, B.A. (2007) 'Promoting well-being: a British perspective', in R.J. Estes (ed), *Advancing quality of life in a turbulent world*, Social Indicators Research Series 29, The Netherlands: Springer, pp 25–40.

Searle, B.A., Smith, S.J. and Cook, N. (2007) 'From housing wealth to well-being: the health implications of savings, spending and debt' (in review for the journal *Sociology of Health and Illness*).

Seavers, J. (2002) 'Young people, money and risk in early adult life', *Research Briefing No 10*, ESRC Research Programme: Youth, Citizenship and Social Change.

Seligman, M. (2002) *Authentic happiness*, New York: Free Press [the questionnaire is accessible online at www.authentichappiness.com].

Sennett, R. (1998) *The corrosion of character*, New York: Norton.

Seyle, H. (1956) *The stress of life*, New York: McGraw-Hill Company.

Shaw, I. and Aldridge, A. (2003) 'Consumerism, health and social order', *Social Policy and Society*, vol 2, no 1, pp 35–43.

Shields, M.A. and Price, S.W. (2003) *The labour market outcomes and psychological well-being of ethnic minority migrants in Britain*, Economics and Resources Analysis Unit, Home Office online report 07/03, www.homeoffice.gov.uk/rds/pdfs2/rdsolr0703.pdf (accessed 28 October 2004).

Shields, M. and Wooden, M. (2003) *Investigating the role of neighbourhood characteristics in determining life satisfaction*, Melbourne Institute Working Paper No, 24/03, Australia: University of Melbourne.

Shin, D.C. and Johnson, D.M. (1978) 'Avowed happiness as an overall assessment of the quality of life', *Social Indicators Research*, vol 5, no 1–4, pp 475–92.

Shriver, L. (2005) *We need to talk about Kevin*, London: Serpent's Tail (first published 2003, New York: Perseus Books Group).

Sirgy, M.J., Michalos, A.C., Ferriss, A.L., Easterlin, R.A., Patrick, D. and Pavot, W. (2006), 'The Quality of Life (QOL) research movement: past, present and future', *Social Indicators Research*, vol 76, no 3, pp 343–466.

Skolbekken, J.A. (1995) 'The risk epidemic in medical journals', *Social Science and Medicine*, vol 40, no 3, pp 291–305.

Smart, B. (2003) *Economy, culture and society*, Buckingham: Open University Press.

Smith, C. and Borland, J. (1999) 'Minor psychiatric disturbance in women serving a prison sentence: the use of the General Health Questionnaire in the estimation of the prevalence of non-psychotic disturbance in women prisoners', *Legal and Criminology Psychology*, vol 4, no 2, pp 273–84.

Smith, C.A., Dobbins, C.J. and Wallston, K.A. (1991), 'The mediation role of perceived competence in psychological adjustment to rheumatoid arthritis', *Journal of Applied Social Psychology*, vol 21, no 15, pp 1218–47.

Smith, G. and Noble, M. (2000) 'Developing the use of administrative data to study poverty', in J. Bradshaw and R. Sainsbury (eds) *Researching poverty*, Aldershot: Ashgate, pp 77–97.

Smith, J., Borchelt, M., Maier, H. and Jopp, D. (2002) 'Health and well-being in the young old and oldest old', *Journal of Social Issues*, vol 58, no 4, pp 715–32.

Smith, S.J. (2005a) 'States, markets and an ethic of care', *Political Geography*, vol 24, no 1, pp 1–20.

Smith, S.J. (2005b) 'Banking on housing? Speculating on the role and relevance of housing wealth in Britain', Paper prepared for the Joseph Rowntree Foundation Inquiry into Home Ownership 2010 and Beyond.

Smith, S.J. and Easterlow, D. (2005) 'The strange geography of health inequalities', *Transactions of the Institute of British Geographers*, vol 30, no 2, pp 173–90.

Smith, S.J., Cook, N. and Searle, B.A. (2006) 'From canny consumer to care-full citizen: towards a nation of home stewardship?', an ESRC/AHRC Cultures of Consumption Programme Working Paper.

Smith, S.J., Easterlow, D., Munro, M. and Turner, K.M. (2003) 'Housing as health capital: how health trajectories and housing paths are linked', *Journal of Social Issues*, vol 59, no 3, pp 501–25.

Social Exclusion Unit (SEU) (1998) *Bringing Britain together: A national strategy for neighbourhood renewal*, Cm 4045, London: Social Exclusion Unit.

Social Exclusion Unit, www.socialexclusion.gov.uk (accessed 26 November 2004).

Spitzen, W.O., Dobson, A.J., Hall, J., Chesterman, E., Levi, J., Shepherd, R., Battista, R.N. and Catchlove, B.R. (1981) 'Measuring quality of life in cancer patients: a concise Quality of Life Index for use by physicians', *Journal of Chronic Disease*, vol 34, no 12, pp 585–97.

Sroufe, L.A., Fox, N.E. and Pancake, V.R. (1983) 'Attachment and dependency in developmental perspective', *Child Development*, vol 54, no 6, pp 1615–27.

Stark, J. (1987) 'Health and social contacts', in B.D. Cox, M. Blaxter, A.L.J. Buckle, N.P. Fenner, J.F. Golding, M. Gore, F.A. Huppert, J. Nicklson, M. Roth, J. Stark, M.E.J. Wadson, M. Wichelow, *The health and lifestyle survey*, London: Health Promotion Research Trust, pp 59–66.

Stehlik, V. (1999) 'Gross national happiness: a respite from a biblical economy or attaining Utopia?', in S. Kinga, K. Galay, P. Rapten and A. Pain (eds) *Gross national happiness*, Bhutan: The Centre for Bhutan Studies, pp 52–8, available at www.bhutanstudies.org.bt/publications (accessed 8 March 2004).

Stewart, H. (2003) 'The day investors said enough is enough', *Guardian*, 20 March, www.guardian.co.uk/executivepay/story/ (accessed 20 May 2003).

Sun, M.H. (1993) 'Psychosocial stress of employed women', *Chinese Journal of Mental Health*, vol 6, no 1, pp 13–33. Cited in L. Lu and Y.Y. Lin (1998) 'Family roles and happiness in adulthood', *Personality and Individual Differences*, vol 25, no 2, pp 195–207.

Talberth, J., Cobb, C. and Slattery, N. (2007) *The genuine progress indicator 2006: A tool for sustainable development*, Oakland, CA: Redefining Progress, available at www.rprogress.org.

Taylor, S.E. and Brown, J.D. (1988) 'Illusion and well-being: a social psychological perspective on mental health', *Psychological Bulletin*, vol 103, no 2, pp 193–210.

Taylor, S.E., Peplau, L.A. and Sears, D.O. (1997) *Social psychology*, New Jersey: Prentice-Hall Company.

Theodossiou, I. (1998) 'The effects of low-pay and unemployment on psychological well-being; a logistic regression approach', *Journal of Health Economics*, vol 17, no 1, pp 85–104.

Thinley, L.J.Y. (1999) 'Values and development: "Gross National Happiness"', in S. Kinga, K. Galay, P. Rapten and A. Pain (eds), *Gross national happiness*, Bhutan: The Centre for Bhutan Studies, pp 12–23, available at www.bhutanstudies.org. bt/publications (accessed 8 March 2004).

Thomas, B. and Dorling, D. (2004) *Know your place: Housing wealth and inequality in Great Britain 1980–2003 and beyond*, Shelter, available at www.shelter.org.uk (accessed 30 November 2004).

Tkach, C. and Lyubomirsky, S. (2006) 'How do people pursue happiness? Relating personality, happiness–increasing strategies, and well-being', *Journal of Happiness Studies*, vol 7, no 2, pp 183–225.

Townsend, P. (1979) *Poverty in the United Kingdom*, Harmondsworth: Penguin.

Townsend, P. and Davidson, N. (eds) (1988) *Inequalities in health: The Black Report*, London: Penguin.

Treanor, J. (2003) 'Rebels humiliate Glaxo', *Guardian*, 20 May, www.guardian. co.uk/executivepay/story (accessed 20 May 2003).

Triemstra, A.H.M., Van Der Ploeg, H.M., Smit, C., Briet, E., Ader, H.J. and Rosendaal, R.G. (1998), 'Well-being of haemophilia patients: a model for direct and indirect effects of medical parameters on the physical and psychosocial functioning', *Social Science and Medicine*, vol 47, no 5, pp 581–93.

Tufte, E.R. (1997) *Visual explanations: Images and quantities, evidence and narrative*, Cheshire, CT: Graphics Press.

Turner, A. (2004) *Pensions: Challenges and choices: the first report of the Pensions Commission*, London: The Stationery Office.

Turner, R.K., Pearce, D. and Bateman, I. (1994) *Environmental economics: An elementary introduction*, New York: Harvester Wheatsheaf.

UNDP (United Nations Development Programme) (2006) *Human Development Reports*, http://hdr.undp.org/ (accessed 2 November 2006).

Veenhoven, R. (1984) *Conditions of happiness*, Dordrecht, Holland: D. Reidel Publishing Company.

Ville, I., Favaud, J.F. and the Tetrafigap Group (2001) 'Subjective well-being and severe motor impairments: the Tetrafigap survey on the long-term outcome of tetraplegic spinal cord injured persons', *Social Science and Medicine*, vol 52, no 3, pp 369–84.

Voluntary Simplicity Movement website, www.simpleliving.net/ webofsimplicity/ (accessed 19 September 2002).

Walters, S.J., Munro, J.F. and Brazier, J.E. (2001) 'Using the SF-36 with older adults: a cross-sectional community-based survey', *Age and Ageing*, vol 30, no 4, pp 337–43.

Ward, L. (2004) 'Babies and jobs: no easy choices', *Guardian*, 25 November, citing Barrett (2004) *UK Family Trends: 1994–2004*, National Family and Parenting Institute.

Waterman, A.S. (1993) 'Two conceptions of happiness: contrasts of personal expressiveness (eudemonia) and hedonic enjoyment', *Journal of Personal Social Psychology*, vol 64, no 4, pp 678–91.

Weber, M. (1976) *The Protestant ethic and the spirit of capitalism*, London: Allen and Unwin. Cited in B. Smart (2003) *Economy, culture and society*, Birmingham: Open University Press.

WHO (World Health Organization) (1979) 'Psychosocial factors and health: new program directions', in P.I. Ahmed and G.V. Coelho (eds) *Towards a new definition of health: psychosocial dimensions*, New York: Plenum Press, pp 87–109.

Wilkinson, R.G. (1996) *Unhealthy societies: The afflictions of inequality*, London: Routledge.

Williams, H. (1973) *Requiem for a great killer: the story of tuberculosis*, London: Health Horizon. Cited in D. Armstrong (1983) *The political anatomy of the body*, Cambridge: Cambridge University Press.

Wills, T.A. and Shiffman, S. (1985) 'Coping and substance use: A conceptual framework', in S. Shiffman and T. A. Wills (eds) *Coping and substance use*, New York: Academic Press. Cited in J.D. Kassel, L.R. Stroud and C.A. Paronis, (2003) 'Smoking, stress and negative affect: correlation, causation and context across stages of smoking', *Psychological Bulletin*, vol 129, no 2, pp 270–304.

World Values Survey, http://wvs.isr.umich.edu/index.html.

Index

Page references for figures and tables are in *italics*; those for notes are followed by n